Practical socia

Published in conjunction witn
the British Association of Social Workers
Series Editor: Jo Campling

| B A S W |

Social work is at an important stage in its development. The profession is facing fresh challenges to work flexibly in fast-changing social and organisational environments. New requirements for training are also demanding a more critical and reflective, as well as more highly skilled, approach to practice.

The British Association of Social Workers has always been conscious of its role in setting guidelines for practice and in seeking to raise professional standards. The concept of the *Practical Social Work* series was conceived to fulfil a genuine professional need for a carefully planned, coherent series of texts that would stimulate and inform debate, thereby contributing to the development of practitioners' skills and professionalism.

Newly relaunched, the series continues to address the needs of all those who are looking to deepen and refresh their understanding and skills. It is designed for students and busy professionals alike. Each book marries practice issues and challenges with the latest theory and research in a compact and applied format. The authors represent a wide variety of experience both as educators and practitioners. Taken together, the books set a standard in their clarity, relevance and rigour.

A list of new and best-selling titles in this series follows overleaf. A comprehensive list of titles available in the series, and further details about individual books, can be found online at:
www.palgrave.com/social workpolicy/BASW

Series standing order **ISBN 978–1–4039–4999–8**

You can receive future titles in this series as they are published by placing a standing order. Please contact your bookseller or, in the case of difficulty, contact us at the address below with your name and address, the title of the series and the ISBN quoted above.

Customer Services Department, Macmillan Distribution Ltd, Houndmills, Basingstoke, Hampshire RG21 6XS, England

Practical social work series

New and best-selling titles

Robert Adams *Social Work and Empowerment (3rd edition)*

Sarah Banks *Ethics and Values in Social Work (3rd edition)* **new!**

James G. Barber *Social Work with Addictions (2nd edition)*

Suzy Braye and Michael Preston-Shoot *Practising Social Work Law (2nd edition)*

Veronica Coulshed and Joan Orme *Social Work Practice (4th edition)* **new!**

Veronica Coulshed and Audrey Mullender with David N. Jones and Neil Thompson
 Management in Social Work (3rd edition) **new!**

Lena Dominelli *Anti-Racist Social Work (2nd edition)*

Celia Doyle *Working with Abused Children (3rd edition)* **new!**

Tony Jeffs and Mark Smith (editors) *Youth Work*

Joyce Lishman *Communication in Social Work*

Paula Nicolson and Rowan Bayne and Jenny Owen *Applied Psychology for Social
 Workers (3rd edition)* **new!**

Judith Phillips, Mo Ray and Mary Marshall *Social Work with Older People
 (4th edition)* **new!**

Michael Oliver and Bob Sapey *Social Work with Disabled People (3rd edition)* **new!**

Michael Preston-Shoot *Effective Groupwork (2nd edition)* **new!**

Steven Shardlow and Mark Doel *Practice Learning and Teaching*

Neil Thompson *Anti-Discriminatory Practice (4th edition)* **new!**

Derek Tilbury *Working with Mental Illness (2nd edition)*

Alan Twelvetrees *Community Work (3rd edition)*

Alan Twelvetrees

Community Work

Fourth edition

 in association with the
Community Development
Foundation

strengthening
communities
for 40 years

First published 2008 by
PALGRAVE MACMILLAN
Houndmills, Basingstoke, Hampshire RG21 6XS and
175 Fifth Avenue, New York, N.Y. 10010
Companies and representatives throughout the world

PALGRAVE MACMILLAN is the global academic imprint of the Palgrave Macmillan division of St. Martin's Press, LLC and of Palgrave Macmillan Ltd. Macmillan® is a registered trademark in the United States, United Kingdom and other countries. Palgrave is a registered trademark in the European Union and other countries.

ISBN-13: 978-1-4039-4999-8
ISBN-10: 1-4039-4999-9

This book is printed on paper suitable for recycling and made from fully managed and sustained forest sources.

A catalogue record for this book is available from the British Library.

A catalogue record for this book is available from the Library of Congress.

10 9 8 7 6 5 4 3 2 1
17 16 15 14 13 12 11 10 09 08

Printed in China

To Ruth

Contents

Practice focus boxes

Preface to the fourth edition

Students often came on the course I used to teach thinking they knew what community work was – usually something slightly different for each of them. But they soon realised that it was many things. When I started out as a community worker in the early 1970s, the only kind of recognised community work in Britain was neighbourhood work. There were no institutional structures within which to deliver community work, 'partnership working' had not been 'invented' and there were no community work strategies or programmes. Today, I think it is helpful to think of community work as a bit like an onion, of which neighbourhood community development work is the centre; but there are several other 'layers' building up the whole onion. However, it is a matter of opinion as to whether the outer layers are community work or not; what I would call community work, another commentator might not. Looked at in different ways, these outer layers can be social work, youth work, service delivery or planning, to name but a few. However, definitions are only important to help us be clear about and think through what we are doing. Thus, this book aims to help readers develop a theoretical framework which is relevant to them, and to be aware of some of the knowledge and skills one needs in order to undertake community work and related work effectively.

I am writing for four main audiences: students; fieldworkers; the managers of community workers and related staff; and funders and sponsors. Chapter 1 is relevant to all. Chapters 1–9 are primarily relevant for students and fieldworkers; Chapters 6 and 8 for managers, and Chapter 10 and the Appendix for sponsors. Having said this, policy-makers and sponsors ideally also need to understand the different dimensions of, and practical issues within community work, so that they can create successful strategies, appropriate job descriptions and sensible management arrangements. There are also several overlaps between chapters; some themes which may not be fully dealt with in one chapter are picked up in others.

I believe that community work has to be institutionalised to be effective. Thus, the last chapter spends a good deal of time drawing on literature, case studies and interviews to demonstrate how community work, at its best, has a major contribution to make to urban and rural regeneration (in particular) and to human service delivery generally. My main purpose therefore is to help you work out how to develop your understanding and practice, at whatever level you work. I also now believe that understanding community work principles should be a 'must' for all human service workers, and so this edition of *Community Work* is written for a much wider audience than earlier versions.

Community work is now so broad that no book can cover everything thoroughly. Instead, I have picked out what I consider as useful insights from my own experience and reading. I have also asked several experts in particular fields to write short pieces or interviewed them. The result is, I hope, a useful guide to community work for a range of practitioners, planners and managers.

Community work is also, in some respects, highly personal, and what may work for me may not work for you. In the last analysis, it comes down to your moral values. So, perhaps the best use of this book is to spark your own thinking, and help you to improve your practice in your own way. Comments on the text would be appreciated and should be sent to alantrees@hotmail.com. I also have my own website: www.twelvetrees-cc.co.uk

Acknowledgements

As I am no longer a fieldworker, I invited a small group of practitioners to work through the 2001 version of *Community Work* suggesting changes. I would like to thank all these people and many others both for their encouragement and their insights, to which I hope I have done justice. I am particularly indebted to: Sue Allen, Jan Bennett, Sarah Bower, Anthony Brito, Alun Burge, Mark Campion, Barbara Castle, Gabriel Chanan, Chris Church, Kerry Davies, Pat Dunmore, Susan Dunsmore, Elinor Evans, Kevin Fitzpatrick, Anna Freeman, Charlie Garratt, Alison Gilchrist, Gwyneth Goodhead, Sandra Goosey, Sara Harvey, Paul Henderson, Jayne Humm, Helen Hunter, Eddie Isles, Neil Jameson, Lina Jamoul, Bill Jenkins, David John, Chris Johnes, Mandy Jones, Avila Kilmurray, Sue King, Andi Lyden, Ruth Marks, Cindy Marsh, Alex Norman, Deborah Norman, Ben Reynolds, Jack Rothman, Ann Shabbaz, Steve Skinner, Clare Twelvetrees, Mel Witherden.

1 | Introduction: What is community work?

Many kinds of spontaneous and autonomous initiatives arise in communities, run in a voluntary capacity by the members of those communities. This book is, in large part, about the process of assisting and supporting such initiatives, essentially by another organisation or worker. There is no agreement among practitioners about the exact use of terms, and some phrases, especially 'community work' and 'community development' are used in different ways by different writers. The terms are also sometimes interchanged by the same writer or used rather loosely. I can, therefore, only say how I generally use the terms, and try to be consistent. Community work is also constantly evolving.

Willmott (1989) emphasises two main points about community. First, communities can either be of a geographical nature or be 'communities of interest', where the link between people is something other than locality, for instance, people suffering from a particular impairment. Second, there is both attachment and interaction between the members of a community. It's also important to understand, as Hoggett *et al.* state, that there are all kinds of competing subgroups and struggles between different sectors for power in a 'community'. Hoggett *et al.* also show that the more you try to examine 'community', the more slippery it becomes (see also Mayo, 1994, pp. 48–68; Henderson and Salmon, 1998). So the word 'community' in 'community work' largely needs to be seen as an adjective, describing a certain approach to social intervention (but see pp. 8–10 on this) rather than having the aim of 'creating community'.

For me, the best way to start thinking about community work (especially community development work) is to consider it as *the process of assisting people to improve their own communities by undertaking autonomous collective action.* Having said this, I use the term 'community work' mainly as an umbrella or 'overarching' phrase to cover, for instance: paid work; unpaid work; doing things for, or to benefit particular communities or groups; and helping

1

groups or communities to do things for themselves. I use other terms to describe specific approaches within what I now believe needs to be seen as the very 'broad church' of community work.

As is implied above, assisting communities to help themselves collectively requires, in many cases, paid workers. These workers are employed in a number of different guises by many organisations and have a range of job titles. Community work may also be carried out by: social workers, housing officers, clergy, adult educators or health workers – in addition to, or as part of, their 'normal' work.

The essence of professional (paid) community work (especially community development work) is to ensure, first, that people, as members of geographical or non-geographical communities get a better deal, and second, that, as far as possible, they bring this 'better deal' about themselves (largely through collective action), developing more skills and confidence in the process. The main rationale for employing staff to facilitate this process is twofold. First, a healthy society needs the active participation of its citizens – imposed solutions to problems without the involvement of their supposed beneficiaries just don't work well enough. Citizen participation is also vital as a means of holding politicians and policy-makers to account. Second, without assistance, many attempts by people to engage in collective action and other forms of participation and influence fail, especially in 'excluded' communities. Note, however, that while 'professional' community development work tends to be mostly directed at disadvantaged communities, the process of supporting local autonomous collective action can be, and is, applied in a wide range of other 'communities' too. For these reasons, if a society is seriously concerned to improve the quality of life for all citizens, ways need to be found of working to create, support and strengthen community groups and to ensure that they are effective, influential, inclusive, democratic and work for just ends.

Different approaches to community work

It is important to try to categorise the different approaches to community work because it is easy to lose our way. However, the 'ideal types' of community work discussed below do not describe exactly the messy reality of practice. Also, there are so many different dimensions to community work and so many things a worker needs to know that you really need a team of workers in order to have enough skills to do everything. However, we almost never have that 'luxury'. Each approach to community work is listed in Figure 1.1 in the form of a continuum. At one end of each continuum is one form of work, while its opposite (more or less) is at the other end. Workers can plot where they are on each continuum either in general, or for a particular piece of work. Most of the approaches described below are worked through in later chapters.

Figure 1.1 Different dimensions of community work

Community development work...................Social planning

Self-help or service approaches.................Influence approaches

Generic community work...........................Specialist community work

Concern about 'process'............................Concern about 'product'

The enabling or facilitating role of the worker................His/her organising role

Community work 'in its own right'..............Community work as an approach or attitude

Unpaid community work.............................Paid community work

---

Community development work 'versus' social planning

Community work, especially community development work, is best understood at neighbourhood level. However, the principles of community development work at that level apply in a number of other contexts, too (see, especially, Chapter 9). Neighbourhood community workers tend to operate in two main ways. The first is to help existing groups and to assist people to form new ones. This approach can most usefully be called *community development work,* and it is this method which is most unique to community work. Community development workers operate as facilitators with people in relation to what *those people* decide to become involved with, helping them realise *their* collective goals. The second main way in which a worker may operate is by initiating projects, liaising and working directly with service providers to sensitise them to the needs of specific communities, assisting them to improve services or alter policies. In this approach, the worker, to a greater or lesser degree, bypasses the community group, if one exists, in order to bring about change. I generally refer to this form of community

work as the *social planning approach*. While all community workers need to be able to work in both ways, some community work
jobs will involve more opportunities for community development
work and others more opportunities for social planning. Inevitably,
in a community work team, some staff will primarily be doing community development work and others, probably the manager, social
planning. There are also many forms of community work which
involve both community development work and social planning (see
Chapters 6 and 9). This applies particularly to partnership working, covered briefly at the end of this chapter and in more detail in
Chapter 8.

Self-help/service approaches and influence approaches

If we examine the role of the community group or organisation with
which the worker is working, we note that some of the community's needs can be met largely from the resources existing within the
community: play schemes, lunch clubs, voluntary visiting schemes,
coffee mornings, sports clubs, festivals. In these situations the group
is involved in a self-help or 'service' approach. Other needs can only
be met by modifying or changing the policies of organisations outside the community or by accessing resources from them. These needs
require 'influence' approaches, which can involve everything from
'consensual' work, through to 'contest' (see Chapter 7).

Generic and specialist community work

'*Generic*' community workers are able to work in relation to any
issue or sector – play, employment, leisure, housing – and with any
group – older people, women, disabled people – whatever kind of
agency they work for. However, service agencies often appoint what
can be called *specialist* community workers (though they usually
have other job titles) whose job is both to improve services and to
involve consumers or client groups in some way in this process. Thus,
in the past three decades in Britain there has been a growing emphasis
on 'specialist community work' by service agencies either with the
whole geographical community on a particular issue (for example,
health) or with a specific category of people (people with learning
difficulties, for instance) (see Chapter 9).

Process and product, expressive and instrumental groups

What is often called a 'process' goal (or even just 'process') is to do with changes in people's confidence, knowledge, technical skills or attitudes, or the development of an organisation. A 'product' goal is to do with the changed material situation – an improved housing maintenance programme or a successful play scheme. Both kinds of goals are important and are intertwined. Different situations tend to dictate whether process or product goals predominate. I was once working with a group to try to prevent a motorway from being built. In order to present evidence at the public enquiry a great deal of co-ordinated work had to be undertaken quickly. If 'process' had predominated and attention had been given to ensuring that the group members developed the necessary skills, the deadline would have been missed. It is often the case that a worker can use a 'facilitating' or 'enabling' approach when process goals are paramount, but uses an 'organising' approach when concerned with product.

Community development work is largely based on the idea that 'product' should be brought about by a process which ensures that the participants in the action have as much control as possible over all its aspects and that they acquire the ability to act themselves (individually and collectively) as a result. However, this approach usually only works if product goals are also met, since group members lose heart if they fail to achieve their concrete objectives. Therefore, in most situations workers have to attend to both kinds of goals.

Community groups which are only concerned with process (that is where the sole purpose of the group is the shared experience, the learning and other social benefits within it) are sometimes called 'expressive' groups. Expressive groups can be contrasted with 'instrumental groups' in which the main purpose is to achieve a 'product'. While all groups have expressive functions, some groups have virtually no instrumental functions. It is important for a worker to understand the main function of any particular group, since an instrumental group needs 'leaders' who can run meetings and organise action, as well as people who could obtain some benefit from being members but who might not contribute towards 'product'. If a worker is working with an instrumental group, it is vital that he or she encourages people to join the group who are prepared (or may be helped relatively easily to develop the skills) to take (instrumental) action, usually via a committee of some kind. Even with an expressive group, however, someone has to organise it, which requires instrumental skills.

The facilitating (or enabling) role and the organising role

The classic community development work role is that of enabler, guide, catalyst or facilitator where the worker goes at the pace of the group and assists its members to work out what they want to do and how to do it. This style of work is also sometimes called 'non-directive'. However, there are times when the worker takes a more directive, leadership or organising role within a group, either informally or even as the chair or secretary, usually because 'product' needs to predominate and because the group members may, at that time, lack the necessary motivation or skills. The worker may also change from less to more directive roles and back several times in one meeting.

Community work in its own right and community work as an attitude or approach

When a generic or specialist community worker is facilitating autonomous collective action in the community as his or her main job (or part of it), this can be called community (development) work 'in its own right'. However, schoolteachers, faith workers, shopkeepers, police officers, community centre caretakers, housing workers and other service providers may carry out their work 'in a community work way'. That is, they show respect to community members, seek to learn from them, try to take their concerns into account when doing their own jobs, and offer occasional advice or help. Thus, the central ideas (i.e. empowering individuals and groups, understanding the needs of others and taking these into account when actions are taken or policy is made) are not unique to community work.

Unpaid and paid community work

People who are active on an unpaid basis in their own communities, including elected representatives, often claim to be community workers. One difference between paid and unpaid community work can be that the unpaid workers are community leaders rather than facilitators. Such unpaid workers generally take roles in community groups such as chair and secretary. However, in Britain, some courses for 'volunteer' community workers or activists now encourage those volunteers to develop facilitation skills. And paid workers sometimes take organising roles, as we have seen. However, the paid community development worker really must have the skills to facilitate. The unpaid worker may be poorer without them, but they are not absolutely mandatory for running community groups. Also, paid workers are usually answerable to a manager or board and have terms of reference requiring them to do particular kinds of work, with the supports and sanctions which go with paid employment. These arrangements both legitimise the work of the paid worker and create expectations about standards of practice which mostly do not apply with unpaid self-selecting workers. A related point here is that it is possible to use 'community development' to describe the autonomous process by which community groups form, grow and act (mostly without any outside assistance) and to use 'community development *work*' to describe the professional activity of supporting this process. In the minds of lay people the two processes are often not separate.

Starting where people are: a paradox

A community worker on a council housing scheme was keen to set up a tenants' association to pressurise the council to repair the housing more effectively. Several tenants agreed to come to a meeting to discuss this. Nobody came. Then, some tenants asked the worker to help them set up a bingo group. While the tenants, presumably, wanted better housing, it looked as if they were not motivated, at that time, to take collective action to do anything about it. As community workers, we are often so enthusiastic about our own objectives for the community (and we can only do the job well if we *are* enthusiastic) that we fail to perceive that the community members do not share that enthusiasm. This mistake is easy to make, partly because community members will often tell us what they think we want to hear.

The paradox is that effective community development work can only take place if the members of the community take some responsibility. Yet, what community members want to do is often different from what community workers think they should do! Community workers who think the community has a particular need but find that, at a particular time, the community will not work to achieve it have three, not mutually exclusive choices. They can seek to meet the need themselves by taking an organising or social planning role. Or they can build up contacts and trust and 'sow seeds' until some community members are ready to 'own' what the worker thinks they should own. Finally, the worker can work with the community on priorities it identified but which were not his or hers.

The centrality of networking

Most models of community development work are based largely on an organisational paradigm, that is the idea of creating, supporting and working with definable community groups in order to achieve specific ends. Thus, most community development practitioners seek to create an 'organised community' with its own, often 'low-level' institutions which can act as agents for change, and do not try to build that vague thing 'community'. There is, nevertheless, something real, although very intangible, about a 'sense of community' (see also p. 1). Feelings of solidarity, sharing, etc. help make life worth living, especially when times are hard, and it is this which 'networks' address.

Sometimes, the real work of a committee gets done or the real impetus for a breakthrough is agreed in an informal chat outside a meeting. While these processes can lead to abuses of power, any good community worker creates and uses such opportunities to move things along, to 'test the water' for a new idea, to smooth a ruffled ego, and for many other purposes. Gilchrist (2004, pp. 28–86) describes what I now think of as the 'networking paradigm' of what community development and community development work are at least partly about.

Getting things done using the 'organisational' paradigm alone is difficult. Organisations have to be built and maintained, develop rules, gather resources, allocate roles, etc. The more complex they are, the more bureaucratic they become. This formality makes it difficult for them to negotiate with each other, especially when there is a change of situation for which there is no precedent, agreed procedures or staff available. Experienced community workers spend much time creating links both between local people and between them and a range of organisations, helping them deal effectively with each other. This 'networking', which community workers both engage in and facilitate, takes place, at least in part, at a semi-informal level, with individuals meeting, to a degree, as individuals, when they may not be operating entirely in their formal roles. If you can get two individuals from different networks chatting informally about an issue, in the pub, on the train, or in the works canteen, there develops a greater flexibility about their interaction, as a result of which obstacles to getting things done begin to shift. This shift may be accompanied, or indicated by the sharing of a joke or a personal story. Shared visions can also begin to emerge from such interactions – they don't often come from formal meetings as the box below shows. You also know you're getting somewhere if the body language of one of you mirrors the other's.

The 'stupid' questions

I was once at a committee meeting where a senior manager who was to run the meeting failed to turn up. As a consequence the lower-level staff talked informally about the issues in question and dared ask the 'stupid' questions which they had not voiced beforehand. At the end of the meeting a member said that this was the first time she had really understood the issues in question and now knew what we were supposed to be doing! The group went on to agree a course of action to which all were committed, I think, because of the open and honest exploration in a relaxed atmosphere.

Networking results in accidental and unpredictable outcomes and could be called 'planned serendipity'. According to Gilchrist, networking is about operating on 'the edge of 'chaos' because networks are by definition, unorganised. But it is on this 'edge' that change begins to happen. Other key points Gilchrist makes in relation to networking are that people's sense of collective identity is constructed within informal groups and relationships. Networks cope relatively well with contradiction and complexity, are a way of ensuring critical opinion is expressed and can create a needed safe space to discuss contentious issues. Co-operation in and between networks relies on persuasion and reciprocity, not coercion and contracts. However, you can't control networks, and they can undermine formal authority. Half the work in all organisations is done through networks and is invisible to management. In particular, networks are very relevant for multi-agency working and provide space 'behind the scenes', where people feel free to say things. Networking is a kind of 'bridging social capital' offering the beneficial 'weak ties' which we all seem to benefit from personally and professionally. Moreover, networking across boundaries helps people gain useful insights from other areas/fields and can result in the creation of alliances across disciplines. Additionally, if a network has provided an experience in the past of good collaboration, there may be more resilience when there are deep-seated conflicts.

The existence of effective networks is probably a prerequisite for the development of effective community groups and projects. Networks are like the clouds of pollen which ensure plants bear fruit. However, you need to be strong to create time to network, because today's emphasis on targets has resulted, to some extent, in the spontaneity and flexibility being squeezed out of community work activities. Make sure you network systematically.

The problem of invisibility and demonstrating effectiveness

It is not easy to observe the painstaking work, often behind the scenes, which has resulted in a community group becoming effective. Consequently, it is difficult to demonstrate, to potential funders, for instance, that community work makes a difference. Community workers don't do the development of the occupation any favours when they emphasise that the community itself has undertaken a project without also indicating that, in order to facilitate it, the worker's role was critical. In order to demonstrate effectiveness it is often necessary to make potential sponsors 'walk the streets' with you. That is, you have to take them to see effective projects and schemes and then carefully talk through with them the reasons why the particular scheme was successful. Community workers need to develop the skills of making community work processes more visible. Also, more research is needed to indicate connections between community development work and increased voluntary action and other outcomes (see CDF/CLG, 2006).

Start–stop . . . start and sustainability

Many community work projects are short-term: three years at most. It will be six months before the project is 'up and running'. It will be another six before much is delivered. And after another year and a half the staff will be looking around for new jobs, with the better staff leaving first! Then, several of the community-run initiatives supported by the staff run down, leaving a disillusioned community.

Three years later, a similar initiative repeats the process in the same area! Moreover, some individuals are excellent at their jobs, others less so. Yet others may be temporarily ineffective through illness or domestic problems. Once in post, the worker may also have to seek to redefine their job description because it was not carefully enough thought through. For all these reasons, community work needs to become strategic, long-term, appropriately funded and integral to the mainstream work of the organisations which deliver it. In Britain, while there has been good progress over the last few years, there is still limited understanding of the above points.

What is community work for?

Values and attitudes

Community work, especially community development work, can be described, first, as a set of values and, second, as a set of approaches linked to those values. The values are to do with justice, respect, democracy, love, empowerment and 'getting a better deal' for people who, in some way, are collectively 'missing out' (see FCWTG, 1999, 2001; SCCD, 2001, for more on values and occupational standards). The values of some community workers seem to be primarily political. Other workers come from pacifism or religion (see Kelly, 1993; Kelly and Sewell, 1996). Yet others seem to come at it from a concern merely to 'do good', for instance, or, in the case of Alinsky (1969, 1972), a concern to make the existing system work better for 'the poor'. In real life, there are many pressures and constraints on a worker. So, whatever their ideology, effective practitioners need to select pragmatically those actions which seem most likely to help the members of a particular community get a better deal for themselves and become more confident and skilled, and which also improve local government or other systems for community benefit. Having said this, however, socialist and feminist perspectives, to which we now turn, have had a great influence on community work thought in Britain and left a substantial legacy.

The contribution of socialism and feminism to British community work

In the early 1970s, a number of research reports came to the conclusion that the main cause of disadvantage was the capitalist system.

These reports drew heavily on a Marxist analysis of society to explain the persistence of poverty. It followed (to some community workers, at least) that, if you were seriously interested in alleviating disadvantage, you needed to work to 'abolish capitalism'. This analysis, together with the sharp growth of community work jobs in the early 1970s in a liberal policy environment gave the impetus for a mini-explosion of attempts, by some, to become a Marxist or socialist community worker. At that time the prescriptions of socialism were largely: nationalisation (at least to some degree) of the main means of production distribution and exchange; worker (and, to a degree, 'community') control; a high taxing state; redistribution and an extended role for the state in service provision. The key characteristic of most of the community work approaches to practice flowing from this analysis was 'oppositional' work, since one was seeking, in however small a way, to abolish an oppressive class-based system. This could include: campaigns, demonstrations and sit-ins; links with trades unions to build more power for change; creating federations of community groups to develop more power for tenants or residents; engaging in political education and propaganda.

However, if you were working, for a Local Authority on a deprived council scheme, how could you gain the space to work in 'oppositional' ways, whatever these actually were? (Many community workers are (still) 'told what to do' by rather directive employers.) Also, since a worker has to seek to achieve specific objectives, evidence was needed that working in 'oppositional', rather than 'other' ways, was more effective at achieving these objectives. Finally, community workers could not reasonably be called such if they did not work, at least to some degree, to the agenda of community members, many of whom would not have been interested in 'oppositional' work.

None of these theoretical problems was, I believe, effectively dealt with by 'socialist' community workers. Also, between 1978 and 1997 there was great governmental emphasis (under Margaret Thatcher and John Major) on competitive capitalism and individual entrepreneurship. Many nationalised industries had been privatised (and the Labour Party which came to power in 1997 did not reverse this general approach). The power of local councils and the resources available for them to spend were reduced, and there was also widespread recognition that local government could sometimes be wasteful, oppressive and bureaucratic. Scope for 'socialist' community work became even more limited. Additionally, it came to be recognised by government that the public, private and community sectors all had to work together to bring about benefits for excluded areas and people. Communities began to be asked for their views, however inexpertly this was done.

Partly as a reaction to the apparently 'macho' and materialistic world view of some 'Marxist/socialist' community workers, from the mid-1970s, several women involved in community work began drawing attention to the exploitation of women by men. Such 'feminist' perspectives also took community work thinking beyond gender relations alone and into issues to do with 'caring' and personal growth (see Dominelli, 2006). Many of these ideas from feminism were accepted (in theory at least) by 'socialist' community workers (and others) and, for a time, it was possible to identify people who seemed to fit the model of a socialist/feminist community worker in that they consciously tried to combine insights from both these perspectives in their practice. Some were 'zealots' who seemed to place ideology above the experience and constraints of practice. Others combined a commitment to their ideology with an ability to act pragmatically, recognising that you had to achieve benefits in a relatively short time for the people with whom and for whose benefit you were working. Yet other workers, who did not start from a socialist/feminist analysis, also took note of such insights.

A wider concern with equality

By the mid-1980s, the 'oppression' of women, ethnic minorities, older people, gay men, lesbians, disabled people and others was firmly on the community work agenda as it was increasingly recognised that certain people are systematically denied opportunities both by the way public and private organisations work and by personal prejudice. From then on, many local authorities (in particular) developed equal opportunities policies and engaged staff, some of whom were once (or thought of themselves as) community workers in order to extend and implement such policies. By about 1990, those community workers who would have been associated with a socialist/feminist approach to practice had tended to adopt as their focus a burning concern to fight against inequality, discrimination and injustice and to build the power of oppressed groups. The initially narrow 'socialist' class analysis had been replaced by a wide-ranging commitment to combat all forms of discrimination and exploitation. So, the inheritors of what can perhaps be called the 'socialist and feminist tradition' of community work now sometimes find themselves working on equality issues in relation to a range of excluded or oppressed groups in the public, voluntary and to a lesser extent the private sectors. However, community workers whose underlying political ideology, if they consciously have one, is not 'socialist/feminist' have generally also taken on board this 'equality' issue, and it is now part of mainstream British community work theory.

The ultimate paradox is that some aspects of a Marxist analysis are, in my view, increasingly relevant today. The global market has meant that, while capitalism has ensured that many prosper beyond their wildest dreams, many others seem destined to have poor (or no) jobs, poor health, poor education and a life of poverty and in some cases oppression (e.g. asylum seekers enslaved into prostitution). As the majority are not badly off, they do not vote for significant redistribution, and prospective governments advocating this would not get elected. This is not to say that the answer is to seek to abolish the global market, nor that nothing is ever done to alleviate poverty and oppression – the answers are not simple.

Society's institutions and the individuals within them tend to develop systems and cultures which reinforce negative attitudes to: 'scroungers', 'disaffected' young people, ethnic minority people, women (in some situations), disabled people, older people. The economic position of 'excluded' people, together with these cultural forces and expectations, also often creates a kind of 'learned helplessness' which prevents them from developing positive self-images and envisioning for themselves a better world where they can succeed rather than fail. Thus, action is needed at different levels and in a range of ways to counteract these economic, social, cultural and psychological processes which produce and perpetuate systematic oppression, exclusion and powerlessness. An understanding of such processes is, in my view, essential for effective community work practice, though the opportunities to address them at field level are, of course, limited.

The value and effects of community work

Little is written about the effects of community work, but a picture of its value is now beginning to emerge.

Individual change

Being involved in (voluntary) community action can help some people grow enormously and lead enriched lives, benefiting not only their community but also their career. Additionally, there is now evidence that people who are part of strong networks have less heart disease and generally recover more quickly from highly stressful situations, than those who do not. However, the direct positive effects from engaging in community action probably mainly occur to the small numbers of people who participate in it. In addition, people often lose money by being involved in community groups; they take unpaid leave or subsidise the group, for instance. Running a group sometimes causes breakdowns, burnout and marital stress. Being involved in community action often causes a person to look at the world in a new way – for example, a woman beginning to question her role as wife and mother – an important but sometimes traumatic process.

However, community work and community action help to spread the idea, by demonstration, that people can become involved in doing things themselves. When people initiate a project, it is likely that they got the idea from someone else. People who are involved in community action probably also provide models for their children, who later become involved in similar activities. But these changes are often indirect, long-term and difficult to measure. A linked point is that no one piece of community action should be viewed in isolation.

Complex outcomes

When I was a fieldworker, several years' work had been undertaken by my predecessor to help establish a carnival committee, within which were several able community leaders. By the time of my arrival, some of these leaders were aware that many other community needs required attention. I encouraged them to think about these, and two of them subsequently became leaders of other community groups and left the carnival committee, which declined somewhat. In encouraging these leaders I had probably contributed to the decline of the carnival, which I had not anticipated.

Community groups can and do achieve significant objectives. But these changes are often limited, and many groups die before achieving much. A dispassionate analyst would probably conclude, not only that the efforts put in far exceed the concrete achievements, but also that not many members of community groups develop personally either. But are there other achievements and why is it that community workers feel so strongly that collective action is good? One answer is as follows. There are often some positive outcomes which are not intended and which are not connected in the minds of most people with the existence of a particular group. Jim became chairman of a parent-teacher association (PTA). At the same time, two students doing practical work with me started a youth club and, when they were due to leave, they found that he was willing to take over. He later started running a junior football team too. The PTA had provided a way in for him, first to fulfil himself more, and second to contribute to the community. More research is needed in order to distinguish such outcomes and the wider effects of community development work (see CDF/CLG, 2006).

Community development work encourages at least some people to believe that they can act, that they can cause positive change. Of the lessons learned by the participants in community action, perhaps the most important are new attitudes, new political perspectives and a broader understanding of how the world works. Grace, a single parent, told me that, since our project had been running, she had learned to stand her ground with the housing department worker and no longer let her walk into the house at will. The carnival committee ran a reasonable carnival for a few years, as a result of which the area appeared on the front page of the local paper for positive reasons rather than because it was a 'debtors' haven'. This must have done much to boost the self-esteem of residents, possibly giving some of them more hope that their life would get better. Goleman (1996, 1998) singles out 'hope' as a key factor influencing people's ability to make the most of their life chances.

Changing policies?

Pressure from community groups alone does not seem to induce a governmental organisation to change a policy completely, though such pressure can help to modify one, especially if community groups forge alliances with other organisations which have greater influence. But community groups also have a longer-term effect. Through running playgroups for thirty years or so in Britain, the pre-school playgroups movement was influential in affecting thinking about play. Also, campaigns against damp in council housing and campaigns for more women's refuges, though often unsuccessful in individual cases, resulted in recognition that certain types of house construction are faulty, and that there is an enormous amount of domestic violence. Similarly, the incorporation of equal opportunities policies in many organisations and also in law, in Britain, has been the consequence, in particular, of campaigns from the women's and black movements. Thus, the major outcomes of community action are often their long-term effects on the climate of opinion and on subsequent legislation or service provision rather than their immediate concrete results.

Evidence-based theory

Putnam (2000) has produced considerable evidence to show that, where there are strong social networks and a wide range of voluntary associations, there is: less crime, better health, more wealth, a better educationally qualified population and many other 'good' things. Clearly, community workers strengthen networks, facilitate the entry of people into community groups and assist in the creation of more (and more effective) local organisations. These networks and organisations can also be thought of as 'social capital'. This is, in summary, 'the capacity of individuals and communities to act directly and indirectly, in a range of ways to influence their surroundings and circumstances for the better, gaining personal benefits, including skills and useful connections, in the process'. Chanan (2003) also produces evidence to indicate that the building of social capital is a prerequisite for the success of neighbourhood regeneration programmes. That is, the existence of locally run organisations, 'staffed' by skilled, knowledgeable and 'network-rich' volunteers, is necessary if the large neighbourhood regeneration programmes are to work effectively and be sustained (see Chapter 10).

Conclusion

The persistence of disadvantage is not merely due to the lack of resources allocated to disadvantaged neighbourhoods. It is also due, in industrialised countries, to housing, education, social services and other programmes not being joined up and there being so many rules and formal procedures that the service deliverers are so restricted in what they can do that they cannot act flexibly to meet social need. The bringing of people together in local partnerships with service providers (see Chapter 8), facilitated by community workers or others, creates an interface between such service providers and the local community which at its best, enables problems to be ameliorated. Community development work is basic in all this, because normally, informed and sustained participation by local people in such partnerships only happens (at least, in disadvantaged areas) when they grow into that through engaging in small-scale activity (e.g. the road safety campaign, the 'litter pick' or the summer play scheme) first. The structures, networks and new accountabilities created in the development and regeneration process also give legitimacy to the community workers who, sometimes via local partnerships, sometimes out of their own initiative, create new projects (social planning) 'bend' existing programmes or find ways around barriers to local improvement (see also Chapters 6 and 10).

Points to ponder

1. Do you agree that the core of community work is 'assisting people to improve their own communities by undertaking autonomous collective action'?
2. What do you believe community work is for?
3. How important should political ideology be in community work?

Further reading

Alinsky (1972) *Rules for Radicals*.
CDF/CLG (2006) *The Community Development Challenge* (this important publication covers many of the theoretical points discussed in this chapter).
Corkey and Craig (1978) 'Community Work or Class Politics'.
Dominelli (2006) *Women and Community Action*.
Gilchrist (1995) *Community Development and Networking*.
Rothman (1976) 'Three Models of Community Organization Practice' (the all-time classic community work theory article).

2 | Planning for effective community work

Community work intervention needs to be carefully planned. It can involve the establishment of a project team of four staff, to run for five years, or one worker in an existing agency, or establishing a comprehensive community work programme in a city or a region. There are also differences between the employment of staff in a statutory as opposed to a non-statutory agency or by a community partnership. This chapter initially discusses setting up the kind of four-person community work team described above, then describes how individual workers, once in post, can work out what to focus on. Finally, it considers 'evaluation'.

Designing the intervention

Pre-start

In some cases, a project is started after a community needs analysis has been completed, which, if it is done well, provides a solid basis for the initiative. Such an analysis can also be considered by agencies and community members, which can lead to wider ownership for the intervention. More often, though, this luxury does not exist. Either way, the most important thing about project design is knowing what you want to do, how you intend to go about it and how this will produce desired outcomes. That is, you need a 'theory of change'. In reality, project design is often 'funding led' and happens hurriedly, because bids for money may only be made for a limited period of time, for instance. Also, because funding from external sources for community work offers the opportunity of injecting more resources into an area, the Local Authority, for example, may support a project without its officers and members understanding the implications. Such mismatches in understanding often result in unproductive conflict later on, when the outcomes turn out to be different from what those sponsors expected.

Unless you clarify several issues when you start, there will be many problems: you may have under-budgeted; key agencies or sectors of the community may not be 'on board'; or you may not be paying enough money to get the quality of staff you need. These issues can be more complicated when a local community partnership is running the project, since the managers are also beneficiaries and, in addition, may have no experience of running organisations and managing staff. It is vital initially (and on a continuing basis) to explain to potential stakeholders (e.g. relevant voluntary and statutory bodies, community groups, funders and potential future funders) what the initiative is expected to achieve and the way it will run, in order to give everybody a chance to think about the implications. Ideally, of course, a project needs a long-term development plan, building on any previous work, and this can grow out of carefully thought-through project design. However, producing such a plan in fine detail 'pre-start' can be a waste of effort. This is because, as workers on the ground will have particular aptitudes, different workers will work in different ways. Also, they will need to develop their own networks and gather some information for themselves in order to 'own' the work. Getting such a plan right also requires resources up front, which are often not available. So the 'pre-start' plan may have to be fairly general, but still convincing!

It is normally useful to explain to those community leaders (or groups) what the initiative is for and to involve them in its development, but, think about what you will do if they don't want it! In some communities, the population has been 'consulted to death', and has never seen any results. They may be suspicious of the authorities, especially if they had been involved in a project which 'went wrong' some years earlier. Moreover, explaining community work to the uninitiated can be difficult, especially if there is no organised group to explain it to. Communities mostly do not ask for community workers and may not understand how community work can help them until they have seen it working in practice. Finally, if it is not certain that the project will go ahead, expectations can be raised and then later dashed. In many initiatives, therefore, any community consultation work has to come *after* the staff are appointed. But then you run the risk of being accused of 'parachuting in' with no regard to local wishes. This is a paradox which is almost impossible to resolve.

Some initiatives now do come from the community itself, however, which sets up a different dynamic. Local people may feel they know and speak accurately for the community, when, in reality, they are likely to have a partial view only. It is vitally important for the worker in such a situation to create the space to do their own community consultation or profile, which may not be easy to 'sell' to the community-led committee.

Developing the project 'proper'

Commit the results of any 'pre-start' work or research to paper, linking the rationale for the project with the specific methods of work, expected outcomes and how these will be monitored, drawing attention to any important implications or likely problems. Consideration should also be given, if possible, as to what will happen after the first tranche of funding runs out. In this whole process you will probably find that certain key players don't want you there. They may want the money themselves; they may have been trying to get resources for that kind of work for ages; your organisation may have a particular image which is not popular locally; you may have alienated them by not consulting them early; they may be sceptical about community work or just unable to understand it; elected representatives may only want you there if they can control the project. So, be prepared for opposition and how you might handle it. You may, in the end, just have to go ahead in the face of opposition and seek to build bridges later. (I have had to do this several times when setting up community work projects.) Note, too, that undertaking project design will take at least a day per week for about a year. But your employer, if you have one, is not likely to understand this and may expect you to carry out many other tasks too, thus preventing you from giving proper attention to project design – a recipe for disaster, later.

Getting started

You may want to form a committee or partnership to run or oversee the project, composed of people who: understand what it is you will be doing; are well respected; can get more support for you; and represent you in the 'corridors of power'. Consider the premises from which you want to work, their availability and cost, as well as what you want to put in them. (This may well be the most time-consuming thing you have to do at this stage.) You will need to: begin to design job descriptions; set up financial systems; decide how you are going to recruit, who should be involved and what interview processes you will use. (If local people are to be involved in recruitment, ensure they fully understand the principles of 'equal opportunities recruitment' and the processes you will be using. If you don't, you could hit problems.) How will professional supervision be provided? Things like organising headed notepaper, designing a logo, developing a brochure, getting a website going can also be extremely time-consuming.

Getting ownership

If a sense of ownership is not developed early with potential future funders, you will be competing with all the other schemes clamouring for their attention later on. Having said this, some funders do not want a 'relationship', in order to preserve objectivity perhaps, but these are a minority. In order to win the support of the major players, especially future funders, try to take them to see similar projects. Prepare such visits carefully, work out in advance what it is you want them to conclude (i.e. how such a project could help the funder achieve *their* objectives), brief your hosts accordingly and ensure that the visitors discuss and reflect on the experience afterwards. Funders also need to have realistic expectations and understand that the community development process is slow, the gains modest and the problems many. At the end of a financial year, they may also want some money spent hurriedly. So, it is always a good idea to have a few small projects 'up one's sleeve'.

You will probably also want the most influential stakeholders on your management or advisory board to ensure that their sense of ownership, once developed, continues to benefit your project. Local residents, as committee members, may also need continuing assistance to develop their understanding of what the project is about; they can benefit from visits to similar projects, just as funders can. In community work, you are on a journey, where you broadly know where you want to get to, but you are not sure exactly how you will get there, and you cannot predict what you will meet on the way. What you attempt may not work and then you will have to reconsider. You will need to take calculated risks. But some bits *will* work. If you monitor things well, you will be able to work out which bits work best (and these may be different in different places). Then you can build on them but only by constant review. All stakeholders need to understand this.

Some practical details

Give attention early on to: developing office procedures; setting up filing and recording systems; keeping appropriate accounts; ensuring there is adequate insurance for the office, mastering employment law, etc. If there is, say, a four-person project, including a secretary, it is often wise to employ the project leader first, followed, as soon as possible, by the secretary, in order to ensure such systems are in place. However, funders often don't want to pay for administrators/secretaries/book-keepers; yet these functions, if undertaken well, make a team doubly effective. So, if you are getting funding from different sources, you will need to seek to 'top-slice' the grant to cover such costs, including management time. In some places small organisations collaborate to buy in book-keeping and other support services, and this can sometimes work well. Funders also tend to want to fund innovative projects and are less interested in supporting a project which has proved its worth over, say, three years and is now about to close! Part of the trick may, therefore, be to design your (new) application so that the project appears innovative.

Project costs

Think about the costs of fire and health and safety regulations, disability access, water charges, rubbish collection, rent and office maintenance, all of which can add up if you are not prepared for them. I have found that, in order to cover everything well you need the 'support budget' – that is, everything except the salaries of professional staff (i.e. not secretaries, book-keepers, cleaners, etc.) – to come to about half the salary costs of the professional staff. I suggest aiming for this figure even if you can't reach it in reality. These issues crop up with all projects, whether there is one staff member or several.

Contact making

General principles

However well a project has been prepared, the workers, once in post, have the task of deciding exactly what to do, even though their general focus will probably have been determined by their job descriptions. As community workers, our job is not primarily to spend money, already allocated, to create buildings, or manage service personnel to achieve specified outputs under our control.

That is, we cannot *make* things happen. Unless we take care to cultivate a sense of ownership in others (with local people and professionals) about what we want *and want them* to achieve, we may find that the natural conservatism and resistance to change of many people will turn into opposition. Initially at least, we cannot know who has the time, inclination, resources and connections needed to undertake a piece of work unless we are systematically making and remaking contacts at all levels.

It is normally best, first of all, to make contact with those who we think will be of like mind, but to meet, later, with people who are not, in order to prepare us for the obstacles we may encounter. When making contact, be clear, first of all, why you are in contact with the other person. Then work out what effect you want to have and therefore what image you want to present and what style you want to adopt (relaxed, challenging, organised, helpful?). Consider, too, how much you will tell people. Some people won't want to see you until you have worked out a plan. On the other hand, you really need a relationship with them, irrespective of your specific project plans. Either way, communicate why you are going prior to the meeting. When in a meeting, remember to pitch your use of language appropriately. I was once on an interview panel, and one otherwise excellent candidate just chatted to us in answer to specific questions. That might have been appropriate in the staff canteen, but not in a formal interview. She didn't get the job, partly because we judged her unable to decide on the appropriate language style for that situation.

As community work could be described as a kind of permanent innovation, we always need to be on the lookout for new ideas, which tends to occur when we are networking. Here is an example. One day a probation officer dropped in for a chat at the neighbourhood centre I ran. We arranged a more formal meeting with his team during which they expressed concern that probationers in the locality had to travel a long way to report to the probation office. After further discussion we arranged to make our centre available once a week for the probation department to use as a reporting centre.

The 'rules' of contact making and networking

By trial and error, I found that the most important principles or rules to follow (whether with professionals or community members) are:

Rule 1: Never pass up the opportunity to make or renew a contact – unless you are fairly sure that to do so will damage another area of work. Also, it is not usually a good idea to ask a new contact for something you want at the first meeting. Concentrate more on finding out how they see the situation and where their self-interest is, thus developing the relationship. You may later be able to relate what you want to do to their self-interest.

Rule 2: Consider what impression you are making. How we dress, for instance, is a statement about ourselves, and people make assumptions about us from it. Consider whether you are having the desired effect on the other person. Punctuality is vital. People may write us off before we start if we turn up late for the first meeting. Equally, people will not take us seriously if we agree to do something and fail to do it. Say well in advance if you are not able to honour a commitment. Be credible.

Rule 3: Learn how to listen and observe. By 'listening' I am referring not only to taking in what someone is actually saying but also to understanding what may only be implied. Is the person just saying what they think you want to hear? What are they conveying about their relationships with others? Most important of all, for initial contacts with community members, what are they conveying about both their motivation and their ability to take organisational responsibility? If possible, be aware of local and 'community' politics prior to developing (or early on when carrying out) your contact making plan. Find out about the different factions. Remember, too, that there are jealousies between departments and organisations, especially within Local Authorities. Picking up on these differences early may help prevent you from putting your foot in it later. At neighbourhood level, be aware of the views of the local councillors. They can help or hinder you greatly.

Active listening means speaking too, since we will often want to steer the other person round to discuss matters *we* want to cover. It also involves assessing or interpreting what somebody has said, perhaps tentatively at first. Because, in this first phase, you are learning and making relationships, you probably won't want to disagree much with your contacts. But, in the end, you can't be 'all things to all people', and you may, on occasion, have to make a point clearly, or at least explain what you can and cannot do, or what is unrealistic for them to expect. Do not give false information about what community work can achieve because you will be creating future problems.

We cannot perceive others accurately unless we are in touch with our own feelings. Do we find this person boring? Do we find we become angry when he or she is talking? Do we feel threatened? It is also important to try to understand what the other person is feeling, to put ourselves in their place. Whatever we want from a meeting (any meeting) – information, a relationship, a decision, money – we are more likely to get it if we can empathise in this way. Notice not only how you affect other people, but also how they in turn react to other parties. At an important meeting I once held with a county councillor, the assistant county clerk looked bored. That indicated something about the relationship between the councillor and that officer, a useful point for me to remember at a later date perhaps.

Notice where people sit, how they arrange their rooms, what newspaper they read, what pictures they have on the wall. Neighbourhood community workers also need to notice what is going on locally. If people appear with theodolites, ask them what they are doing. Know which shops are closing, which houses are vacant, which planning applications are going to the council. You need a systematic information gathering system too. Read the local paper and other relevant ephemera, e.g. church magazines. A community worker operating in a community with a massive drugs problem would need to learn about that scene. We also need to guard against becoming too parochial. Workers doing similar jobs in other parts of the country will have discovered many ways of dealing with situations which you are meeting for the first time; find ways of learning from them.

Rule 4: Create opportunities for establishing personal contacts. For neighbourhood workers the rule could be rephrased: *Walk, don't ride.* Walk around the area regularly, but in a planned way, e.g. during fine weather or summer evenings. If you are not working at the neighbourhood level, put yourself in situations where you have time to meet people informally but in a systematic way.

Rule 5: In order to get, we must give. People give best if they get something in return. It may be useful to encourage them to talk first about what interests them: their work, their hobbies, sport, a recent holiday, their family. It can also be useful to learn about the interests of the person you are meeting beforehand so that you have a good chance of creating some rapport quickly by mentioning certain topics. You know you are getting somewhere if you find yourself swapping stories (about virtually anything) because that means people are opening up a bit. Most importantly, we need to be genuinely interested in the people we are meeting, and their work. When

I was a neighbourhood worker I contacted a local head teacher, explained my role and made tactful suggestions that he and his staff might get more involved in the community. Nothing doing! Much later he complained to me that some parents would not visit the school on open evenings. I eventually asked whether he thought they would come to our neighbourhood centre if a teacher was available there. He became interested, and eventually an agreement was made to use it. Only when I could help him was he prepared to listen to me. *Rule 6: Do not believe everything people say.* A member of a community group would sometimes tell me privately that they were going to resign soon, but never did. While they were talking to me it might have been their full intention to resign because they were particularly aware at that moment of the frustrations of being a group member. But at other times they would have looked at their membership of the group in different ways and become more aware of the disadvantages of leaving; so, when it came to the crunch, they did not resign. Store such information until it is corroborated by information from other sources or until intentions do indeed become actions. People often avoid telling the truth to save face when under pressure, or will assert the opposite of what is actually the case because they want to convince us that they 'always consult widely', for instance. This also raises the issue of at what point we should challenge people if we believe they are not telling the truth. My inclination is not to challenge unless it is vital.

A community profile (or needs analysis)

The main purpose of a community profile is to discover things about the 'community' in order to help you to act strategically to benefit it. You may also find the information useful for a funding application or, later, for an evaluation report. The easiest way to start thinking about a community profile is with reference to a geographical community. Some community profiles relate to small neighbourhoods, others to whole counties. Yet others may relate to a 'community of need'. Nevertheless, whatever the context, the principles covered here can be adapted to most situations. Two types of information are required for a community profile: hard and soft. Hard information consists of quantified data and can be obtained from official reports such as the census. Soft information is more subjective and consists largely of opinions.

In the process of undertaking a community profile, we make contact with many people, and some of those contacts are likely to be the starting-point for action. We may discover that several local people are concerned about the lack of play space and are prepared to do something about it, for example. The community profile stage may then overlap with the action stage. We may also be under external and internal pressure to get on quickly with the job and, therefore, to skimp on the community profile. When I started out as a neighbourhood worker, I worked largely from the basis of contacts left by my predecessor and never stood back, reviewed my overall strategy or systematically developed my own contacts. I made many mistakes as a result, such as setting up a tenants' association which nobody wanted! I also recommend that workers do community profiles themselves rather than bringing in consultants, because of the contacts and knowledge you gain along the way.

Gathering information in the worker's own agency and in other organisations

It is useful to start by discovering the views of one's colleagues, the management committee (if there is one) and staff in related departments and their expectations of you, the worker. At the same time it is necessary to read agency records, and to look at relevant reports and planning documents. If we know how the area has been perceived over time (and what people's pet projects are or were), we should be able to predict more accurately how our own agency and others will react to our proposed work. We should also know whether a certain approach has been tried and failed.

Planning sections of Local Authorities will often make reports and plans available. Contact such officials personally – they are usually pleased to provide such information. Obtain from agency staff their perceptions of needs in the area: who holds power, who to go through to get things done, who may be sympathetic to your approach, who you should get on your side. Talk to a range of people from different levels and varying perspectives. At the same time, it is necessary to ask people if they can suggest further contacts in other organisations or in the target community.

Gathering hard information

It is normally useful to know the size and age structure of the population and other demographic data. Some of this information will be in the census which should be in the public library. It is useful, also, to be able to work out trends, whether the black ethnic minority population, for example, is increasing, which may mean referring to previous censuses as well. It could also help to know how the figures for sickness or infant mortality compare with the area as a whole and with the country as a whole. However, the information may not be compiled in such a way as to break down in the way that you require it. Figures, relating to unemployment or health, perhaps, may cover a different area from that with which the project is concerned.

An understanding of the socio-economic structure is useful in analysing the needs and problems of a community – the type of prevailing industry, where people tend to work, what kind of pay they get, whether local employers are contracting or expanding, unemployment rates, the nature of deprivation (e.g. level of child poverty, numbers of disabled people). It can be useful to find out whether the housing is 'social', privately rented or owner-occupied, its age, the degree to which houses contain basic facilities, patterns of overcrowding and of multi-occupation. Information about the Local Authority's housing policies may also be useful – their allocation and transfer policies, whether they are privatising council housing, for example, or what their role is in relation to homelessness. We should use our own initiative too. School rolls may provide information about the child population, and it might be possible to find a head teacher who can provide information that reveals year-to-year changes which the census does not.

Gaining softer information

Find out which councillors represent the neighbourhood and who the 'heavyweight' councillors are. How strong are the various political parties on the council? Much of this information can be obtained from the town hall information office, reading the local paper and from talking with politicians, officials or activists who have been around for a long time. It is useful to observe a council meeting or read past council minutes. Information also needs to be obtained (ideally through personal contact) about agencies which are located in or which serve the area. On the statutory side, these include: health centres, police, youth centres and public transport. Non-statutory and community organisations include: voluntary organisations employing professionals, such as the National Society for the Prevention of Cruelty to Children; commercial organisations, such as working men's clubs, and commercially run opportunities for leisure-time pursuits, such as bingo halls; faith groups and political organisations; tenants' associations and playgroups; traditional organisations, such as the Women's Royal Voluntary Service, and organisations for disabled people (which may be part of a national structure); local regeneration partnerships; city/county wide organisations such as arts groups, play associations, business development forums or community safety partnerships. This information can be discovered in a library and by asking around. In Britain, councils of voluntary service often have directories of voluntary organisations, too. And buy a street map.

Get a feel of what it is like to be a local resident. Travel around a bit by bus or approach estate agents about accommodation. Also, take advantage of what comes naturally to you, personally, in contact making. One colleague, a keen churchgoer, built up contacts by regularly attending church. Another, a 'youth community worker', stresses that, when working with young people, it is important to explore 'hidden worlds'. Go to the places the young people go, at a time they go there (behind the castle, by the boatshed, on the allotments, on the 'Harbour Road', late at night). Consider issues to do with safety, too, and not just your own physical safety. Think carefully before putting yourself in a situation where you could be accused of harassment. You should let colleagues know where you will be, ensuring you take a mobile phone with you, or even telling the police in advance, if the situation was potentially a dangerous one. A connected issue is how much you tell people about who your employers are, assuming you are employed. Some workers take the view that it is not necessary to spell out your role, and that you can establish better relationships with local people if you do not say you're from the Local Authority, for instance. I suppose, in some informal situations, e.g. chatting in a pub or at a public event, this is just about OK. But my view is that, as you are there for a purpose and your aim is to act with others to improve conditions in the community, it is usually best to come out pretty early, if not immediately, with the reason for making contact.

Try to discover what the people you meet think are the needs of the community or the key issues which should be addressed. What is their position in their organisation, if they are in one, and how much influence do they have? What are they touchy about? What was tried in the past and what was the result? Who have they got good contacts with? Who do they respect/not respect? It is vital to have such 'soft' information, because, when you want to make something happen, acting on assumptions which turn out to be faulty can mean the failure of your project. Conscientiously record the information you obtain, because the next stage is to try to marry it all together and develop an analysis which will lead to action. We should also be clear from the beginning why we are doing a community profile and the kinds of things we expect to be drawing conclusions about, though, in reality, this clarity often emerges as one goes along.

'Snowballing'/chain referral

Our contacts with other professionals may provide us with the names of several people who are or were active in the community, and it is important to follow them up. To introduce ourselves we can usually mention the person who referred us to them. But think, too, about how you describe yourself. It may be inappropriate at an initial meeting to say that you have come to help them join with other community members in taking action on issues they are concerned about. But over time we need to find ways of conveying this, perhaps by giving examples of concrete ways in which we could help. One way is to engage them in general conversation and gradually slip in the points we want to make. At this stage, however, we mainly want general information; we want to pick their brains about the history of community action in the area and what is currently going on. Always remember that, while we will wish to encourage some of our contacts to become involved in community action, attempting to 'push' people into this before they are ready generally doesn't work. At this stage we are students; we are learning.

Many people are happy to talk about themselves, and the problem is often keeping them on the subject of community needs rather than their other interests. So we often need to steer the conversation to some extent. If you consider that public transport is inadequate, you might introduce the subject by asking whether it is easy to get into town and back. That way you are guiding but not imposing a rigid structure. An opportunity may also occur for workers to demonstrate their commitment. If, for example, the contact says there used to be a playgroup run by Mrs. X but, since it closed, the equipment seems to have got lost, the worker could offer to visit Mrs. X to try to discover the whereabouts of the equipment. Actions like this are often more important than mere words in conveying what the worker is there for. But take care that you do not spring too quickly into action, thus neglecting your strategic planning tasks and giving the impression that you are there to do things *for* people rather than help them do things themselves.

The danger with 'snowballing' is that we may become familiar with only one network, since people often put us in contact with people like them. So, make contacts in other ways too, by attending places where people naturally congregate, outside primary schools at the end of the school day, for instance. Other commonly used places are pubs or post offices, but there are many more possibilities. However, when making contacts by going to such places, one is also meeting with an unrepresentative group – women with young children, for example. Are the people one is meeting representative enough? Other factors affect this type of contact-making too. Some community workers might feel unhappy chatting in public houses, or meeting mums outside school. On the other hand, some workers might be personally drawn to using certain methods of contact making through personal preference rather than because this was the best way of getting to know people. It is important to think about the methods we choose.

Door-knocking

Planned door-knocking is another method to consider, but it takes a great deal of time. If you want open-ended discussions with as many residents as possible, you are likely to be in some houses for well over an hour. If you have to return later to houses where the occupant is initially out, it can take weeks to contact even half the residents in a street. I once asked a student on placement to make contacts in this way in a street of 200 houses. It took six weeks and resulted only in two major contacts. Also, try to keep focused. 'I found myself re-hanging an old lady's curtains once', one of my colleagues told me. One way to ease the first meeting with people when door-knocking is to put a leaflet through the door a day or so before you call, stating who your are and what your business is. It is amazing how this can break the ice.

Sowing seeds

Contact-making does not necessarily produce quick results. People participate when *they* are ready. The fact that a community worker has contacted them at a certain point may well provide them with more knowledge than they had before. You may have sown seeds which begin to germinate at a later date, perhaps next year when their children go to school and they have a little more time on their hands. It is also important not to make up our minds about people too quickly. A student on placement made an initially favourable contact with a vicar who promised a lot of help. On the other hand, a local councillor was very suspicious and was mentally 'written off' by the student. Later the vicar showed himself to be only interested in getting people into church whereas the councillor became helpful when she realised that the worker had a genuine commitment to the area. Many of the people with real power and commitment will not co-operate until you have shown yourself trustworthy and useful.

Surveys

A colleague once asked some local employers to give their employees a questionnaire about local needs and issues. The same approach can be used with school children taking a questionnaire home to their parents, and, of course, by putting questionnaires through doors, in post offices, etc. (assuming they are completed and come back!). But surveys are time-consuming. Work out beforehand whether the survey is being used as a means of gathering 'soft' information relatively systematically and as a means of getting into the area, or whether the task is to produce a more objective measurement of need. You can't do both with the same questionnaire. An 'objective' survey must be carefully designed. It will need to be closed-ended, with questions like 'Do you mainly shop: in this street?/in this estate?/in town?/elsewhere?' The task is to get clear answers to questions which can be quantified. But if you are using the survey to contact residents and acquire soft information, you will ask 'open-ended' questions such as 'What do you think of the shops in the area?' You will probably want to complete it personally with respondents, and you will want to encourage them to 'talk around' each question. If you opt for an 'objective' survey, get an expert to assist you.

Asking people what they want – the dangers

In Britain, in 1994, certain disadvantaged communities qualified for European Union (EU) Structural Funds, which could be spent on many things a local community wanted, though not on leisure centres. But, when asked, local people often did want a leisure centre.

This issue became problematic because the EU was, on the one hand, saying the local community had to decide what it wanted, but at the same time imposing limits. It was quite difficult for Local Authority officials, who were not trusted much anyway, to explain this. More generally, if you just ask people what they want you sometimes get an enormous and unrealistic 'wish list'. So you have to find some way of getting across that people won't get everything they ask for. Substantial skill is needed to get this right. A more realistic approach goes something like this.

> Central government says we have to do A, B, C.
> This will cost £N.
> That leaves £X over, which we can decide how to spend
> For £X, we could do D, E or F, and here are the pros and cons of each.
> What is your preference among these and do you have any other preferences which we can look at together?

Focus groups

A further way to discover views about needs is to invite people to a small group discussion, ask them a series of questions and record their answers. Such 'focus' groups (see Stewart and Shamdasani 1991) are now sometimes used to produce information for community profiles. You need to learn about how to organise these and plan them carefully to get useful information, though.

Broad and narrow angle scanning

When undertaking a community profile, Henderson and Thomas suggest initially undertaking a 'broad angle' scan (2002, pp. 66–80) which provides general information. The subsequent 'narrow angle' scan provides more detailed information relevant to specific issues. It is important to distinguish between the two because one can go on gathering information indefinitely. It is necessary to undertake a community profile as economically as possible and to know when to stop!

An 'issue' profile

The principles for undertaking a community profile in relation to a community of need are the same as for a geographical profile, namely: gathering hard and soft information from agencies dealing with that community; and gathering (mainly soft) information from *personal contact* with community members and, in some cases, their 'carers'. In order to start on an 'issue profile', try a 'brainstorming' exercise; this usually produces a good list of sources of information. There are national agencies such as: Women's Aid, Shelter, Mind, and so on, and contact with them can produce not only hard data, including information on relevant laws, but also guidance about how to set up particular projects. More difficult to obtain, however, is statistical information for that 'need community' which relates to a particular county or city. However, relevant Local Authority departments are an obvious early port of call as are local support agencies, if they exist, which specialise in work with or for that group. See Hawtin *et al.* (1994) for more on community profiling.

A 'do-it-yourself' community profile

This is a process where a worker brings together a group of people who are as representative as possible of the locality (not always an easy process) and helps them produce a questionnaire. Local volunteers are then guided in a door-knocking and interviewing process, and the completed questionnaires are used to produce a needs analysis. The task of the group is then to act on the needs identified. See Henderson and Thomas (2002, pp. 243–261) for some excellent guidance here. A similar process, 'Planning for Real' (see www.nif.co.uk), is based primarily on the creation of a physical model of the community. Local people are then encouraged to move the parts of the model around, saying what they want where. This can be an extremely motivating way of discovering how local people want their community physically improved. Walker (1998) describes similar processes where people are brought together in a public meeting, helped to create a mission statement and invited through a brainstorming process to identify community needs and then to prioritise the most feasible and desirable projects. While such approaches are useful, they need to be seen as only one tool among many in the community development process and not a substitute for it.

From community profile to analysis and action

A community profile is a tool with which to build an analysis as a basis for action. The information obtained has to be ordered, emphasising not only the objective needs of the community but also the more subjective perceptions of its members and others. Unemployment may be an enormous problem, for instance, but it may not be possible to help the community organise to do something about it. If one or two residents expressed the desire for a parent-teacher association (PTA), you would need to ask yourself whether there would be much support from other residents or from teachers, whether becoming involved with a PTA would fit in with your priorities and those of your agency (and, if not, perhaps to refer them elsewhere), whether the necessary resources were available, and so on. List alternative possibilities for action from all the information you have gathered. Each alternative should contain an assessment of its own advantages and disadvantages. You can score them if you wish. Then make a choice about which alternatives to select. The main factors influencing the decision are:

- your own relatively objective assessment of needs (based on hard and soft data);
- what your agency expects;
- your own ideology, value system or skills – what you *want* and *feel* able (or are equipped) to do;
- the likelihood of success, and
- what at least some community members want to get done and seem motivated to work on.

There may be good reasons for not going with the option which comes out 'top', but, by writing things down, you are giving yourself the opportunity of being as objective as possible and forcing yourself to think through some of the issues.

While community workers should write down their community profile and discuss it with their manager before acting on it, community work can also proceed in a more opportunistic way. A couple of local people seem interested in an idea and, with the worker's help, call a meeting with friends to discuss it. In no time at all a group gets off the ground. Community work will always happen like that, and it can be excellent practice. But it can also be bad practice because, if workers are under external and internal pressure to get something done, they may be desperate to create a group of any kind. You only realise later that the two residents who seemed keen to set up the group are fervently disliked by the rest of the community, or that you are spending all your working hours helping one group stay together while there are potentially more fruitful avenues to explore for which you no longer have the time.

Also, relatively scientific approaches to intervention are now beginning to be developed which indicate which approaches to a particular problem have been shown to be most effective (see Chapter 10). As knowledge develops in relation to what works, it is the responsibility of the worker, to bring that knowledge to bear.

I conclude this section with some advice from two experienced workers:

> Grow things slowly; don't rush in; don't put all your eggs in one basket; something may still be relevant if only two people want it; keep your ear to the ground; mix with as many people as you can; remember that you can't leave a group entirely to itself (initially at least) and that you cannot control what it does.
>
> (Ben Reynolds and Helen Hunter, personal communication)

Evaluating community work

The most important thing to do when designing an evaluation is, if possible, to predict what 'success would look like'. So, give thought, in the project design phase, to what it is you want to change and measure, For instance, if the project is aiming to set up more community groups, or get more local participation, or change certain policies, you can design a scheme to measure these things. At best, evaluation design (while still using professional expertise) is undertaken through an interactive process with the community so that the evaluation itself relates to the changes its members want. That can be difficult to do, however, especially 'up front' before the community is organised and you have your own resources fully in place.

Baselines

If you want to identify changes, you have to have a measure of where things are before you start, namely, a baseline. A well-understood baseline is, for instance, the number of school children getting examination passes at a certain level. In community work, though, we usually want to measure more intangible things, and it can be hard to find (or create) the right baseline type information. Also, even if you are able to get figures to construct relevant baselines for the things you expect to change, these figures are likely to be affected by many other factors besides the contribution of your project. While there is now an explosion of data on the internet, and while public bodies collect vast amounts of data, via consumer surveys, for instance, there are problems with demonstrating impact if repeat data aren't available in an appropriate timescale. If you have used census figures, in Britain, you may have to wait ten years to obtain 'repeat' data. So, when you develop a baseline, choose the data carefully, and think about how they will be collected in, say, three years time, and whether they will be in the same form. In reality, the baseline may not be measured again unless you collect exactly the same data *yourself* later on or there is good agency commitment both to evaluation and good record-keeping. In practice, baselines are rarely constructed and then re-measured later in community work, though they should be. Community profiles are rarely useful as baselines because they are not normally constructed (and the *process* recorded) in such a way as to be exactly repeatable some years later. Community work needs to become more professional in this respect.

The 'percentage meter'

To construct this, you need first to get community representatives to work out up to fifty statements describing how they would like the community to be, such as:

● Local people are active in community affairs.
● Local Authority departments are keen to know residents' views.

Then you ask groups of respondents (adults, children, older people, or professional workers) individually to rate between zero and one hundred the degree to which they believe each statement is true. You then average the replies and discover that, for instance, 'local people are active in community affairs' is regarded on average as, say, 30 per cent 'true'. In this way you build up a picture of the quality of life as perceived by various beneficiaries or stakeholders. The exercise only takes about ten minutes to carry out, though a day or two to prepare and process afterwards. The percentage meter shows up perceived strengths and weaknesses in a programme, and is easily repeatable at regular intervals. Try this out yourself. It is quite easy, and good fun.

A longitudinal approach

An important method to use, if you have the resources, is the 'longitudinal' approach. Here you survey the same sample of people more than once over a period of time. This method is good at measuring change relatively accurately, but it is expensive, and you need a large enough sample to cope with the numbers that drop out in subsequent surveys.

Action research

Also, for learning lessons, an 'action research' approach can be very useful. Here a researcher works alongside the project, investigating various aspects of it, normally at your request, and feeds back lessons about what is or is not working, so that you can modify your approach as you go along.

Proxy measures

In community work, the really important goals may be difficult to measure. Therefore, one has to select other things – proxies – which can be measured and which approximate as closely as possible to the desired goal. For instance, a volunteer visiting project designed to decrease the loneliness of elderly people could not easily be evaluated. If, however, several elderly people were applying of their own volition for such a volunteer, then this measure could be a possible indicator (or proxy) of effectiveness.

Monitoring

Monitoring involves collecting quantified information on a day-to-day basis to indicate what is being done – number of client contacts, numbers and types of groups worked with, and so on. These data later help you draw conclusions about the value of the work (i.e. evaluation 'proper'). Once you have decided 'what success would look like', you can work out what data to collect and how to collect them, which will help to tell you whether you have attained that success. Thus, the types of monitoring data gathered are determined by the requirements of an evaluation proper, the success of which, in turn, depends upon the relevance and accuracy of those data.

The 'goals' model

Evaluation which is concerned with measuring concrete objectives specified in advance is often referred to as the 'goals model'. However, inappropriate goals have often been required of community projects by funders. Therefore, in order to apply this model effectively, it is necessary to undertake a good deal of preliminary work. The evaluator (internal or external) helps the staff (and/or community) to identify the most appropriate goals for a particular time period and then to develop the means to measure whether those goals have been achieved. If community workers can identify, early on, appropriate things to measure, it is probably more likely that funders will accept these rather than imposing inappropriate ones.

The unpredictable

One community project leader makes a great deal happen. Another alienates politicians. Yet another has particular skills and uses these to develop innovatory schemes. Or: anticipated funding does not materialise and the project has to change tack; new political masters change the emphasis and thus the goals of the project halfway through; a powerful champion emerges who uses their influence to ensure the project receives special assistance. Good evaluation has to pick up such factors as well as other 'unanticipated' outcomes.

Process, objectives, outputs and outcomes

Many evaluations of community projects, quite correctly, tell a story and describe a *process*, covering: the need for the project, how it was started, what it did, what happened and so on. This is essential. However, as is indicated above, projects also need to specify their goals or *objectives*. This needs to be done at a general level – 'to involve more local people in community groups', or 'to provide more play opportunities for small children', for example – and this objective setting may take place every year or two. But it also needs to be done more often in a specific way – 'to establish a playgroup in the community centre in the next six months' or 'to recruit more members for a community group by the end of the year'. The information you gather in order to carry out your evaluation should tell you whether you are achieving your specified objectives. When these objectives have been achieved, they can be called *outputs*. However, you then need to work out whether the outputs achieved have made any difference to the wider situation you wanted to change. For instance, an output could be the building of a community centre, which is easy to monitor. An *outcome* could be whether the centre had, for instance, increased community activity – less easy to measure. A major problem is that outputs rather than outcomes are often measured. All these points can be linked by the 'theory of change', as discussed below.

The 'theory of change' approach

Taking a 'theory of change' approach can help to demonstrate the impact and achievements of community work because it develops a hypothesis about how and why an intervention works (see Connell and Kubisch, 1998). The elements of the approach, when brought together, provide a sound basis on which both to predict and evaluate the impact of community work. The approach also relies on the project's stakeholders (i.e. those who will do the work, fund it, or benefit from it) being involved in developing the 'theory of change'. They work together to agree what the long-term outcomes of the initiative should be and then work back to the intermediate outcomes, early outcomes and the strategies and actions needed to bring these about. Thus, a theory is developed about what action is required to bring about the desired change. In this way we make explicit the implicit ideas we have about what needs to be done. This approach requires much input at the beginning, but, once developed, determines the outcomes of the initiative, the milestones and the targets, and even the work programme. Reviewing progress relating to the 'theory of change' must also be worked into the timescale of the initiative (Jayne Humm, personal communication).

Triangulation

Generally, in order to evaluate community work projects, it is necessary to use a combination of approaches: case studies; examining data produced by the organisation as well as other records and reports; interviewing managers, staff, beneficiaries, funders and other agencies; in addition to using the 'goals method'. It is vital here to get views on the project from different sources, which is called 'triangulation'. Then one has to put the information together and try to form a coherent picture of the effectiveness of the project. In doing this, don't ignore information which does not fit with the view (which usually begins to emerge early on in the process in one's own head) about what *one would like to be able to conclude*! Often, research like this results in paradoxical or ambiguous conclusions – that certain objectives have been achieved at the expense of others, for example. But that is the messy real world of community work.

Other factors

Your evaluation needs to take account of the likelihood that beneficiaries, project staff and sponsors may all be wanting something different from a project, so be clear who you are evaluating 'for'. While outside evaluators may be used from time to time, a project team needs to give attention to evaluation too. Responsibility for internal evaluation has to be allocated to a staff member or members and time given. Otherwise, when the pressure is on, this will slip. For staff working within the project, I recommend that a minimum of 5 per cent of everybody's time should be spent on record-keeping, monitoring and evaluating. If you want to learn serious lessons for wider application, no less than 10 per cent should be ring-fenced for evaluation. Good evaluation is time-consuming (and poor evaluation is not worth bothering about!). So, spend a lot of time up front; decide the few things which are really important; plan it; keep it as simple as possible; and stick to it. While, for sponsors and funders, the most important questions are usually to do with effectiveness and value for money, for project teams the most important question is 'what, with hindsight, would we do differently?' Thus, one is learning the lessons for future action.

Conclusion

Projects mostly fail because they are poorly thought through at the start, there is no clear theory of change and no coherent project design. Often, certainly, community work is so poorly funded that there is no time, finance or staff resources for good thinking through. But if we are to succeed in the longer term, we have to get this right more often, recognising the various problems in the way. For more on evaluation, see: Ball (1988), Voluntary Activity Unit (1997a and b), Taylor (1998), Eyken (1992), Feuerstein (2002), Dept for International Development (2002), Kellogg Foundation (1997), Roche (1999), Rubin (1995).

Points to ponder

1. What are the most important things to remember about community work project design?
2. What are the main reasons why community work projects fail, do you think?
3. What are the main things you have to take account of in setting up a community work project?
4. What is a 'theory of change'?

Further reading

Carnegie (1936) *How to Win Friends and Influence People.*
Henderson and Thomas (2002) *Skills in Neighbourhood Work.*
Wiseman (2003) *The Luck Factor: How to Change Your Luck and Change Your Life.*

3 | Helping people set up and run community groups

It's so difficult to get all of it right, I'm surprised anybody ever sets up an effective community group.

(Ben Reynolds, personal communication)

Community groups are set up in different ways: sometimes a worker makes contact with individuals who gradually come together; sometimes one or two individuals approach a worker; or there is a requirement (in order to access funding perhaps) for a group of a particular kind to be formed; or an existing group decides to set up a sub-committee; sometimes several existing groups come together to form a federation. Sometimes the worker is the leader of the group but other times more its servant. And, of course, most groups form without the assistance of a worker.

When you are setting up 'autonomous' community groups, the most relevant concept is that of 'working alongside' people, though it takes many different forms. You are working with people as far as possible to *their* agenda, and you are always looking for ways of helping the group to be effective. Therefore, it is important to assist people to realise early on that, as far as possible (and within certain limits) you are there to 'help them do what *they* want to do'. This process is not conflict-free (within a group, between the group and the worker and between the group and the wider community, for example); hence you need many diplomatic skills and political awareness.

Why set up community groups?

Getting something done usually requires the power and legitimacy of an organisation. That is why community workers spend time helping community members set up and run organisations. Note, though, that it may not always be necessary to set up a group. There may be existing groups who could act on their own or link up to act on an issue or to create the desired benefits. Alternatively an individual community member might take things forward. Or you might be able to act with other professionals to reach an objective. It is important not to rush into setting up a group. And always know why you are doing it.

Intensive work to set up a group

Effective community groups tend to have in them or associated with them people who are undertaking the functions listed below, even though they would not necessarily consider themselves to be community development workers. The most important stages for a worker when helping establish an autonomous community group (that is, working generally 'outside' the potential group, not as a member) are:

1. Contacting people and identifying general needs.
2. Bringing people together, helping them identify specific needs and assisting them to develop the will to see that those needs are met.
3. Helping them understand what will have to be done if those needs are to be met.
4. Helping them identify objectives.
5. Helping them form and maintain an organisation suitable for meeting those objectives.
6. Helping them identify and acquire resources (knowledge, skills, money, people, equipment).
7. Helping them evaluate alternative lines of approach, choose priorities and design a plan of action, thus turning strategic objectives into a series of smaller objectives and tasks.
8. Helping them divide these tasks between them and carry them out.
9. Helping the members of the group feed back the results of their actions to the whole group which then has to evaluate those actions and adopt modified objectives.

The process discussed above is rarely a linear one. In this process, the worker is:

● attending at least some group meetings;
● working with (potential) group leaders individually;
● doing some things *for* the embryonic group.

It is as much art as science, where the worker is using intuition, guess-work, making judgements, switching roles, using trial and error, applying their own particular relationship skills, and managing conflicts and pressure from various quarters. At the same time group members are learning (or not learning!) from what might be new experiences for them. They also have their own lives to lead; the group is, for most, unlikely to be their enduring passion, though it can be for some

Bringing people together

Let us now assume that you, the worker, have carried out your needs analysis and have some idea of your own objectives. You are in contact with a number of community members and others, and you want to move from the information-gathering and contact-making stage to the action stage. On, the one hand, the information-gathering and contact-making stage can merge, almost imperceptibly, with the action stage, and if your objective is to build community groups in general, you may take this approach. That is, you will start at the top of the list above, because, within reason, it will not matter what the focus of the group you establish is. On the other hand, these stages can sometimes be clearly demarcated in the sense that you gather your information, make your contacts and make your analysis, pause, and then consciously work to set up a group on the issues which you judge to be the most appropriate. In this situation you may need to take more of an organising as opposed to a facilitative approach. Similarly, if you have a more specialist brief, you will consciously seek out individuals whom you judge to be able to contribute most effectively to the issue which you wish to work on. In both these cases you will probably start a bit lower down the list above. Either way, at some stage, the group will concentrate on 'X' and the worker will primarily be interested in working with people who share that interest.

You may spend months making contacts without finding an issue or activity on which community members seem prepared to take action. Conversely, you may discover that there are many such issues, but no consensus, or even diametrically opposed views. Generally I would counsel against taking up issues which divide the community, though this is sometime unavoidable, because you will run the risk of losing your legitimacy with some people. If there seem to be no burning issues which people are concerned enough about to get involved in, you will eventually have to consider whether there are any other (social planning) ways to make something happen (see Chapter 6). On the other hand, you may find that a number of residents are concerned about the same issue. At this point you will need to work out whether you are prepared to help people organise to address it. If your answer is 'yes', you will probably need to allocate about two days per week for the tasks outlined below. A worker who set up a successful women's group on an isolated housing estate spent many weeks visiting a large number of people individually, in ones and twos (some five times) before setting up the group.

Identifying and strengthening motivation

When you are trying to discover if people have the motivation to become involved, you undertake a mixture of tasks. You try to identify points in the conversation when your contact expresses a concern about community problems, such as the bus service. You then try to keep the conversation on this subject, probably by asking questions. 'What you said about the bus service – does anyone else feel the same?', 'Why do you think it is that the bus service is so poor?', 'Has anyone ever tried to do anything about it?', 'Have *you* ever thought of doing anything about it?', 'Would you be interested in meeting with a few others to see if anything could be done about it?' It might only be through a process of several meetings that you set the community member thinking that they might get involved to change something, and the majority don't reach that point. Nevertheless this is your main objective. 'Hey, maybe there is something I could do after all' is the kind of feeling you want to evoke. In all this, you are a 'leader from behind'. Even if you try to be totally objective and 'non-directive', you will be giving off subliminal signals all the time about your preferences. There is nothing wrong with this and, indeed, we are paid to use our professional judgement. But be aware how you, probably as a high status outsider, may be having influence. Also, people may tell you what they think you want to hear, and you may come away thinking they are committed to doing something when they are not.

Focusing on one issue – next steps

As some of the individuals with whom you are in contact become motivated to take action on a particular issue, you then need to see how far other people are interested in *that* issue. The next step is to bring people who seem to share a particular interest together. Often two or three keen people will be happy to meet to discuss the idea further. This may well happen without your suggesting it and, if so, that is usually a good sign. They also need to understand it is *their* project, and that you do not want to be seen as the leader. Let us say that you are in contact with three women individually who have expressed interest in doing something about children's play. One way of moving ahead is to try to get them to arrange the first meeting between themselves rather than doing it yourself, which also tests their commitment and ability. (You'd then have to work out whether to brief any of them first.) In practice, however, community members may have insufficient confidence to set up a group themselves, and such circumstances may dictate that you arrange the meeting. Many successful groups start that way. However, if you play a major organisational role in setting up the group yourself, you will need to move it from dependence to autonomy later on – not easy if they see you as the leader. So, if you do take a leadership role make sure you explain that, while you will organise the first meeting or two, you expect the group members to organise the subsequent ones themselves, and that you will assist them in this.

Remember to create a good environment for the meeting. If it is going to be different from what some of the people there expect, explain this to them beforehand. In meetings where people have varying expectations and ways of behaving, be aware, in particular, of cultural differences, e.g. black ethnic minorities may have a different way of communicating, especially in mixed sex groups. Business people tend to have more of a 'cut and dried' approach than local community members. Try to avoid the use of acronyms or abbreviations which are only known to some of those present (or 'translate' them), and be aware of the type of language used (e.g. professional terms – 'service level agreements', 'in-service training', etc.). If you are running the meeting yourself remember that, depending how you present an issue and whose views you ask for first, people will tend to agree with the first speaker. So, in order to get a variety of perspectives discussed you may need to try to ensure that people who probably have differing views speak directly after each other. It can also be useful to seek to agree 'ground rules' first of all, e.g. listening; one point at a time; respect for different views; no swearing; length of meetings, etc. Remember that the issues which are troubling people often come out in a private chat after the meeting. So, hanging around to pick up such things and general gossip is vital. Also, you cannot deal with all issues in a meeting – you have to sort some of them out afterwards. When people get together, they sometimes just 'chat'. So, in order to get the group to focus on the needs which they are (ostensibly) meeting to discuss, you can throw in ideas, ask questions, make statements, tell them what you think they should be doing or provide information. Assuming you are not running the group, try to make sure that the person who is doing so also understands the need for the group to develop an appropriate focus. Beware of getting the group to focus too early though, because this can frighten people off. Conversely, leaving it too long will also result in some members disappearing! It's a matter of judgement.

It may take several meetings to get an embryonic group to focus on needs and objectives, and they may all be interested in doing different things. Or, personality problems may emerge, making co-operation difficult. Try to keep up the momentum. Make sure that a date is arranged for the next meeting, before which you meet the members individually, if you can, and plan with some of them what the meeting is to achieve. Conversely, if you have decided that you do not wish to continue with this group, you can 'forget' to suggest a date for the next meeting! (It is not particularly ethical to do this intentionally, I suppose, but, on the other hand it often happens naturally if people, including the worker, are not very motivated to continue the group, and it can provide an 'easy way out'.)

Know what *you* want the meeting to achieve, though this could change during it. Ideally, too, ensure that people coming to it are clear in this respect, though their objectives may be different from yours and each other's. But you will all be in a fog if several people have unstated and different assumptions about its purpose. If you and those present don't have this clarity, you may, after the meeting, be asking yourself 'Why did I waste two hours of my life on that?' At the end of, and even during a meeting you may summarise where you think the group has got to, because people often have different interpretations of what actually happened.

The people who are meeting together may already know each other, and that makes it easier for you. If they don't, you may need to encourage informal interchange and make people feel comfortable. Most of us are pretty scared in a meeting of more than three or four people, especially people we don't know. With a group of strangers there may be a 'testing out' period, and it might well take such a group quite a time to 'gel'. Ensure that a cup of tea is offered, and think about what casual subjects of conversation they are likely to respond to.

Expanding the membership

Many groups start with two or three people and gradually build up. When there are very few members, everyone should try to recruit more. The worker, especially, should try to bring in more people because existing members will tend to recruit people they know. Unless care is taken to recruit widely, community groups can become, or become seen as, cliques. Indeed, they often contain members of the same family.

When the group has focused on one area, you will want to recruit people with a potential interest in that. At this stage, the worker, or the group, may try to get an article in the press or on local radio, or get posters put in shops. However, few people will come to a group where they know no-one. They also need to know what is in it for them. Consequently, if you hear of people who might be interested, call to see them or try to get a member of the embryonic group to do so. Personal contact is the best method of expanding the membership.

Deciding what to do

A group tends to become a group and start working out its specific objectives when it numbers about six, and in many ways this is the ideal size. Big groups often have too many people in them to make decisions easily; some people may feel intimidated or excluded (unless everybody has their say, which creates other problems in large groups – e.g. lots of tangential issues raised and overlong meetings). However, members often become despondent if they only get attendances of six or so, and the worker then has to find ways of convincing them that they are doing OK. People new to groups may also want to achieve too much too quickly. The group has agreed to focus on 'play', and one member says in early July, 'Let's run a summer play scheme.' The rest agree and decide with enthusiasm that it should start next Monday and run daily for six weeks! Your role is to find a way of helping groups adopt realistic objectives, such as, in this case perhaps, a one-week play scheme at the end of the holidays. Otherwise you may have to do a great deal of organising yourself!

The law

The police once called at our neighbourhood centre and greeted me with 'We believe you have illegal gaming going on in these premises!' The bingo group had been giving money prizes for which we had no licence! Also, a drugs and alcohol worker was once imprisoned, in Britain, for not complying well enough with the law in relation to preventing drug taking on the premises for which she was responsible. So, be aware, at an early stage, of how the law may impinge on what you want to do.

Choosing priorities

After the group has decided, broadly, what to get involved with, you must help its members identify and choose between different priorities – to run a play scheme or press the council to provide fixed play equipment, for example. Also, how much money would be needed for a play scheme and how would it be obtained? How many helpers would be needed and who would recruit them? What are the time and skill implications of this for the group members? Whose permission would be needed if the group wanted to use the school playground and who will find out? Try to get the group to face such questions. However, it is their enthusiasm which keeps them going at this point, and it is important not to extinguish that. You've also got to let them take risks, and your view may not be correct anyway. I once advised a group not to buy an old minibus because I didn't think they had the money or the organisation to run it. But they did, and managed it very well.

Most people generally think about 'projects', often relatively narrow ones, and not outcomes. Your job is to ask questions like 'What do we actually want to achieve?' and 'Will doing X help us achieve this?' Also, try to get group members to think about where the proposed project fits (or not) with what others are doing to achieve these outcomes. Issues may also arise about which you know little. You need to be honest about what you don't know, and offer to discover appropriate information if group members cannot, or to put the group in touch with somebody with relevant expertise.

Failure

The secretary of a community group I once worked with decided to hold a sponsored walk to raise money. I knew he was organising it inappropriately and tried to encourage him to make better preparations. He didn't, and it was a disaster. Only a few walkers turned up and no-one paid the money they collected to the group. That community leader never ran another sponsored walk!

Groups sometimes fail to achieve their objectives. Consequently, as well as trying to ensure they don't fail, our role is, perhaps, to prepare them that they might fail but to keep up their enthusiasm and seek to ensure they learn from any failure. This is important if we find ourselves supporting something which might very well go wrong. It is tricky, though, to explain this 'up front' because groups don't usually like to discuss potential failure. However, it is usually harder to learn from success, so groups may sometimes have to fail if they are going to learn.

Here are two worker styles:

(A) Never mind the problems – let's go for it.

(B) We may be able to achieve this. However, we must make sure that we do X first. And, after all that, it may not work. The power to make it work is yours, though I can help. Nothing much will happen unless you do something yourselves.

The internal (and possibly external) pressures on you will make you want to be worker A, in which case you will probably be rushing round madly trying to prevent failure and probably creating dependence. However, you may be wiser to be worker B. Think also about the style you will adopt, how you will do things and what your stance will be, for example, when people want do something which you think won't work. Know, too, when you are being directive, overtly or subtly, and when you are being genuinely facilitative with no particular end of your own in mind apart from assisting the group with its own agenda.

Community groups and money

We may not be too bothered personally if we find out that the treasurer of the tenants' association is keeping accounts on the back of an envelope! But we would be worried if we discovered that the books did not balance and the rest of the committee was accusing them of embezzlement! This kind of thing is quite common and can result in the death of a group. While my work with community groups was mostly 'non-directive', I eventually became quite directive about account keeping, especially when activities involving cash were taking place on premises for which I was responsible. Treasurers should know how to keep proper accounts *before* things go wrong, as it is then often too late to rectify the situation. The group also needs to agree who decides on expenditure – the treasurer, the whole group, the officers? Managing money is not very difficult, as long as one is methodical. There are now several handbooks which cover this field. Or get a book-keeper's advice. A related point is that, while it may not be hard, today, for community groups to obtain small amounts of money, it takes longer for them to learn how to use it wisely.

Contractual work

A funder agreed to provide £3,000 to a community organisation for a study into the feasibility of establishing a community business, on the basis that its members agreed to undertake some of the work themselves. They also had to agree to restructure their organisation, with a consultant's help. The money was released in three tranches of £1,000 in stages as the agreed tasks were completed.

Professional community workers should generally understand the types of organisational arrangements necessary to achieve effective democratic collective action in relation to the issues with which community groups are concerned. In situations where it is vital for a particular structure to be adopted and for the group members to have certain capabilities, the worker may need to agree a contract with the group, to *train* them perhaps in how to organise themselves. You cannot, in a non-directive way, allow the group to proceed in an unfocused manner if they aspire to run something serious and complicated and which may involve large sums of money. As community work becomes more established and community groups adopt sophisticated goals, 'contract working' may develop considerably. This kind of relationship between a community organisation and a support worker or agency is potentially important, since, in theory, it enables the dignity of the members of the group to be maintained in that they know what they are getting and can control it, at least to some degree, rather than being under the control of the worker. See the box below and Hyatt and Skinner, 1997, for more on contract working.

Views of a 'community consultant', by Ben Reynolds

'When advising or setting up a community organisation or enterprise you need to access (through intensive networking) gatekeepers and holders of expertise who have information, contacts, advice, goodwill and access to resources. These could be in the economic development department of the council or the youth service. They could be a politician, a business leader or almost anybody. However, I find that, where there is the most need, there are usually the least resources.

I may be paid to do "X" for an embryonic organisation but I see all kinds of other needs which require my assistance too. But I have to say "no". Some people bring me in and say "Do this job and finish it – that's all we want." Others are more interested in using the interaction to help develop their organisation. The biggest frustration is that you are paid to work on a particular issue, but you soon realise that there is another massive problem staring the client organisation in the face which they don't want to look at (the "elephant in the corner"). Do you raise it or do you ignore it? But, how do you say to a group "You are a shambles; you don't have the knowledge or skill to do that"? Also, no matter how you improve people's skills, you don't easily change attitudes. Ideally you raise such issues with the chair or trustee (if there is one) of such an organisation who then takes them forward. But this doesn't happen much, in my experience. Sometimes you have to point out that the organisation is "going nowhere". This is often because of personalities. Small community organisations with totally volunteer boards suffer most from this. The more professional organisations have systems to deal with it. These are not "quick fix" issues. They are also about organisational and cultural changes.

If you have a passion for a cause, think carefully before becoming a community consultant because you will only be able to work on little bits of it. Also, take care not to have your own axe to grind. Use your professionalism to apply your expertise impartially.'
(Ben Reynolds, personal communication)

Social audit

When developing and managing private non-profit bodies I suggest you use a 'social audit'. This is a systematic, regular and objective accounting procedure that enables organisations to establish values and criteria on which they can plan and measure performance. The Social Audit Toolkit (Spreckley, 1997) is designed to assist social enterprises to do this and to communicate effectively with stakeholders.

Community capacity building

Skinner (1997, pp. 1–2) defines community capacity building primarily as:

> Development work that strengthens the ability of community
> organisations ... to build their structures, systems, people
> and skills so that they are better able to define and achieve
> their objectives and engage in consultation and planning,
> manage community projects, and take part in partnerships
> and community enterprise. It includes aspects of training,
> organisational and personal development and resource
> building organised in a self-conscious manner reflecting the
> principles of empowerment and equality.

(See also Armstrong, 1998, Nugent, 1998, and Nye, 1998, for other descriptions of approaches to capacity building.)

A major characteristic of effective capacity building is that the community organisation has to 'own' the process. The consultant/trainer helps the group identify its needs. He or she structures the members' learning around these, linking this process with its aims, providing guided learning through group-based activity. Skinner emphasises (1997, pp. 64–84) the importance of the organisational development aspects of capacity building. Here the focus is on strengthening the community organisation itself rather than on the skill development of individual members, by, for instance, building team relationships, designing a constitution and developing management systems and action plans. He also stresses the need for capacity-building plans based on reviews of individuals' training needs and the organisation's development needs.

Community capacity building cannot be carried out at all if the group does not recognise the need for it, and it always has to be negotiated with the group first. Capacity building should also, argues Skinner, focus on creating or strengthening the community infrastructure, including: providing resources, improving networking opportunities, creating participative structures, ensuring community development support is provided and building the capacity of professional organisations (1997, pp. 85–104). See also Skinner (2006) for more on 'agency capacity building'.

Training

Members of disadvantaged communities can be reluctant to participate in training courses, even when run in their own neighbourhood or centre. This may be because they have had bad experiences at school, be barely literate and afraid to reveal this or merely unaware of the gaps in their knowledge. Simpson (1995a) argues that successful training for community groups can normally only be provided if it arises from and is followed by community development work. Trainers who are merely interested in getting their subject across or ensuring the 'trainees' gain qualifications rarely make good trainers for community groups. A prior understanding of 'where the group is at' is needed, and trainers may have to adapt their material substantially if it does not fit with what the group members are ready for. One trainer discovered that the local mums, who had been successfully encouraged by a community worker to come to his word-processing course, were so scared that he decided not even to switch a computer on during the first evening! He chatted, building trust with the women, about their school experiences, the nature of the voluntary work they were doing, why they thought computer skills might be useful, etc. Next time, they were happy for him to start the course, and they 'flew'.

If the right kind of relationship is developed by the trainer and if the content of the training is negotiated in an unthreatening way, confidence builds, the participants become more open to receiving the training, and in due course, attending conventional courses. The most effective courses are often those where experiential learning, small group exercises and guided visits (which are reflected on afterwards) are used. Ensure too, that you make appropriate arrangements for those with caring responsibilities, covering transport and other out-of-pocket expenses. However, it can be difficult to find the right kind of course, which is practical (i.e. not too theoretical), at the right level, relatively brief and gives people skills they can use virtually the next day. Consequently, you might need to devise and run such courses yourself.

I have sometimes noticed the following sequence occurring. Women become interested in running local ventures, such as playgroups. Then, they realise they need education and training to develop this work more effectively, and they ask for non-vocational type courses. Next they see the need for vocational qualifications. Finally, some of the men become interested! So, when organising training for both men and women you may need to be aware of different gender expectations. For instance, men seem to want training to lead to something concrete, e.g. a job, while women may be more concerned about their own development *per se*. Ethnic minorities may also have differing expectations.

The training needs of community groups vary from committee skills to business plans, from how to supervise staff to how to recruit volunteers, from how to manage a building to how to keep accounts, and more. By starting from the perceptions and needs both of the individual and the group, many of the blocks to involvement can be overcome.

Organisational and interactional skills

If a community group decides to ask the Local Authority to provide a playground, the worker should immediately begin to think of the practicalities, some of which are mentioned earlier. The group members will think of some of these points but there are likely to be gaps in their thinking. For instance, they may decide that a particular action will be taken but omit to decide who will do it. Our job is partly to advise on these *organisational* questions. Additionally, though, we need *interactional* skills, that is, the ability to form relationships with other people in such a way that they will seriously consider our advice. We use both sets of skills to help the group do *its own* analysis, planning and organisation. We must be able to empathise with the people we work with while retaining a degree of detachment. We must not be so full of what we want to say that we do not see Fred and Joe exchanging angry looks or notice that Joan has been very quiet that evening. We need also to be aware of the background and concerns of the people with whom we are working because, then, we are less likely to make inappropriate comments. While some of these skills are the normal skills of effective living, taken together, they are substantial.

The worker's role in meetings

During group meetings your job, as a facilitator (see Brookfield, 1986, for more on facilitation), is to help the group members move smoothly through the business more or less at their pace. First of all, make clear the role you see yourself playing, what you can and cannot do and that your objective is, ideally at least, to help the group get off the ground and then to withdraw. You may well have met with some members beforehand to plan the meeting. New members, or members who are not within the 'inner circle', will have less knowledge than those who have prepared the meeting, and you will want to make sure that they also understand and contribute to the proceedings. Try to predict what the difficulties will be, and work out with the group's chair, beforehand if possible, how to deal with these. A group may sometimes take half an hour to reach a decision you could have taken in three minutes. However, that is one way that people learn. While part of the role of a facilitator is to give information, another important aspect is asking questions, such as: 'Does anybody know if we need to get permission to mount a demonstration?', which, without either telling them what to do or embarrassing them, prompts people to think of things they hadn't previously considered and generally to clarify their own thoughts.

If you do conceal your own views, you may be perceived as ineffectual. Rather, state your opinion simply, clearly and only once if possible, while indicating that it is up to the group to make its own decisions. However, you will sometimes need to argue the case for a particular approach. There may also be times when you are sure the group is about to make a mistake about which you want to spell out the possible consequences. Also, think about what you don't tell people, and why.

In practice, the group's chair often brings items to the meeting and talks to these (really the secretary's role), rather than primarily chairing the meeting, and possibly eclipses others in the process. If possible, try to separate these two roles out. Ideally, many groups need members with other roles, too, including minutes secretary, membership secretary, publicity officer and treasurer. However, there are often too few people to fill these roles. It can also be a good idea to write down, and keep to hand, some simple procedures (bullet points) about how the group will run, role of chair, etc., which you can give to and discuss with the group at an appropriate time. But don't overdo it; people don't generally read (or certainly take in) more than a page. In the early stages of a group everybody may be involved in deciding about everything, but, after a time, work can be routinely delegated. For example, the treasurer may be able to spend, say, £50 without asking the group and just report back afterwards. Subgroups of two or three can usually deal with things quickly.

Be aware that, if you let people decide on something, they won't always make the decision you want. A colleague let a youth group decide what to do about smoking in the youth centre. 'I let them make the journey of deciding. But they didn't decide to ban it.' However, as it was a rule of the building's owners, she had to forbid smoking! While community workers must be aware of 'rules' and know the consequences of not following them, we should also have ideas for getting around at least some of them.

During the early meetings of an Age Concern group, Marion used to say things like, 'I've run a bingo session in my house. Here's £20.' Although not previously sanctioned by the group, Marion's actions did no harm. But other independent actions can be disastrous. One of our tasks is to teach group members how to liaise with each other between meetings, to sound out ideas, to plan together and to divide tasks among them.

Work with individual group members

You will often need to spend time with a group's key members, helping them work out an agenda, implement decisions, and so on. Sometimes a member agrees in a meeting to perform a task which they can't do. They may then give a lame excuse at the next meeting. For instance, a member might have agreed to write to the housing manager on a particular issue. However, the worker knows that this member is not accustomed to writing letters of that nature and so decides to offer help. People new to community action sometimes talk a great deal about what they plan to do but do not get around to carrying it out. I spent quite a bit of time with Eric, because he was always talking about the needs of old people in the area. Eventually I gave up hope that he would ever act. Then suddenly he started doing things; it was as if the talk was a preparation for the action. (But some talkers never 'do'.)

Some community group leaders speak with assurance even when they are unsure and are actually making mistakes. Such people can be difficult to work with because they don't admit they need assistance. I often found myself almost colluding with such leaders when they blamed others for problems for which they themselves were responsible. Any attempt by me to try to point out where their own actions had created the problem was so often met with a denial that I gave up trying to influence them directly. When I wanted to influence one such community leader, I used to say privately to his wife (also a group member) something like: 'I've been wondering whether the group should try such and such'. Sometimes her husband would approach me a month later and say 'Alan, I've had this great idea...'. Other group members rely too much on the worker. To take the example of writing a letter to the housing manager, some people will always try to get the worker to do it. In such a case, try saying, 'This time I'll do it for you. But let's work on it together so that next time you can do it yourself.' If you have initially spelt out that your role is to help the group become independent, your task should be relatively easy.

Some group members do lots of work but alienate others. Such members are often initially tolerated. But sometimes they go too far and the other members take them to task, at which point they become angry and threaten to resign. Some group leaders may feel threatened when new people join the group, particularly people with ability, and, in effect, try to exclude them. They may also be suspicious of a community worker. If you have any choice, think carefully whether a particular person is somebody through whom and with whom you want to work before you encourage them to take a leadership role. It is not easy to change a difficult situation later. With community members who are damaging the group, *you* may have to try to find ways of getting them to leave, because, while group members moan about them, they don't usually do much to change the situation. (There are of course moral issues here, and it depends, in part, on the nature of your contract with the group.) You can try holding one-to-one meetings with the person to hear their concerns, and seek to get them to see the damage they are doing and to suggest they either change or leave. Or you could try supporting other group members, outside the meeting, to require either that member's resignation or changed behaviour. You could even, as a last resort, confront them in a meeting. Also, the more formal a group is, with rules of procedure, the more possibilities there are to get rid of people, at least in theory. Maybe we need to be a bit tougher in community work, too. However, sometimes it's better to have a troublemaker in the group than outside. 'Had I tried to get rid of two difficult members I would have lost their "following" – a whole street , and I could have been criticised for manipulation' (Anthony Brito, personal communication). Whatever you do, think about it carefully, and discuss it with your supervisor.

Structuring the group

Community worker 'A': 'We stopped having minutes and an agenda for our community forum. While this created a helpful informal atmosphere we struggled without an agenda and we drifted back to one.'

Community worker 'B': 'Not having an agenda and going off at tangents can be useful, but you need to take time at the beginning to clarify things, e.g. "We need to achieve this, this and this", and to allow, say, 15 minutes for the discussion on each item, coming back at the end to what we are going to do.'

Generally, if the meeting's chair knows their job, they will make an unstructured meeting run well. If they don't, there will need to be a strict agenda – and the meeting still may not work! Committees were invented to help groups take decisions in the most effective and democratic way. Whatever structure a group adopts, it must be designed to take the kinds of decisions and actions which that group needs to take. If, for instance, a group is to be handling large amounts of money, or mounting a complicated campaign, clear accountability, delineation of roles and division of responsibility along the lines of a formal committee are necessary. On the other hand, a broad-based forum which exists to involve many people but with no executive powers needs a different structure. It is also important to agree processes *before* you get into a situation where, for example, somebody has to be elected chair and there is no agreement how to do this. If you are concerned that some members may be afraid of a formal committee structure but think that something is needed to stop meetings degenerating into unstructured chat sessions, you might suggest they make a list of the items for discussion at the beginning of the meeting and that someone keeps a record of decisions. Only later might you say that those were an agenda and minutes. You also need to make sure your eventual constitution offers the space and flexibility for you to do what you want to do, rather than it being a 'cage'. Be clear exactly what you want it for.

Delegation and leadership succession

All community leaders eventually move on. So, somebody has to give thought to how new leaders will emerge. If they are to come 'through the ranks', they need to learn through having work delegated to them. But, dividing up and delegating tasks requires thought about which tasks would be suitable, bearing in mind the abilities of the person who is to carry them out. You may need to help existing and potential leaders work together in order to ensure appropriate learning and delegation. After a year or two, one or two original members may have departed, and then groups often lose momentum. Consequently, you will need to think about how to get new people in and how to integrate them. Here your continual networking is vital, because it is often the only way to identify potential new members. I once asked an accountant if he could recommend anybody to help a group with book-keeping. He was very busy and so I did not expect him to volunteer. But he did. I had unintentionally used a 'soft sell', but it worked.

Rotating roles, 'collective working' and co-operatives

Some community workers advocate non-hierarchical organisation (I am thinking here of small organisations with paid staff, and the roles they take on, rather than the roles of management committee members). On a simple scale, organisations can work without hierarchy, having, perhaps, equal pay, equally shared responsibilities and status, no clear manager, and with all having the same say in decision-taking. But there are problems if staff disagree, if some don't pull their weight while others with more knowledge, skill or responsibility are effectively taking leadership roles and working long hours, and when decisions need to be taken quickly. Non-hierarchical groups tend not to be effective at achieving complex tasks. The problems they throw up can also take many hours to resolve by consensus. Also, I have never seen frequent role rotation work well in community groups. There may be one member who is quite good at chairing meetings. Thus, the meeting may be best chaired if they do it for, say, two years. The problem is even bigger with the roles of secretary and treasurer, where continuity is particularly important. Remember, too, that the outside world likes to deal with one spokesperson for an organisation. (See Edwards, 1984, and Landry *et al.*, 1985, for some of the pitfalls involved in establishing non-hierarchical forms of organisation; Stanton, 1989, for a thorough and positive account of collective working; and Freeman, 1970, on the 'Tyranny of Structurelessness'.)

Leadership, participation and expertise

In any group an 'inner core' tends to dominate, and the rest may feel excluded (sometimes called the 'iron law of oligarchy'). Therefore, consider ways in which all members can be involved, so that they feel part of the group and are less likely to drop out. On the other hand, one person, as a minimum, has to ensure that the group's tasks are completed, and you may have time to work only with him or her outside meetings. Organisations now have to allow for consultation and influence both laterally and vertically, organisations such as Local Authorities are seeking and often failing to find such ways of operating and of relating these to traditional management. A great deal of work needs to be done to find ways in which organisations, of all kinds, can be democratic, effective and humane. Any successful enterprise, whether a community group or a Local Authority, needs leadership, participation and expertise. These three are all in tension, however, and if any one of them is too dominant, the whole enterprise suffers. Try to ensure all are in balance.

The need for hard resources and technical assistance

Community groups' needs may include: photocopying facilities, Criminal Records Bureau checks, insurance, ICT equipment, a room to meet, information, and help from professionals such as architects. When a group is starting off it may also require a small amount of money, and it is useful if community workers have 'pump-priming' funds which they can make available. The provision of hard resources also helps convince people that the worker really is on their side. In Britain there now exist several agencies which give 'technical assistance', sometimes free of charge, to community groups. Find out what exists in your area and how it can be tapped. For helpful booklets, contact national support agencies such as, the Federation for Community Development Learning, the Community Development Foundation, or Community Matters. A word of caution, however: the fact that something is written down does not necessarily mean that group members will be able to use it; you may need to help them.

Creating a constituency

Public meetings

When a new group proposes to act on behalf of the community, its members often consider it necessary to ensure support by holding a public meeting, of which a major purpose may be to elect a committee. But public meetings can go wrong, resulting in: a poor turnout and despondency among the group members; an unruly meeting which the organisers cannot control; or a meeting monopolised by one or two dominant individuals (a local councillor, perhaps), which fails to achieve its objectives. (Perhaps it is better not to invite your councillor to the public meeting but go to see them with a couple of community members separately.) There are also a number of other factors which cannot be easily anticipated – the weather, and popular TV programmes, for example.

Publicise a public meeting by putting notices through doors and in shop windows, through announcements on local radio, by a loudspeaker van perhaps, and most important, by word of mouth. Use your imagination – sometimes schools will give children notices to take home. Making practical arrangements is sometimes tricky, such as when you find the only room available is a primary school classroom with tiny chairs or that you cannot use the tea-making facilities. Considerations like the layout of the chairs are important. Most likely you will want the chairs in a semi-circle, so someone must get there early to organise things. Also, how do you balance the democracy of a public meeting with control by the organising group? If possible, one of the existing group members should chair the meeting. But they may be reluctant to do this, and not very good at it.

If an inexperienced community member is going to chair the meeting, you will need to spend time helping them prepare for various eventualities. Also think about the most appropriate role for you. If you are electing a committee at a public meeting it is imperative for the embryonic group to have some names in advance to put forward, especially for officers, because sometimes totally unsuitable people are nominated or there are no nominations. At the same time, the process should be seen to be democratic. If a meeting is seen as rigged, support may vanish. Before one important meeting (not a public meeting) I had prepared with a keen group member 'our' nominations for secretary, treasurer and chair. Instead of asking for nominations for each office, as a result of which everyone could have made suggestions and during which either of us could have suggested 'our' nominations, he took out the sheet on which I had written these and said, to my considerable embarrassment, that these were the people he and I thought should take the offices! I had failed to prepare this person adequately because I had *assumed* he would know how to handle the situation.

Legitimacy comes from 'doing'

You can't expect, nor would you want, the whole community to attend the normal meetings of community groups. But, if people know of the group, believe that they will be heard or can participate at some level, if they understand that they can use the organisation to take up issues of concern to them, and if the organisation is effective in achieving its goals, this creates legitimacy. This is usually about as far as you can get with regard to local democracy. The best way of preventing community groups from becoming out-of-touch cliques is if the members have continuing personal contact with the rest of the community. By all means have annual meetings. But such meetings are often not well attended. Another way is for the group to arrange representation according to streets, though each street representative may not report back to their neighbours. Other groups collect subscriptions or run a door-to-door lottery. Public events, such as exhibitions, jumble sales or summer fetes often publicise the group, arouse interest and create legitimacy. But it all takes time and organisation.

A newsletter

I once asked residents whether a local newsletter would be a good idea. They said 'yes' but did not say they would run it. A newsletter may well be a high enough priority for a worker to do it if local people cannot. Having said that, some local people will write articles for a newsletter, but the worker will probably have to edit it, and organise printing and distribution. Note though, that producing one copy of a one page (two sides) newsletter took me a week, spread over two months. It also takes time for a newsletter to become well known, so magic results should not be expected. It should be kept simple and come out at regular, though not necessarily frequent intervals. Otherwise it becomes a millstone. Getting it delivered is tricky too, and using volunteers often doesn't work. A local playleader agreed to deliver newsletters to 500 homes – great. Two months later I called to see her about something else. On the top of the wardrobe I saw my 500 newsletters! In the same vein, Ben Reynolds told me: 'I just got an irate call from Mr X saying that hundreds of copies of the newsletter had been dumped in his garden.' For more on newsletters, see www.newsletteraccess.com.

Relationships with the 'outside' world

I once felt like a killjoy explaining to a group why it would be difficult to overturn the policy that a Parks Department football pitch could not be hired on a Sunday. On the one hand, it is sensible to explain such formalities in order to prepare people for the response they will probably get if they tackle the outside world in the 'wrong' way. On the other hand, there is no substitute for people learning through direct experience that the way they want to do something will not work and that other avenues must be explored. Try to create situations where the group will learn not just that a particular approach will not work but why. In the above example, it might have been a good idea to get the Parks Superintendent to come to a meeting to explain the policy to the group rather than doing it myself. Make sure you are personally 'up to speed' with the relevant policies, however. You may also need to explain to groups that 'progress chasing' is often necessary to ensure they get answers to phone calls or letters.

Community groups may initially deal with the authorities inappropriately – with simple aggression, for instance – which can alienate councillors and officials and bring no benefits. Over time, however, most groups can be helped to learn how to deal effectively with power holders, but you may need to assist them to work out the best ways of getting their message across. Having said this, sometimes meeting an angry community group is a good wake-up call for officials and councillors.

There will be times when your group sends a representative to another organisation. However, the 'representative' may not know what it means to do this. For instance: there may be conflicts of interest; they may not realise they should represent 'their' group's views and not their own, report back, etc. Make sure you brief them.

'Professionals' in groups

There is a different dynamic when a community group contains professionals such as housing workers or teachers. They may also talk a different 'language'. (An example of this is that the leader of a local Age Concern group was highly amused when the area director of Social Services said to him, at a meeting 'Write to me on that.') Professionals may not be good at understanding where local people are 'coming from' and may lack the patience to explain simply how they see things and why they operate as they do. At worst they may show a lack of respect to residents, who, as a consequence, feel 'put down'. On the other hand, the exchanges which groups with 'outside professionals' attending them can create are often productive. Residents learn from professionals, for example, the problems of operating a refuse collection service, and professionals learn from residents, in an immediate way, how people perceive community needs. If a professional dominates a community group, imposes their own agenda and doesn't respond to tactful hints, you may need to have a word with them privately. Make sure, too, that, when professionals come to a community group, they know that the group is autonomous and that they are guests, not part of the group. Of course, you may, on occasion want to bring in somebody with technical knowledge to give advice. But it doesn't always work, because the advice giver won't know the local context and 'where group members are at'. So brief both the group and the expert first.

Work with existing groups

Our relationship with groups which come into existence without our help is often not as intimate as with those which we help to create. If you have contacted the group for a particular purpose, remember that it is easier to help a group strengthen its work in an area in which its members are already interested than to get them to change their focus. Also, where a group has asked you to help with a specific problem, it is relatively easy to say you are prepared to do A or B, but not D or E. While we should aim to have such agreements with all groups, it is more difficult when we set up new ones because the members may not initially be ready for such a 'contract'. By contrast, the existing group will already be running itself, so the worker will probably not be drawn into carrying out the myriad activities which are necessary to help a new group get off the ground.

When contacting an existing group, try to find out what they are doing well, what their challenges, are, what they may need help with. Often, there will be actions which the members are taking or not taking which are preventing the group from moving ahead, and, ideally, we need to point such things out. But, in order to do this, we really need to have negotiated an agreement to do so when we start off working with them. However, we may also fear, perhaps correctly, that, if we point out what group members are doing which is problematic, they won't want us to work with them (or not like us!). Of course, being tough is easier if you come in for, say, two months and then go away. If you have to live with the consequences in the locality it may be difficult. But, groups need to face reality if they are to become effective.

Working with moribund groups

How not to revive a moribund group

Once, when I wanted to revive a community group, I discovered that it existed in name only. I decided to work with the sole member, the 'secretary', to re-establish it. However, he was not popular, and his presence had probably prevented other people from continuing in membership. I was concerned about hurting his feelings if I made no effort to involve him, so I told him about meetings, which he came to, but I did most of the organising work with other individuals myself. I wasn't really clear what I was doing, and the group never got off the ground – basically, I made a mess of it. In this kind of situation think carefully and consult with your manager before you act.

When a group was declining, I sometimes asked the members whether it should be disbanded. This normally resulted in people deciding to carry on, perhaps because they could not face the fact that the initiative had failed. I now believe that I should have tried to get them to explore the issue more seriously, examine different alternatives and, perhaps, to face some stark realities rather than simply asking the question. In another case, with a group I only occasionally attended, I eventually told its members I would not be attending any more, explaining why. If you believe that a group should disband, I think you should find the right time and then state that, in your view, the group should cease to exist, and explain why, but also listen to arguments why it should not. You would then probably either withdraw, perhaps unilaterally, or work, with the agreement of the existing members, to help it wind up.

Leading and 'doing for'

Two community development workers tried to help 'traveller' families organise to put their case to the Local Authority for the provision of basic facilities. No organisation emerged after two years' (though somewhat intermittent) work. Consequently, the workers set up some activities, including a literacy scheme and a summer play scheme. As well as providing needed services, their objective was, in part, to show the travellers that something positive could be done, and thereby to engender within them the idea that they could act for themselves, though the workers recognised that this might never happen. Also, it is easy to deceive ourselves that it is really local people themselves who are running a scheme whereas in reality they see us as the leader. When I set up an anti-motorway action group, which local residents certainly wanted, I gathered people together and we started various actions. Only when I discovered that I was doing all the work did I realise that, although I saw the group as theirs, they saw it as mine! They would follow, but they would not lead. So I led because 'product' in this situation was more important than 'process'.

Creating larger organisations and the role of professional staff

The example of a community association illustrates the issues facing large voluntary community organisations (i.e. those composed entirely of volunteers). In Britain, community associations bring together representatives from existing local groups and sometimes statutory bodies, as well as representatives direct from the neighbourhood, into a 'council'. They take up or promote a range of issues or activities, and often run a community centre. If a community association is to be set up, the following questions need considering. Which groups and organisations should be asked to send a representative? Do you want councillors? If so, should they vote? Do you want businesses? What kind of representation should Local Authority departments have, if any? Should professional workers be members or just attend? Should individuals be allowed to join the council? Should you try to run everything through the council or should there be an executive committee and sub-committees? How will any sub-committees differ in practice from similar but independent community groups constituting the organisation? How will financial control be managed (e.g. will the table tennis group have to get permission from the council to buy new balls)? How do you ensure that the various parts of the organisation communicate with each other? Should there be individual subscriptions? How do you get local people to participate in an organisation which has had to develop formal procedures in order to manage itself?

In such community organisations, usually two or three people will run the organisation between them. In theory, decisions are democratic. In reality they are often taken outside the formal meetings by these individuals. In my experience, making a large community organisation function effectively in an area without a great deal of organisational expertise generally requires the services of a professional worker.

'Umbrella' organisations, that is, those composed of people representing a range of interests and organisations, tend to move at the pace of the most conservative, and it is easier to prevent action being taken than to initiate it. Those umbrella organisations which consist of the same type of constituent group (such as federations of tenants' associations), where there is considerable agreement both about the problems and the means by which to solve them, are on occasion able to muster a considerable amount of power. However, in one city a federation of tenants' associations was established. But its main member associations concentrated on the problems of houses made of steel which were now corroding. The other constituent associations whose members lived in brick houses eventually left. A complex community organisation also tends to become remote and act as a buffer between 'simpler' community groups and the authorities, which may expect these always to go through it. It is also difficult for members of an umbrella organisation to give time both to the community group which they represent and to the umbrella organisation, thus increasing the likelihood that it will be dominated by an out-of-touch clique. It requires considerable (skilled) time to ensure the links are kept between umbrella organisations and their constituent groups. Getting the terms of reference right at the beginning in federations or umbrella organisations is also important, because it is vital to ensure that no one group dominates.

If you are assisting a large totally voluntary community organisation, you may find yourself both making proposals to, and implementing decisions for the group, i.e. acting almost as its 'chief officer'. There is a conflict, however, between playing that role and the 'enabling' role. If you are (effectively) the 'chief officer', there are many executive tasks to undertake which involve heart as well as head, and actions taken must sometimes be defended, which makes it difficult to stand back and advise. (For more on such roles and issues, see Chapters 6 and 8.)

Withdrawal: from intensive work to 'servicing' to 'exit'

As our main job as community workers is to assist in the creation of autonomous community groups, we need to know how and when to withdraw. However, while we can and should withdraw from particular groups, there are often other needs requiring our attention in the same area. Also, with high need communities, withdrawal should probably never happen completely. Such communities need continuing support, particularly if those who have gained confidence and skill leave, to be replaced by other disadvantaged people.

For a neighbourhood worker it is possible to identify three types of withdrawal, though the principles are the same for each. These are:

1. withdrawal from an intensive role to a 'servicing' role;
2. withdrawal from a servicing role;
3. leaving that neighbourhood altogether.

Withdrawal is often handled badly. This may be because workers: get satisfaction from being in the centre of the action; feel lost if a group is no longer dependent on them; or feel frustrated with a particular group. It is often easier not to face such (sometimes uncomfortable) feelings. But only if you deal with them can you withdraw in such a way as to benefit the group and community. The emotions of the group's members also need to be taken into account. In the early stages of withdrawal you are: carrying out your old role of servicing the group; preparing, probably, for new challenges elsewhere; and seeking to identify others who can take over certain of your functions. It takes great effort to devote extra attention to the group when you have left it behind mentally. It is during withdrawal that your policy of having an agreement with the group will pay off. If you have given the impression that you will be around for ever and that you are just an ordinary group member, you should not be surprised if the members are angry when you tell them you are withdrawing. However, it will be easier if you have emphasised that your job is to help establish an independent group and if you have discussed your role with its members.

When should you withdraw? The initial period of intensive work, if successful, sees a marked development in the effectiveness of the group. But, even if a worker continues to work intensively, the rate of improvement tends to slow down. It is likely, also, that your aspirations are for the group to achieve a higher level of functioning than is possible. When the group's growth in performance begins to level off, you can either continue to work intensively with it or withdraw to a servicing role, which you would obviously discuss with the group first. (See below for more on this.) If you withdraw to a servicing role, the group might continue in existence at more or less the same level of functioning, or it could decline or even grow. In deciding whether to withdraw, either completely or from an intensive role to a servicing role, you need to work out which scenario is the most likely. There are other factors, too. Perhaps a group is starting somewhere else to which you could be of use, but you do not currently have the time to work with it. Sometimes, the desire among community workers to preserve groups at any cost may inhibit the formation of other groups. Community groups tend to spring up for a particular purpose and then decline. Alternatively, if one allows this natural process to take its course, the groups with which one is working may never become fully effective. If you judge that a particular group is likely to play a part in your future vision for the community, you will probably be unwilling to let it die.

When withdrawing, you should, if possible, help the group establish contact with a range of individuals who can offer help. You could also seek to train an active member to fill your role, or try to link the group with similar groups. Given the frequently short-term nature of community work posts, a role for all workers, from the start, should perhaps be, initially, to identify such support mechanisms and seek to ensure that all the groups with which we work use them.

When you are servicing rather than working intensively with a group, you may attend some meetings, and you may still provide limited assistance. But the group is less dependent on you. It is now increasingly up to the group to ask for advice, and you need to ensure that the members understand this. The worker becomes more of a consultant, reactive rather than 'pro-active'. Once you are in this 'reactive' role you should be wary of becoming involved intensively again. Quite often a crisis would arise in a group just after I had withdrawn and I would feel pressure to take up my old role. Be pragmatic, but understand that, unless you resist that pressure, you may never succeed in withdrawing. You must also find ways of demonstrating that you still regard the group's work as important because, whatever people say, they may feel that they are being betrayed.

When you have withdrawn completely, you will probably wish to maintain a minimum of contact, perhaps by occasionally telephoning the chair to hear how the group is getting on. When you move away from the neighbourhood you may have to withdraw quite quickly from a group with which you have been working intensively. Ideally, we need to inform the people with whom we are working as early as possible that we are thinking of moving on so they can consider the implications. Then, when we have obtained another job, we should try to give ourselves plenty of time to withdraw, say, three months, and talk it through with care with those community and group members with whom we are working.

Project closure

Simpson (1995b) eloquently describes the closure of a whole project. In this project, closure was planned for twelve months ahead. All the staff stayed until the end, and, since the Local Authority had agreed to take over some aspects of the work, closure was not traumatic.

But it was still time-consuming. Other projects may be closed down because the funder has failed to renew funding, perhaps late in the day, in a situation where some staff have already left, where those remaining are in conflict with each other and where, consequently, no real work is carried out for several months before the close-down. Morale is usually at rock bottom and there is probably no will to devise a good exit plan. I've lived through one of these closedowns and it isn't fun. Simpson (1995b) lists the following points which, ideally, should be taken into account when closing a project:

● Plan an exit strategy a year in advance, alert others about the timescale, and withdraw gradually.
● Make a list of what needs to be done and when: disconnecting telephones; winding up the photocopier lease; letters of thanks, disposing of files, closing bank accounts, etc.
● Seek to ensure the work you are undertaking is replaced by other organisations.
● Have the withdrawal strategy on a chalk board and review it regularly.
● Keep sponsors, management committee and community groups informed and, if possible, involved.
● Ensure an evaluation of the work is completed, consider what dissemination activities might be useful and carry them out.
● Ensure that staff redundancy procedures are understood and the time is taken to implement these properly.
● Agree the principles on which the disposal of assets will be decided before deciding their actual disposal, preferably in written form at the beginning of the project.
● Bear in mind that project closure can be a particularly painful process as the equipment in the office starts disappearing before one's eyes!

Conclusion

Facilitating the development of community groups: is both draining and exhilarating; makes you laugh and cry at the same time; requires objectivity but is also an art rather than a science; allows you to let your hair down sometimes but also requires you to be very organised; is repetitive but gives scope for creativity. It is also highly personal – you will need to find your own style.

Points to ponder

1. What are the most important things to take account of when setting up and working with autonomous community groups?
2. What skills do you need?
3. When should you start thinking of withdrawing from a group?
4. Should you develop a contract with a community group, and what should this consist of?
5. In a regeneration scheme, in which the Local Authority was investing many millions of pounds, a particular resident was putting all sorts of unrealistic and unfair obstacles in the way and, in effect, stopping the scheme moving ahead. He was not popular in the community, though he had a small following. The Local Authority consulted with several key players and then said they would not continue with the programme with him on the group. He left. What is your view of the Local Authority's action?

Further reading

Freeman (1970) *The Tyranny of Structurelessness.*
Goetschius (1969) *Working with Community Groups.*
Henderson and Thomas (2002) *Skills in Neighbourhood Work.*
Skinner (1997) *Building Community Strengths: A Resource Book on Capacity Building.*

4 Community groups: dealing with practical issues and problems

Understanding community participation

You work for two years with little success trying to organise a group to take up a range of social issues. Then a newspaper article suggests some waste land may be used as a gypsy site. Overnight an organisation forms in the same area and quickly organises a 24-hour picket! The basis for bringing people together is self-interest. Even when people are altruistically motivated, personal interest will dictate their area of involvement. Our first job is to understand their motivation and self-interest.

As well as divisions of class, gender, age and race there are many more subtle differences between groups of people. For instance, Jamaicans might prefer not to mix with Grenadans. If the first people who join a particular community activity are from one 'sub-group', the 'roughs', for instance, the 'respectables' will not come and vice versa. Whatever activity is started, it will quickly attract an image which, in effect, prevents other people from participating. In addition, people often think of their 'home area' as encompassing only a few streets, and, perhaps for that reason, it is common for meetings of neighbourhood groups to be attended only by people who live less than a quarter of a mile from the meeting place. All these factors tend to inhibit wider attendance and increase cliquishness.

For some people in bad housing, improvement means a transfer, but for others it means refurbishing existing property; all the members of a community sharing a problem may want different solutions or to achieve the agreed solution in different ways. Often, only those whose approach is adopted stay in the group. Previous unsatisfactory experiences in groups can also inhibit participation, and people easily become cynical. 'We tried this before, and nothing happened' is a common, and understandable response to an invitation to get involved. The forces keeping people in community groups are, thus, relatively weak.

There is some evidence that really poor people (especially women) may join together in collective action if the situation is bad enough (see, for example, Gallagher, 1977; Piven and Cloward, 1977). But, normally the worker will have to work slowly by providing simple services, arranging social activities for example, gradually building up motivation and confidence. Other barriers to participation are a lack of contacts, knowledge, education and position. Those with these advantages are more able to participate effectively. Broadly speaking, poor people do not have such advantages, especially if they live disorganised lives.

Participation by local people in activities run by the community itself (e.g. fun days) is sometimes called horizontal participation. Participation in seeking to change policies which are primarily the responsibility of government can be seen as vertical participation. Some examples of the latter are: campaigns of many kinds; joint Local Authority community working parties on crime prevention; tenant consultative committees; and parent representation on the managing bodies of schools. Vertical participation (especially at a high policy level) usually requires local people to sit in (boring) meetings month after month, read long papers and come to terms with the differing points of view of many vested interests. If you have stayed the course, you often get only the tiniest bit of what you originally wanted. There are very few local people who have the stomach and skills for that, and they tend to get to that point after several years of working on smaller more local issues. But the vast majority prefer to stick with horizontal participation. Don't confuse the two. (Note, there is also what I call 'low-level' vertical participation, when beneficiaries of a service are asked their views on something that can quite easily be changed, for example, the opening hours of a youth centre.)

Vertical participation is also problematic, both because government often purports to consult when it really wants to get support for what *it* wants to do and because community groups sometimes think their view will prevail when they are merely being consulted or even informed. Also, local people are sometimes 'consulted to death' but, understandably, become disillusioned when 'nothing changes'. Think clearly when involving community groups in (especially high-level) vertical participation because they can be used merely to legitimate decisions which would have been taken anyway and which may not be in their community's interest. In reality, community workers themselves often play a major (social planning) role here in that it is they who feed the community issues through to the policy-makers and sit on the 'boring committees'. This, to me, makes a great deal of sense, and it is often the best way to go about ensuring effective vertical participation, at least vicariously.

Understanding and influencing group processes

Helping groups make decisions

Community groups often find it difficult to take even small decisions. I have been to meetings where hours have been spent discussing, for example, how many coffee cups should be bought. Some group members (probably unconsciously) hope to take every decision in the whole group and by consensus. A worker needs to try to get a group to agree about member roles, i.e. who can decide about what, and which matters have to be brought to a meeting for decision. Another way to help a group deal with this kind of thing is to encourage members to vote occasionally. That is, we need to seek to apply simple management techniques to their decision-making and implementation processes.

Group A discussed making a grant to group B but decided, I thought, to defer the matter until the next week. At the next meeting the matter was not mentioned until a member raised it, only to find that the treasurer had already paid over the money! You need to anticipate such problems and, perhaps, intervene to ensure that everyone knows the decision, particularly if minutes of meetings are not well kept. However, when an important item comes up unexpectedly, you might try to have the decision deferred to another meeting, when people will have had time to think about it. There will be other occasions when a group continually postpones a difficult decision, and you may have to work both with individuals and with the group as a whole to help the members face it. Remember, too, that people do not always act 'logically'. Let us say that the chair takes the minutes of meetings. A suggestion that there should be a separate minutes secretary, which would be in the chair's own interest, might well be rejected because it could be perceived as criticism. Many needs are met in groups which are not to do with the stated aims of the group. If the stated aim requires a meeting once a month but the group is meeting weekly, the reason may be that the more frequent meetings cater for expressive needs (see Chapter 1), which even the members do not recognise. When working with any group, workers can usefully ask themselves which needs it is meeting and for whom, since meeting the unstated needs of some members may cause frustration for others.

With some groups you may find it difficult to get a word in at all. One way to deal with this is to mention to the chair beforehand that there is a particular point you want to raise. If a group does not accept an idea from the worker, this does not necessarily mean the members have forgotten about it. We should be patient and continue 'sowing seeds'. We never know when they will bear fruit. Note particularly that, if you are raising something completely new at a meeting, however logical you are and however well prepared you are, the group may not pay much attention. It may take two or three meetings for them to come round to the idea.

Making meetings work

Few people will attend meetings regularly which go on after 10pm, so, try to ensure they are kept reasonably short. Also, the thoughts of members often do not coincide with items on the agenda: they might prefer to speak of a personal experience, gossip or tell a joke. Some allowance should be made for people to express these feelings, which helps a group to 'gel'. Otherwise, the decision-making process may feel rather sterile. However, meeting such needs may conflict with effective decision-taking. Some group members are good at ensuring tasks are effectively undertaken; others are better at meeting 'expressive' needs. Try to promote the right balance. Note, also, that emotions affect decisions in groups. For example, there may be opposition to a sensible proposal purely because it was made by a certain person; or, if there are bad feelings between group members, a significant point may be 'lost in vitriol'. Good points can also be ignored if they are made by an inarticulate person.

You also need to be clear what kind of meeting it is – a 'business meeting' where good focus and organisation are vital or, say, a community forum, where ideas can be expressed loosely and where you want people to 'think outside the box' and to network.

Groups often concentrate on the tasks they enjoy rather than what they 'ought' to be doing. It is good if you can find some tasks which are fun and easy to do, since groups often begin to 'gel' when the members work together. One such occasion was when the carnival committee I worked with spent several evenings turning two roomfuls of groceries into 1,200 Christmas parcels for old people! It is also interesting to note that this group had as its original purpose running the carnival – it only decided to give Christmas parcels when it accidentally made a profit. Later, the members spoke as if the main aim of the carnival was to raise money for that purpose. That is, the group had changed its focus without its members realising this. The role of the worker here might be to help members see what is happening and decide if this is what they want.

A few group members will take it seriously and do most of the work, including the boring but vital jobs, while others just turn up for the fun bits or don't do any work. Showing those who do all the work that you recognise this and them is important, because they may not get much positive feedback otherwise – often just criticism.

Some group members keep 'going on' about the same point even when they are clearly in the minority. In some situations, it is useful to give them proper space to have their say, put it to the vote, and, assuming they lose, ensure that the decision is minuted, so that, if they complain, the chair can point out that the matter was discussed, voted on and finished with. Also, try visiting such individuals at home to sort such matters out.

Chairing meetings

If an inexperienced person is selected as chair, you will need to train them, before they take up the role if possible. Incidentally some 'professionals' are awful chairs, so make sure you learn this skill too. If you have to chair the meeting because nobody else wants or is able to do it, explain that you are only doing it on a temporary basis and will help somebody else to take over as soon as possible.

Over-involvement

A local volunteer may become so involved in, say, running a youth club, that they open it every night, find that they cannot cope, and have to reduce it to one day, thus creating frustration in the young people. When problems arise, emotionally over-involved people are likely to react as if they had been personally insulted, blaming the people for whose benefit they are supposed to be working. The enthusiasm turns to a sense of martyrdom, and often the person gives up. Be prepared for people to get over-involved and the likely consequences.

Keeping calm

I rarely see a calm community worker – they're usually rushing around with too many projects on the go at the same time, leaving lots of loose ends. They also get pressed into doing things *for* groups when they should really be facilitating.

(Bill Jenkins, personal communication)

When groups organise events, crises sometimes occur. The man providing transport for the older participants does not arrive, but Jane is going that way to collect the ice cream and agrees to do the job. Then she finds she has to go to the other side of town and forgets. We can have a calming effect on others if we can appear calm. Similarly, if you speak confidently, even if you do not feel it, you will raise the confidence of those around you. Whatever the mood of the group, keep a level head and try to create balance. You are thus helping people, sometimes by example, to develop the skills and attitudes to run things themselves. 'My role is to say "Hang on a minute, let's not get carried away with this" (which can be either unwarranted despair or over-enthusiasm' (Anthony Brito, personal communication).

Knowing your group members

Some people 'switch off' in groups, just as others may talk too much. Some call a 'spade a spade'. Others keep quiet but get work done. Some criticise (the group and/or you) from the sidelines. Others like to be in charge. Understanding them and their styles will help you assist the group. To do this, go to the pub occasionally with them afterwards, if that is what they do, or go on a trip from time to time if they organise one. One community leader was keen for me to see where he worked – a shoe factory – and organised a tour for me. I went because it helped build the relationship. But keep such activity in proportion. While it will help you do the job; it is not *the* job.

Perceptions

The neighbourhood office which I managed also ran an advice service. Consequently, we became tagged with a 'welfare' label, as a result of which some residents refused to come to our building. Because, as a community worker, I succeeded a 'motherly', female worker, some of the women with whom she had worked became quite resentful that I was not prepared or possibly able to give them the same attention as she had done. Find out how you are perceived by keeping your eyes and ears open, and develop a range of contacts (including colleagues or staff you manage) whom you can ask for feedback.

Our presence in a community may have a symbolic value for people. The fact that I was *their* worker and the neighbourhood centre was *their* project probably helped several people in the neighbourhood I worked in to feel that someone cared about them. Dora never came to our advice centre, but I was told she kept a list of opening times in her purse. One effect created by the newsletter which we ran was a feeling of pride among some residents that their estate had a newsletter while others did not. We ignore at our peril these intangible aspects of our work, because what goes on in people's heads can make the difference between success and failure (see Goleman, 1996).

Making mistakes

The adventure playground in the community where I worked was having to be moved from our estate to a new site between it and a neighbouring one. We had done some door-knocking on the neighbouring estate to inform people, but this was not very thorough, nor had they been consulted beforehand. When some residents there opposed the move, I tried to retrieve the situation by spending time with the key protester. I admitted that we were at fault since we had not discussed the matter with her community earlier, and I told her how she could oppose the move of the playground, at the same time saying that, as its chair, I could not support her. When we have made a mistake it is normally best to admit our error and meet the criticism head on. We will have fewer problems in the long run if we are as honest as possible in this respect. I've often learned by getting it wrong, and sometimes more than once!

Dealing with conflict and prejudice

The prominence of certain community leaders often generates negative feelings locally. Some community leaders heighten antagonism, by making sure that it is always their photograph which appears in the paper, for example. Also, consider the following story. Two bingo group leaders once had a vicious argument in another committee over a trivial matter. The real issue was that they each saw the other as a threat. Subsequently, one of them informed the police that the other was running bingo illegally. Think carefully before you get involved in such situations, and remember the first rule for any kind of intervention: 'make sure you don't make things worse!' Also, consider whether you can build conflict resolution procedures early on into the processes groups adopt because, when the conflict arrives, it is often too late to agree a procedure.

When people living in poor circumstances come together for the first time they often express anger, usually against the authorities. Help them articulate their discontent and work through it. It is often a necessary step on the way to effective action. Note, however, that people who are constantly critical of others can be difficult to work with.

A worker with tenants living in appalling accommodation found that personality differences between members were jeopardising the group's survival. He confronted the group and pointed out that, if the members continued to disagree violently, they would never succeed in their campaign. His point was accepted, and the inter-personal conflict subsided somewhat. But he had a high status in the group, and the members were strongly motivated. Remember, too, that most people avoid conflict if they can. An agreement, made by a group member prior to a meeting, to raise an issue, might come to nothing in practice if it meant challenging the leadership. (See mediation in Chapter 8, and also Goetschius, 1969, pp. 93–5.)

Be prepared that local people may formally complain about you if you are not working in ways they want. 'Sometimes, if you play things right, you can get the community "eating out of your hand". But then something goes wrong and you turn into "Mrs Badwoman" overnight' (Sara Bower, personal communication).

You may also have to deal with hostility from councillors, or officials, so learn to apply the principles of assertiveness. When criticised, you are likely to experience a thumping heart, hot face ('flooding', see Goleman, 1996). We need to 'manage' those feelings and deal with the issue calmly because, when we're agitated, we can't think straight. One way of dealing with situations involving personal criticism of you (if you can manage it!) is to listen carefully to what is being said by the other party, acknowledge that this is what they feel and to say you will let them have your response later when you have had time to think about it calmly. If any criticism is deserved, apologise. However, at times it can be appropriate to 'allow' oneself to get angry. If done extremely rarely and with good reason, showing you are upset or even losing your temper can be effective in getting your point across and getting people to behave differently.

When community groups first pressurise the authorities, councillors and officials may become angry and try to force the group to give up (perhaps via the community worker – especially if he or she is an employee of the Local Authority). But if groups can be helped to persevere, the authorities sometimes come to recognise that the group is doing a useful job and tolerate a certain amount of conflict. On the other hand, such conflict can also cause resentment lasting decades. As we are dealing with individuals, people tend to take criticism personally and have long memories. Note also, that organisations tend to 'close ranks' if one of their number is criticised, even though others in that organisation may have a similar view of that person.

You generally need to show respect to people whose views you do not share, while making clear where you are not in agreement (if necessary) and trying to find common ground. But, what about dealing with prejudice?

Sometimes the people we work with make what we consider to be prejudiced statements about immigrants, gays and other minority groups. Such statements can certainly be challenged on the spot (not easy for most of us I think), but silence can also communicate disapproval. Also, if you do not know how to respond at the time, you can think about it and raise the matter later. Or, you can say something like '*I* don't like to hear remarks like . . .'. More generally, community work is ultimately about (largely social) justice, and, you may need to take opportunities to make this explicit. Also, ideally, the people with whom we work need to 'buy in' to these values. We are not working with them with no reference to the wider 'good'. If, for example, a community group opposes the establishment of a hostel for recovering mentally ill people and your sympathy, in this case, lies with the 'authorities' not the group, I suggest you explain to the group what your position is and the terms on which you will work with them, withdrawing if necessary.

There are always dilemmas, though. The election was a few weeks away and the local action committee invited the political parties to say how they planned to improve the area. The British National Party (far right) wanted to come. We allowed them to. If a racist group wants to run a Christmas party for local children, what do you say, and who is 'you'?

Manipulation

At the beginning of a meeting with housing officials, a housing worker paid a compliment to one of the residents. That resident told me later that she felt this inhibited her from criticising the housing department in the meeting. Ernie had let it be known that he was thinking of resigning from a particular committee. Fred, knowing I was in contact with Ernie, told me that he and the treasurer would resign if Ernie did, his unstated objective being to get me to prevent Ernie from resigning. Because emotional factors are brought to bear, such pressure can sometimes be difficult to resist, but the best response is either a carefully thought out one or no response at all.

A counselling role?

When you find that the only issues some people are prepared to talk about are personal problems, you can find you are assuming the role of social worker. The main role of a community worker with individuals is to help them learn how to undertake (mainly collective) action for community benefit, so you should normally steer clear or refer them elsewhere. You can get into difficulties if you are mixing the two roles. Nevertheless, there are times when it is reasonable to act as a counsellor, especially (perhaps only) with residents with whom you are already working as a community development worker and who seek your help in a crisis.

Getting groups to evaluate, and learning by doing

Sometimes, when groups make mistakes, the lessons are obvious and the members change their behaviour. However, facing the need for such a change may be so threatening that they are afraid to look at their mistakes, inventing rationalisations to explain them away. Ideally, therefore, you need to agree with the group to review progress every six months. But, they may not want it. Also, who should do it and by what right? Further, what if the main problem is Joe who dominates meetings or Jane who promises to do everything but never does? I've not known this done well in small community organisations. It isn't easy criticising people with whom you work closely with, who you've kind of 'grown up' with. As they are volunteers, you arguably don't have much legitimacy to take them to task, and they might leave if you do. 'We usually we just ignore the fact that some members do poor work' (Anthony Brito, personal communication). Having noted this, the growing emphasis today on evaluation in British community work should make it easier for us to structure this into our work with groups.

Without periodic reviews, or even with them, you will have to use other methods. If you consider that the group is not effective because Jack is doing all the work without prior approval by the committee, you might raise this either with Jack privately, or with other individuals or even in the group meeting. If you have a good relationship with the group and if the commitment of Jack and the other members is high, they may be prepared to collaborate to solve the problem. Otherwise, you may create friction to no avail. You might, therefore, have to restrict your role to making minor practical suggestions when the opportunity arose. Also, when something which a worker predicted would go wrong does go wrong, check out, afterwards, whether the group members now understand how to avoid making the same mistake again. But do not expect them to say you were right after all. Your satisfaction must be in seeing the changed behaviour. (See also Goetschius, 1969, pp. 106–111, on helping a group to evaluate.)

Using the media

> I once worked to develop 'Tunetown' which encouraged 'budding' musicians, especially many 'excluded' young people, to develop their skills, helped them get gigs and generally to develop the live music scene. However, we were too modest in shouting about what we did, and the work was taken for granted.
>
> (Ben Reynolds, personal communication)

The media can sometimes help your cause a great deal, so you need to work out ways to use them. If reporters have been invited to a community event, they may not attend. Or they may highlight a minor remark, making it seem as if the group is criticising the council. Reporters also often try to talk to people whom they consider will be articulate, such as community workers. However, they can gradually be 'trained' to talk to local people. The chair of a parent-teacher association who was interviewed on the day of a well-attended fete criticised the community for lack of support, and his words appeared as a headline the next day! So brief your local leader beforehand.

In order to control the information you give the media, have a short press release prepared, and take this, plus a photograph, to the local newspaper office. It pays also to establish contact with the news editor, some time prior to major events taking place, who will provide advice on how to get the best coverage and make a story newsworthy. Remember also to supply newspapers with regular items of (good) news which may prevent them from printing articles which negatively stereotype the community.

With local radio, be prepared for a variety of questions. While people mostly become used to speaking on the radio fairly quickly, they may need support to start with. There are now a number of simple handbooks on these subjects. There are also training courses on public speaking and media presentation.

Relationships with politicians

A friendly councillor is a great help to a community group, while an unsympathetic one can be obstructive and destructive. Therefore, community groups must try to get councillors on their side. Local politicians place great store on the fact that they were elected, and many are suspicious of unelected community organisations. They may see community workers as a threat because we are involved in supporting activity which can challenge the council. Or, they may pay lip-service to community participation but speak against it in private. Contact with community groups and workers can help councillors better understand the perspectives of local people and argue their case in the council. But councillors have many pressures (and limited power anyway), and they will not always be able to represent the interests of the community group effectively. There is a particular danger with friendly councillors. If they are generally helpful to a community group, its members may too readily accept the situation when the councillor says that nothing can be done. So, the group should still make its own representations rather than relying entirely on the councillor.

In Britain today, Local Authority officers and councillors have to collaborate with a range of other organisations to seek solutions to complex problems, in conditions of considerable uncertainty. The need to work in such ways is not always well understood by councillors, and community workers have an important role in assisting them to see how collaborative ways of working can assist everybody. Well-organised communities can also assist the council in bids for central government funds.

Members of Parliament, while more remote, can sometimes intervene to good effect in local matters. A letter from an MP to the leader of the council, particularly if it draws attention to a procedure which had not been properly followed, can sometimes ensure that a case is re-examined. It is important to try to establish relationships with potential councillors or MPs *before* they are elected.

Personal politics

If community groups are *perceived* as pursuing party political goals, and if workers are *perceived* as politicians 'in disguise' either by our managers or by elected representatives, they may receive less co-operation from officials and from councillors in general (not merely from those in opposing parties). Community work can legitimately be described in a variety of ways to fit in with the major ideologies, and it is usually possible to 'sell' it in terms which are acceptable to most political parties.

Living in the area

If a worker is working across a large area, it is usually sensible to live in it. It is different for a neighbourhood worker, though. When I was a fieldworker, my wife and I lived for a time in a council house which served also as office, advice centre, and meeting place for groups (we also shared the toilet!). Some advantages were that I made contacts easily and appreciated the needs of other residents who also identified with me because, to a degree, I was one of them. However, in this situation you can feel guilty you are off duty and a group is meeting without you. Some people call at all hours, often on trivial matters. What happens if you are ill or on holiday but at home? You may not be able find the 'space' to write reports. There is also the danger, when deeply involved in day-to-day work, of losing the objectivity necessary for good practice. I only did serious thinking about my work when I was away from the building for a whole weekend or more. The pressures on a partner can also be considerable. We moved out after two years but I continued working there. I do not think the work suffered as a result. So don't feel guilty about not living in the area if you think you (or your family) can survive better by living outside it. If you don't live there, planned local networking is vital.

Some paradoxes of buildings

Sometimes 'community houses' are provided, especially on council housing estates, for community groups, but community members often underestimate the problems of running them. If *you* are responsible for even a small building, note that cleaning and caretaking must be arranged, wages paid, repairs undertaken, neighbours (sometimes) placated and a booking schedule organised. There may be conflict between various users. The creation of a user committee can sometimes help, and some of these tasks can be delegated. But it still takes some time to liaise with the user groups and to manage the caretaker, cleaner, etc. Some community buildings have bars, which can also be a minefield.

Community groups seeking to obtain a large community centre often underestimate the management and running costs. They then have a huge shock when it opens. So, try to ensure that a group with this objective understands in advance the problems it is likely to face. A development plan, which specifies what you want to do, how you want to do it, what it will cost, and how you will pay for it, is a 'must'. With a good plan and adequate help, community groups can sometimes run such buildings more efficiently than Local Authorities. A related point is that community groups are sometimes expected to become self-funding through trading, particularly if they have a community building – in most cases, an unrealistic aim. However, with a proper business orientation, a group with an appropriate building could raise a greater proportion of its running costs, say, 30 per cent rather than 10 per cent (see also the section on community economic development in Chapter 8).

Advice centres

Some community workers believe that a good way to initiate community involvement is to set up an advice centre, on the assumption either that residents will run the service or that individual advice work will generate collective action. However, if you run an advice centre, you will need to be in the building during opening hours. For every hour the centre is open, you spend another hour collecting information, keeping up to date on legislation and taking further action on some cases. This will all detract from work with community groups. Some advice centres are 'drop-in' places where people are encouraged to stay as long as they like. This approach, while sometimes excellent, also has disadvantages. How does a worker in such a centre generate a relaxed atmosphere and, at the same time, preserve confidentiality? Some people may become upset because they feel that certain individuals are monopolising the place. Or, you may feel you are doing useful work just because you are in contact with people all day, without working out what you are trying to achieve – 'mindless activism!' In spite of these difficulties, advice work, when well thought through, represents one of the successful innovations closely connected with community work.

Information and communication technology (ICT)

ICT has helped many 'excluded' people gain information, contacts, confidence and skills. The opportunities for disabled and relatively immobile people (e.g. in rural areas) to interact, gain and share information are hugely improved by electronic forms of communication, some of which are designed specifically for people with impairments. However, for probably most 'excluded' people it is the nature of the relationships they have with friends, outreach workers or other professionals which enables them to utilise any available equipment. The relationships, coupled with appropriate training, make the technology 'user friendly'. The availability of the equipment alone (in libraries or community centres, for instance) may not, of itself, encourage many 'excluded' people to access it. Having said this, some hitherto 'excluded' people take to computers like ducks to water, virtually unaided, and use them to make their 'journey into the acting community'.

Also, such technology offers new ways of consulting, especially with young people, e.g. chat rooms, texting, pop up surveys, etc. Use your imagination here, but don't assume everybody has a computer.

Conclusion

This chapter has focused largely on what workers need to do in order to assist community groups. However, if you don't focus on yourself, too, you will never be truly effective. This is what we turn to next.

Points to ponder

1. What are the key factors to bear in mind about citizen participation?
2. What do you need to do in order to make a meeting work?
3. What kind of conflicts are you likely to experience in work with community groups, and how do you expect to deal with them?

Further reading

Allen and May (2007) 'Setting up for Success: A Practical Guide for Community Organisations'.

Arnstein (1969) 'A Ladder of Participation'.

Goleman (1996) *Emotional Intelligence: Why It Can Matter More Than IQ*.

Laber (1997) *Group Process: Working Effectively by Committee*.

Zimmerman (1997) *Robert's Rules in Plain English: A Readable, Authoritative Easy to Use Guide to Running Meetings*.

5 | Survival, personal development and reflective practice

Surviving agency pressure

I spend half my time visiting my staff in out-posted locations preventing them having breakdowns.

(Community work manager, personal communication)

Employers can, broadly, require their staff to do the work which they, the employers, determine, though good employers recognise that their best asset is the intelligence and goodwill of employees. However, community workers nearly always have three 'masters': their employer, the community (or a particular group) and their own conscience. There are times when the employer wants a worker to act in ways which the worker believes will not benefit the community or will conflict with what the community seem to want. We need to understand how we are being used; otherwise we can be drawn unwittingly into undertaking work which does not benefit the community.

A worker employed by a Local Authority, of which the planning department proposed to build a community centre, brought local people together to discuss the plans. Some residents wanted to submit proposals for a different type of building in a different place. But the Local Authority was not prepared to discuss alternatives, and the worker found himself being used to 'sell' the existing plan to the residents.

There are four broad options for dealing with agency pressure (all of which you will use to some degree):

1. Simply conforming to agency expectations. Although this is fairly common, it constitutes bad practice if it is the main approach we take, especially if used without thought.
2. Getting into overt conflict with your employers on the issue. If you go down this road, you need to be pretty sure you will win.

Most likely you will be told to toe the line, and, if you persist, you may find yourself disciplined. Paradoxically though, the time to make a stand is often at the beginning, and you can sometimes earn respect by doing so. But you may be 'on probation' for the first six months, which can also make self-assertion difficult.

3. Working clandestinely. Here, you do what *you* decide to do, try to avoid being held to account, only 'play the game' of being supervised, don't keep (totally honest) records and merely create an outward show of doing what the agency wants. There are major disadvantages in making this one's main way of working. First, you will not receive agency support and may become isolated. Second, you will, in the end, be discovered and stopped. Third, if we avoid being accountable to the agency, this means we have given up the battle to make it change. Finally, if there are no records or agency backing for our work, our successors are unlikely to take up the same issues, and much of our work will have been in vain.

4. Accepting the realities of how the agency uses you but working to change these. This is the mode we will mostly use. But it requires persistence, compromise, playing a waiting game and a good deal of effort to argue the case for the kind of work which we think should be undertaken.

Resisting project closure

Richard, a community centre warden, was about to lose his job because the (central government) funding would run out in three months. The education department which administered the project wanted to transfer it to the social services department who would have dismissed Richard and used the building for other purposes. The project was tightly controlled by three councillors who had little contact with the centre. What to do? Early on in the project Richard, aware that the funding was time-limited, should have produced information to show what a useful job he was doing and how this work assisted with the objectives of the Local Authority. This information would have described some interesting pieces of work, using statistics to show, for example, increased use of the building. He could also have made sure that a flow of this material went unsolicited to councillors, residents' groups, the local Member of Parliament, etc.

Richard could have attempted to involve the councillors in the work of the centre; frequent contact with the user groups might have helped them identify with the centre's objectives. He should have sought to convert people of influence in the Local Authority to his cause and obtained the assistance of other members of the management committee with this. He might have considered getting strong user-group representatives and sympathetic outsiders onto his management committee. He should have prepared outside parties for the approaching danger – residents' groups, churches, officials from other departments, sympathetic councillors, and the MP. Taking care not to be 'discovered', he could have asked a sympathetic person to break the story to the local newspaper. Finally, having heard that there was a proposal to transfer the centre to the social services department, he could have prepared an alternative plan showing how the needs of the area could be better met if *his* proposal was implemented. That way, he would have been taking the initiative, and his superiors would have had to fight to some degree on his ground.

Building protection and creating space

You can be exposed in this work, so you need to build protection. Ideally this should be from the person to whom you are directly responsible. If your supervisor has approved your action beforehand, and this action turns out to have been beyond the limits set by the agency, he or she takes the main responsibility. Also, establish relationships with people who have influence as soon as you start work – they may be able to help protect you if problems occur. Creating the space to work in ways we think are appropriate requires careful thought. If, for instance, you have made yourself highly regarded in the agency by undertaking everything asked of you, your superiors may be prepared to accept, later, that you spend, say, 15 per cent of your time in areas of work which are less important to the agency.

Work plans

Within the framework of the overall project/team plan (see Chapter 2) you, the worker, need a plan, which should be reviewed regularly. Such a plan gives you the advantage when discussing your proposed work with senior managers because they will need to react to *your* plan. Design it, if you can, in such a way as to give such managers what they want. If not, the project will eventually lose high-level support. We must be able to present our case well to power holders, convince them that the project assists them achieve their goals, and educate them about community work.

Getting out at the right time

There is also the question of what action to take if the employing circumstances are oppressive.

> Most of us have a point where the dissonance between what we are having to do and what we are strongly committed to doing clash so that we become stressed and lose faith in our ability and our work. A colleague, advising me when I was working for an oppressive organisation, said: 'Leave now, while you have something to take.' We should not ignore how connected to values our work is. I have seen many excellent colleagues leave the field disheartened because they didn't prioritise 'themselves' over a reluctance to give up on a job that wasn't leading in a direction that benefited them or the community.
>
> (Sue Allen, personal communication)

You may also sometimes feel that you've gone about as far as you can go with a job. While you still feel committed to it, new blood may be necessary to take it further. It is surprising how often new opportunities open up when you do decide to move on.

The stresses of the job

These include:

- job insecurity and the sometimes constant struggle to get funding renewed;
- the need to do lots of different things – 'keeping many balls in the air';
- the need to relate one minute to a youth club member and the next to the Social Services Dept director – 'emotional gymnastics';
- surviving with fewer staff than you really need;

- coping with isolation, the lack of support and not having a professional bureaucracy to shelter behind;
- the frustration of working for an employer who does not understand and may to some degree be opposed to what one judges needs to be done, coupled with being exposed to pressure (from elected representatives, for example);
- the slow progress in work with community groups which often go over the same ground meeting after meeting;
- irregular working hours, which can be an advantage but may take its toll on your private life;
- the pressure for concrete results, which may be inappropriate;
- the emotional effort of constant innovation; always having to step back and think carefully about what one is doing, rather than undertaking routine work;
- having to try to please everyone;
- constant uncertainty (handling this well is one hallmark of an effective community worker).

If we do not find functional ways of relieving these stresses, we may find ourselves:

- taking on too much, failing to say 'no', rushing around without any strategic direction;
- failing to plan, acting purely intuitively, allowing ourselves to be manipulated;
- getting depressed and physically ill (burning out);
- over-reacting under pressure;
- avoiding difficult situations;
- wasting time by chatting or moaning much of the day.

Towards more effective, and reflective, practice

Developing a theoretical framework is your first protection and means of handling pressure, so that you have a clear focus and know where you are trying to go. Take time to think through what you are doing, and make sure you have a reasonable work–life balance. You won't make good decisions if you don't. And make sure you read around your subject regularly. You take 'hits' in community work (see Bill Clinton, 2004, on this), and you'll need all the help you can to bounce back.

Ideally, community workers should only be employed in teams. If there is only one worker, the work stops temporarily if he or she is ill, has serious personal problems, or leaves. Also, the stresses on a single worker are greater than on a team, where members can provide mutual support. However, many workers do work alone, and what follows is designed, in particular, to assist them.

We often need someone to listen to us, to 'be there' and perhaps to assure us that we are doing a worthwhile job, particularly when there are few concrete achievements to see, or there is pressure to work in ways which we do not agree with. This kind of support can come from family or friends. However, we also need someone to help us stand back and look critically at our work. But how is that to be achieved? If your manager has community work knowledge and/or shares community work values, that is probably the best way. But many workers are managed by someone without this, which, together with the fact that they are also accountable to him or her, may prevent the growth of sufficient trust. (For managers, see Chapters 6 and 8 on professional supervision.)

Another possibility is finding an outside consultant to provide critical support. However, such a consultant must be able to empathise not only with the community work task but also with the situation of being an employee within that particular organisation. When arranging such a consultancy a worker should seek to devise the terms of the contract so that the arrangement terminates after, say, six sessions, unless the worker wants it to continue. Otherwise it is easy to slide into a useless routine which everyone fears to break. The contract also needs to ensure that the consultant serves the worker and not the agency, so that it is clear where his or her loyalty lies. (Agencies also sometimes engage consultants for whole community projects, in which case it is vital for the consultant to be clear whether he or she is advising the employer or the workers.) You can also get support from other community workers in the same locality; all workers should try to meet regularly with their peers, either individually or in a group. However, these types of meeting may not give you *critical* support and can become 'moan sessions'. Some such groups engage a consultant to help the members look at their work. This can work well as long as the consultant knows their job and there is commitment among the members to work at professional self-improvement. Networks of community workers are also important in ensuring that we learn from each other and don't 'reinvent the wheel'. Finally, I received a great deal of support from some of the members of the communities in which I worked. My relationship with some of them became more that of colleague than anything else, and, just as they used me for support, so I sometimes used them.

Community workers are, to some degree, licensed critics. Even if only by implication, we are criticising the status quo when we help people organise to change it. In order to develop effective practice, we must identify what *knowledge* we need. We also require specific *skills*. Third, there are our personal *qualities*, and this is by far the most difficult area. We may have a tendency towards shyness or impatience, or be over-reluctant to challenge others, for example, which can prevent us performing certain functions well. Many of us are afraid to face our weaknesses and therefore neglect to work on them. Sometimes we have to learn to live with and compensate for them; I have always been rather inarticulate when caught off guard, for instance. When examining ourselves it is vital to look at our strengths first; otherwise our confidence may ebb away completely. (Remember, *everybody* has weaknesses, not just you!)

Many people active in community work share one particular Achilles' heel – lack of assertiveness. The main form of this is not wanting to displease other people. Assertiveness is not aggression, nor manipulation, nor passivity. It is to do with working out what one feels, thinks or wants in a given situation and communicating this respectfully, confidently and unambiguously to others. It links also with communication skills, such as making statements beginning with 'I' rather than 'you', which are more likely to defuse potential conflict situations. An example would be 'I felt embarrassed when you did such and such'. It is particularly important for us to be able to 'say no' because we work in unstructured situations with many different pressures on us. (I once agreed to discover information, which I thought was unnecessary, for an inter-departmental working group because I was not assertive enough to state that if my colleague wanted that information, he should find it out himself.) The assertive practitioner is able to push problems which other people expect him or her to solve back to those for whom it is a problem! There are now many books and courses on assertiveness and related areas.

We are told we use, perhaps, 1 per cent of our brains, and we all tend to believe certain negative things about ourselves, e.g. 'I can't sing'. We create 'comfort zones' which psychologically restrict us to living only with particular perceptions of what we can achieve. Yet, we are capable of much more than we have ever dreamed of if we truly want to achieve it. A number of programmes can now assist us to become more effective, both generally and in achieving what we want with other people. These programmes are particularly relevant to community workers, not only because we continually have to learn to do new things, but also because much of our work is to influence and motivate others. Such programmes often emphasise developing positive views of ourselves, envisioning desired outcomes from our actions, 'deleting' the negative programmes in our heads and communicating in ways which ensure others listen to us. Notwithstanding its rather unappealing title, Neuro Linguistic Programming has much to offer here, but see also Black (1994) who has produced a set of mental exercises to help develop personal power; Covey's *Seven Habits of Highly Effective People* (1999); Carnegie's *How to Win Friends and Influence People* (1936); Wiseman's *The Luck Factor* (2003) – about 'making your own luck' and highly relevant to community workers; and Goleman (1996, 1998) on 'emotional intelligence'.

When planning your work, especially when undertaking new activities, write down in advance all the tasks which need to be carried out and what they are meant to achieve and check these with your supervisor. Having a prioritised daily list of things to do is, in my view, also vital. Today there are many courses and technical aids for work planning, but to do it well primarily requires appropriate attitudes and self-discipline.

Even if the agency does not do so, individual workers should record their work with care. If you discipline yourself to write down what you planned to do, what you did, what actually happened, what you thought about it and what your future plans are, you are, first, forcing yourself to reflect, evaluate and, to some degree, plan ahead, and, second, making a record of what happened. You need to be clear though, who/what you are recording for – yourself, your boss, your colleagues, an evaluation? Devise a method of recording which suits you. One way is to keep a daily (or almost daily) logbook to promote your learning/reflection. (I did this for five years as a fieldworker and it became the basis of this book.) This can also be an invaluable tool during supervision because you may reveal in the written word other points besides those you mention in discussion. It is also sometimes worth doing a 'process recording' of one meeting you attended and examining it carefully afterwards. This is a recording which covers chronologically, and in detail, everything that happened, including your thoughts and feelings, as well as non-verbal communication. It helps you understand group processes and develop self-awareness.

Provide your employers with summaries of all your work on at least a quarterly basis. I say 'summaries' since, to be of use, records must be retrievable. Every so often the record should also contain a review of the stage which the activity has reached, and a consideration of your role, including, for example, whether you should become more involved or begin withdrawing. Ideally these summaries should relate to the overall project plan and to any wider evaluation. When considering recording, community workers are likely to think, principally, of recording their work with community groups, but this approach neglects many aspects of our work. For instance, in a project in which I once worked, we developed a community contact-making scheme which needed careful monitoring. In another, a major piece of work was to try to establish better relations with local schools.

The Centre for Reflective Community Practice provides information about different ways of engaging in this. 'Reflective Practice is an active process of witnessing one's own experience in order to take a clearer look at it ... By developing the ability to explore ... our own experience and actions we suddenly open up the possibilities of purposeful learning ... from our own work and lives' (Amulya, n.d., p. 1). (See also Raelin, 2002, and Rolfe et al., 2001.) Amulya goes on to describe different dimensions of reflective practice, for instance:

● individual, collective, and organisational;
● routine (e.g. daily) or occasional e.g. at special team meetings;
● to problem solve;
● to improve practitioner effectiveness;
● to improve organisational effectiveness.

She suggests that reflective practice is driven by questions, dialogue and stories because these help us to 'gain visibility' on an issue and to 'excavate learning' from experience. So set up a system to ensure you engage in it.

When you are preparing to leave your job, bring your records up to date in order to help your successor decide priorities. Summarise the stage you have reached with each piece of work and suggest objectives which he or she might wish to adopt. Consider leaving your successor a list of key 'players', with a few comments about how they might help or hinder his or her work. Finally, we need to 'debrief' and reflect on our experiences when we leave a position so that we do not take old baggage into new situations. Find someone to help you do this.

Points to ponder

1. What do you see as the main stresses of community work?
2. How do you think it is best to overcome these?
3. How should you record your work?

Further reading

Covey (1999) *Seven Habits of Highly Effective People: Powerful Lessons on Personal Change.*
Goleman (1998) *Working with Emotional Intelligence.*
Lombardo *et al.* (2000) *Collaborative Leader: Asserting Yourself Appropriately.*
The Centre for Reflective Community Practice: www.crcp@mit.edu

6 | Social planning approaches to community work

Social planning 'proper' encompasses many activities, such as economic planning, health service planning, transport planning, and is mostly nothing to do with community work. Therefore, 'social planning' within community work needs careful defining. Community workers undertake many activities besides acting as facilitators in relation to community groups. These activities range from doing minor things *for* groups all the way to planning and implementing large-scale projects with limited or no reference to community groups. I use the term 'social planning' to describe all these activities, though terms such as 'inter-agency work', 'programme bending' and 'mainstreaming' are also used.

The idea that community workers work with 'the community' in a neutral way on issues determined by that community is simplistic. We inevitably seek out persons with whom we think we can work and who want to undertake the activities which we believe are the most valuable. Nor, on the whole, do communities choose us to work for them. Thus, virtually all community work includes elements of social planning, since the worker or agency plays a large part in deciding where the worker should work and what activities he or she should become involved with. There are three main types of activity which constitute a social planning approach within community work: (1) doing work *for* groups as opposed to acting as a facilitator (dealt with in Chapters 3 and 4); (2) acting as an *advocate, or broker* with other organisations on an existing group's behalf; and (3) *direct* work: setting up projects or working with service providers and policy-makers without much or any reference to a community group. Only the last of these could properly be called social planning; the first two are, perhaps, stages towards it.

Acting as an advocate for a group

An example of advocacy

I once helped the secretary of an organisation for disabled people get the installation of a telephone paid for by the Local Authority after the organisation's application had been refused. The case had not been presented well, and inappropriate legislation had been cited. The application was only granted when I wrote to the Local Authority citing the appropriate legislation. In theory, I could have helped the secretary write another letter appealing against the decision, but that might have taken some time, besides which the secretary had rather given up the struggle. It was also important to get the decision reversed quickly.

Acting as advocate runs the risk of making groups dependent on the worker. It is so often quicker to do the job yourself, and the outcome is so obviously to the immediate benefit of the group, that 'product' seems more important than process. But, advocacy doesn't on its own help the members of a community learn to get things changed themselves. A related danger is that the worker becomes a buffer between the community group and the target organisation. I think I acted in this way during the incident mentioned in Chapter 3 (p. 66) when I explained to the members of a group that it was no use seeking permission to use a football pitch on a Sunday because Local Authority policy forbade this. When its members did not accept what I said, I found myself trying to 'persuade' them! I was, in effect, protecting officials from having to explain their policies to the community. Community workers can also become pessimistic about the possibilities of change and overestimate the difficulties. Often a great deal can be achieved when the group members are enthusiastic and apply pressure themselves.

Ideally, advocacy on behalf of a community group by a worker should only be undertaken with the knowledge and consent of the group. The aim should also be that the group learns to act as its own advocate. However, community workers who are in contact with a range of officials and politicians have many opportunities to influence political and administrative processes to the advantage of the communities with which they work, and it makes sense both to take such opportunities and to seek proactively to create them. But keep the group informed about what you are doing, so that they know the processes which need adopting if they are to act as their own advocates.

Direct work: setting up projects and working with service providers

A director of social services once said to me, 'It's useful to have neighbourhood workers like you employed without a particular service responsibility because you have the time to look at needs on the ground and find better ways of meeting them.' That is how community workers spend much of their time, and here are two examples from my own experience. There were a number of very large families in the neighbourhood, and I thought that a locally based Family Planning Association (FPA) clinic might serve the needs of the local people better than the city-centre one. So, liaising with the FPA, local GPs and health visitors, I arranged for family planning advice to be provided at the existing well-baby clinic. If I had wanted to take a community development approach to this problem, I could have spoken with local people to see if they agreed that there was a need and were interested in working together to get such a clinic. This process would almost certainly have been a longer one and may not have worked, since, when a worker starts with an issue or activity which interests *him or her,* it is not always possible to ensure that an autonomous community group forms to take it up. A tenants' association, which I had helped establish, collapsed. It had been concerned with influencing the modernisation of council houses, and I thought it important that its work should be continued. So I carried out a survey of tenants' satisfaction with the houses which had already been modernised, and I fed back the results to the housing department in order to seek to influence policy. (Incidentally, as a result of this initiative, we established a joint tenant/housing department liaison group in relation to the modernisation.)

I once suggested to a Local Authority councillor that legislation made it possible for council tenants to turn their estates into housing co-operatives. His reply was, 'We'll give the estates over to tenants any time they want. But they want a good service and not to be bothered with running their estates themselves.' In general terms, I think he is correct. I primarily want to enjoy myself in my spare time and not to 'work'. But I also believe that, unless the beneficiaries of services influence those services, they deteriorate. As 'consumers' are sometimes not able or prepared to participate in influencing such services, it makes sense for community workers themselves, sometimes, to work with other professionals to improve them. By virtue of our ability to build (and help others build) organisations, our ability to communicate and our knowledge of and contact with the people of the communities we serve, community workers are in a good position to influence service development. Legislative changes, the frequent (often short-lived) availability of funds for specific purposes, and new fashions in social policy all require 'social entrepreneurs' (read 'community workers') who can work with others to create appropriate organisations and initiatives and who are concerned to meet the needs of, largely, excluded people.

The case for taking a social planning approach is based on the reality that: helping community groups obtain real power is difficult and slow; the disadvantaged people with and for whom we mostly work want better services *now*; and finally, our own meal tickets are generally provided by a state which, at least ostensibly, wants us to develop/improve services and conditions for high-need communities. So, we need to use similar skills to those we use in the community development process to work with other professionals to improve policies and provide better services for such groups.

Liaison with professionals, or inter-agency work

Many issues bridge several service areas. Therefore, workers who are trying to effect a change will often need to participate in inter-agency groups (see later for a discussion of partnerships and partnership working). These may be temporary working parties or semi-permanent structures. Sometimes no such group will exist but the worker will be networking widely in order to understand key issues, develop relationships, or facilitate (or lay the basis for) a policy change. It is vital, therefore, to structure liaison with other professionals into your work plan. Corina (1977) concluded that contact with middle rank officers was one of the most effective ways of obtaining influence on Local Authorities. Similarly, Levin (1981) describes the process by which a Local Authority took a decision to build a major housing scheme. There was no point at which the decision to go ahead was really made; by the time it was approved by the council there was no other option, and the Local Authority gradually became committed to it. Only by being involved on a continuing basis would it have been possible to affect the course of events.

Judith Bevan, a community development project manager, met bi-monthly with all the deputy heads of the Local Authority departments to ensure that good co-ordination happened in relation to the communities with which her project was concerned. Similarly, when establishing a comprehensive renewal strategy for a deprived valley, Caerphilly Council first put into place an interdepartmental co-ordinating mechanism. Remember, when organising meetings of Local Authority officers with community groups, to get the right level of officer. If you get a strategic director ensure you discuss *policy* in a well-organised way and don't waste their time discussing trivia. Then (or beforehand) work out the practical details with lower-level officers, who make things work on the ground.

Mainstreaming, programme bending, and changing bureaucratic procedures

Mainstreaming

A further education college obtains a two-year grant to employ an outreach worker to ensure community groups in 'Lowtown' are assisted to attend classes in computing, by running the classes in a local community centre, where residents meet anyway. This outreach work is successful and results in more local people getting qualifications. But, after two years the money runs out, the 'outreach' service disappears and Lowtown residents no longer get their local classes. If, however, a local community development worker, the outreach worker, or the local people themselves decide that they want this service to continue, they might make representations to or work with the college so that the outreach function becomes a permanent *'mainstream'* service.

Programme bending

Going back a stage, let us assume the college's computer courses only take place on the college campus. A community development worker, aware of the need for local people to benefit from such a service, might work with the college to develop the outreach course described above, i.e. in the local community centre. The worker would be *'bending the programme'* to ensure it benefited the local community.

Changing bureaucratic procedures

Let us now assume that the college had a rule that further education classes could not take place without 10 students, but that the community worker knew there were only five takers for the course. He or she might then work with the college to find ways around this rule. The recent community regeneration literature emphasises that the biggest block to small area regeneration is the rules, restrictions and auditing procedures of large organisations. This *'bureaucratic procedure change'* is one of the most important contributions community workers can make to neighbourhood improvement.

An example of bureaucratic procedure change

Jan Bennett, a regeneration manager, oversaw the major re-development of a rundown village, with new school, shops, post office and community centre all in one complex. Because this was one entity the rating office decided to charge business rates on the whole development. So, Jan worked with the rating office, politicians and the council to disaggregate the rates so that non-businesses would not have to pay.

Social planning, programme bending and community development work – the magic mix

We can now see the link between community development work on the ground and the contribution of bigger programmes to local improvement. The evidence is emerging that, unless there is a long-term community development programme, the 'big programmes' will run the risk of not meeting the needs of the poorest residents. There will be no link between the large-scale 'top-down' programmes and the people they are supposed to benefit. Even if high-quality community development work is carried out on the ground and community groups are strong, that alone may not improve the life chances of local people much. The big programmes need to be linked to and informed by community groups, locally run institutions and regeneration partnerships in which local people are involved.

This combination of community development work and social planning/programme bending offers, in my view, the main hope that the deprivation of such communities will, in the long term, be substantially lessened. *Effective services will only be provided in excluded communities through continual contact by service providers with an organised and informed community, assisted and mediated by highly skilled professional staff.* I return to this theme in the final chapter.

Service strategies and influence strategies in social planning

Certain 'social planning' initiatives consist of pressure group (influence) work where the driving force is professional workers, some of whom may be working in a personal capacity. Other social planning approaches are, primarily, service strategies. A group of professionals from a range of agencies might initially campaign for and then obtain resources to establish accommodation for homeless people and create a new agency. Community workers (and people with community work skills) play a range of roles both within such groups and by supporting them from outside. Also, many agencies are involved both in service strategies and influence strategies. For instance, Age Concern groups in Britain set up projects such as hospital discharge schemes, but they also participate in campaigns to influence government policy. However, organisations cannot usually obtain public or charitable funds specifically to run campaigns. Thus, the majority of projects set up by means of a social planning approach are 'service' projects.

The 'professional' neighbourhood organisation

A powerful force on the estate where I once worked was an organisation, initially established by the vicar, for professionals to work together, though it later included community group representatives. I became a member but also acted as its 'executive secretary' in that I carried out what it decided should be done. Similarly, a worker on a council estate in Cardiff set up an action group of professionals, with sub-committees on particular subject areas, which designed and implemented different schemes. Corina (1977, pp. 74–8) gives an interesting example of area councillor committees which consisted of councillors, officers and residents, and which were able to discuss policy matters *before* the council took firm decisions. Newcastle had

Priority Area Teams, which are similar. Today in Britain neighbourhood renewal partnerships are emerging, which go under a variety of names, of which the above initiatives can perhaps be seen as forerunners.

From social planning to community development?

The way into community development work for many workers may be through initiatives which are initially of a social planning kind. A 'Take Care' project aimed to repair the homes of poor elderly owner-occupiers using unemployed local people. However, the project leader also set up a number of community groups consisting of older people in order to: oversee the scheme in each locality; discuss their general needs; and to raise these with service providers. If you are employed in a social planning role, figure out ways of doing community development too.

Dilemmas of social planning

One main reason for adopting a social planning approach is that there are so many needs which require meeting and, often, so few members of the community who are prepared and able to work to get these met, that it is unrealistic to expect them to take up everything. A community worker in the USA was helping residents of a trailer park to buy their homes collectively and set up a management co-op. They were reluctant to do this until the worker told them they could employ somebody to collect rents, undertake repairs, and so on. They had, quite understandably, balked at the implication that they would have to undertake all the work on an unpaid basis. If we have assessed needs correctly, and if we set up the project properly, there is likely to be considerable community support for schemes which we initiate in a 'social planning' way.

The dangers of social planning in community work

Community workers engaging in social planning run the risk of merely getting done what *they* want to see done, fail to develop 'community capacity' and, at worst, ignore what members of the community want. They may also find that overseeing the projects they set up *for* the community takes all their time. A community worker identified a need for youth provision and set up a youth club one evening per week. It went well, so he opened two, three, four, five nights per week. Then he found he had become a youth worker! Perhaps it was correct to start a club one evening per week to show how a need could be met. But he should then have spent time trying to involve faith organisations, residents, or the district youth officer, for example, in creating a mechanism whereby others would take responsibility so that he could move on to something else. However, getting others to take responsibility is difficult. We may have unsuccessfully argued the case with potential funders for resources. So, we decide to run a 'demonstration' project, perhaps in our spare time. Only then may our agency take an interest and adopt it as a matter of policy. However, many agencies will allow us to develop a special interest, but let it die when we leave. If we want it to continue, we must also work to structure the change we have initiated into an agency programme. Crucially, if we want to implement a change which will involve another party, we must involve that party and help it develop a sense of ownership at an early stage. They will have done the thinking with us and will not feel they are being presented with an 'all or nothing' decision later on.

Politics, power and social planning

Social planning in community work depends on the ability to manipulate political processes. We often find ourselves making applications and seeking to *persuade* resource holders to support what *we* want to do. However, this works best if we can discover the self-interest of those resource holders. What is it *they* want? If we can find ways of helping them deploy their resources to meet the needs *they* identify, we may be in business.

There may be no chance of getting the resources to run the programmes we consider important at a particular time. But try to get issues on others' agendas. When I wanted to get Local Authorities in Wales interested in community development, I established a relationship with the director of their association. Later, I asked his organisation to co-sponsor a conference on the subject. Without his assistance I would not have been able to attract them. If you do not have direct access to the people with power, establish good relationships with those who do; they may do some of the work for you.

From fieldworker to project manager

This section is aimed at the first-time community work manager; it contains several relatively simple 'do's' and 'don'ts'. (For management on a larger scale, see Chapter 8.)

Let us now assume you manage a small team of community workers; they mostly do the community development work and you mostly do the 'social planning'. While fieldworkers are usually effective advocates for 'their' work on the ground, they may not easily see that, on occasion, the needs of another project may have to take precedence. Or they may all wish to innovate in different directions at once. Managers, on the other hand (as 'multi-dimensional planners') need to ensure that individual workers develop their work consistently in agreed directions. Managers need to take a wide and long view, 'keeping their fingers on all the ends'. When I was a university lecturer, I once spent a good deal of time involved in local projects. I later decided to use this time, instead, to develop short courses for practitioners. Managers, after appropriate consultation, need to make such strategic decisions and ensure that the strategy is adhered to. However, a strategy to concentrate on one area means that other areas must become a lower priority.

Whatever is being planned, you need to take account of the following:

- *Who wants it?* Smiley (1982) recounts how every member of his family thought the others wanted to take a trip to Abilene, though did not want to go themselves. However, they only discovered this after a disastrous day out. It is always useful to try to work out who wants a particular project and why. Often, nobody wants it!
- *What need will it meet?* If the proposal is, for instance, to run a newsletter, what is it hoped that this will achieve? What will be different from the present situation if the newsletter is established? Think about ends before you think about means.
- *What alternative means to the end are there?* Once there is clarity about the end, alternative ways of reaching it should be evaluated. If there are high numbers of isolated elderly people in an area, what are the different ways of reducing their isolation?
- *Who else has tried this and what were the problems?* We often go into a particular project mainly because we *want* it to succeed,

unaware of the pitfalls. These can sometimes be avoided if we discover from other people or from books how such a project can be run, rather than 're-inventing the wheel'.

- *Will it work?* Always estimate the chances of success. There is usually little point in lying down in the road to stop a motorway being constructed if the proposals have been through *all* the legal steps and have been approved. Most of our projects should have a better than even chance of success.
- *What resources are required?* Resources include money, equipment, people and time. What resources are needed, and where are these available? Are they adequate? If resources are too few, there is a danger that we will cut our coat too skimpily. Also, most projects take longer to get going than we think. Try to plan the time it will take accurately (then double it!). It's also useful to have a small budget for unexpected costs.
- *Who is the engine?* At least one person has to be determined to make a project work and 'burn the midnight oil' if necessary. If there is no other 'engine', the community worker may need to become the engine and hope, perhaps in vain, that another leader emerges as the project gets going.
- *Obstacles.* Does the project run counter to an existing policy? Are those whose co-operation is needed too busy, or apathetic? Do certain powerful people have a vested interest in its failure? If so, can they be converted or bypassed? Resnick and Patti (1980) make some excellent points about the importance of predicting resistance in organisational change and preparing one's response to that resistance. Familiarise yourself with the internal politics both of your own organisation and likely target organisations *in advance* of any project, since you will then have a good eye for spotting both opportunities and problems.
- *Where is the expertise?* A further obstacle can be lack of agency expertise. There is always a slow learning curve for any organisation which starts a new activity. To run a new complex project (without exceptionally good advice) in a field where the agency has no existing expertise is usually disastrous.
- *Who else should be consulted or involved?* Potential supporters can easily be turned into opponents because we have failed to involve them early. In our keenness to get moving we may forget to ask ourselves who else could appropriately be involved.

● *The need for allies.* Any new project needs allies. But allies also have to be in place well before the project starts, which underlines the importance of permanent networking. Allies may also provide useful 'inside' information which helps our case. Sometimes, however, that information is secret and we cannot use it freely without compromising them.

● *Have clear, agreed objectives before you start.* It is surprising how often, some time into the project, it emerges that different players discover they were expecting different things from it. Take time to get this agreed 'pre-start'.

● *What kind of organisational structure is necessary?* New non-statutory projects need constitutions and, possibly, to register as a charity or a 'limited liability' or 'community interest' company. Questions such as the composition of the management committee will need to be considered, and there are two conflicting needs here. Effective decisions are best taken by groups of fewer than seven. But a small group often has to have wider legitimacy, which usually means occasional meetings of a large group which, in theory, sets policy. In reality, however, a large group cannot even set policy easily. Its ability to do so depends on how well the small 'executive' group prepares the decisions for the wider policy-making group to decide about. Another dilemma is whether to have all constituent organisations send 'their representatives' to the management committee, in which case there is likely to be some 'dead wood', or to seek out committed and able individuals. A related point is how to be representative in a real rather than a tokenistic way (for instance, the all-male white group which then co-opts a token woman or black person). A way round this is to consider *at the beginning* all the interests which should be represented and to ensure that the invited membership reflects as far as possible the kinds of diversity necessary. See Holloway and Otto (1985), for useful tips about organisation, and Forbes (1998) for assistance on constitutional and legal points.

● *Publicity?* Who do you need to tell about this, why, when, and how will you do it? Often forgotten until a crisis occurs.

● *'No' can be a very good answer.* After doing careful pre-planning, most of us feel reluctant not to go ahead, even if it looks a high-risk project. However, failure at a later stage would be even worse. So it is no disgrace to pull out if feasibility work shows the project is not likely to be viable.

● *Feedback mechanisms.* Once they get going, all projects throw up unforeseen problems. Therefore, good feedback mechanisms have to be in place to reveal potential problems quickly, so they can be corrected before they become serious.

Local staff?

One problem encountered when hiring staff for community-based initiatives is that local people often want to hire somebody from the neighbourhood. They may not recognise either that this could infringe the law or that, in order to hire good staff, it is best to cast the net as widely as possible. There is no simple answer to this one, but be prepared for it to come up, and try to work out in advance how best to handle it. Don't assume there will or will not be anybody in the local community who can do it.

Agency/project maintenance

Agency maintenance ranges from attending the mayor's banquet to raising funds, and from making sure the staff get their pay on time to ensuring the central heating is working properly! While managers do not have to undertake all the above mentioned tasks themselves – though in an emergency they may have to sweep floodwater from the basement – they need to ensure systems are in place whereby all this gets done. It may be necessary to re-negotiate resources each year, possibly adapting the project slightly. Or there may be changes in, say, the political make-up of the council, which means that the funders need re-convincing that the project has value. You need to ensure too that the structure of the organisation remains appropriate to the tasks in hand. Don't underestimate the time it takes to 're-engineer' committees.

In statutory agencies public relations largely means ensuring that those in the higher echelons, and politicians, know about and appreciate the value of the project or service. In non-statutory organisations, the emphasis needs to be on showing the wider public, politicians and potential funders the value of the work through well-produced reports, press releases, open days, talks to other organisations, etc. (See also 'Running a council for voluntary service', Chapter 8.)

Interdependence and the sequence of actions

I once helped a community group prepare and run a jumble sale. They got lots of items to sell but failed to publicise it and so didn't make any money. Both the interdependent actions and the sequence of actions in any project need to be properly worked out. To take the latter case, if you are planning a conference, the venue needs to be booked before publicity material is issued, and enough advance notice needs to be given for delegates to apply to their agencies for funding. Take account of such considerations when setting the date; otherwise time can run out.

Day-to-day work also needs to be planned properly. How many meetings have you gone to where no record is kept of decisions, or somebody has come with a poorly thought-out idea which has been discussed for an hour before people realise the matter has to be deferred to the next meeting? Or the chair not knowing what they are supposed to be doing? How often have you taken part in a meeting without being clear why? When we are pressed, even thirty seconds' thought about our objectives in advance of the meeting can help. Community workers also often find themselves on management committees, the main purpose of which is to set policy, hire and manage senior staff and review progress. Make sure you gain relevant knowledge in this respect, preferably prior to taking such positions.

People management

Supervising professional community workers

A major task of any manager is to *resource* his or her staff by: ensuring they work in reasonable conditions; being available when they want advice; valuing them and their work, giving them the space to take risks, knowing when to offer help; being concerned about their long-term development, even when this may take them out of the agency; utilising their talents, listening to their ideas; developing the team. But there is another side to supervision.

A senior community worker managing several staff thought that the reports of one of them seemed odd. So she checked up, to find that he had missed many group meetings and had been fabricating his records! Some of us are slow at writing reports; others regularly annoy our colleagues. Yet others fail to plan with enough care. It is the responsibility of the manager to ensure that the service to the community is as effective as possible, which means combining the *resourcing* role with the *quality control* role.

It is not easy to work out if a community worker is effective or not. So, managers need to put systems in place which help them get the best possible 'handle' on their staff's work. New community work managers tend not to find quality control easy. But, if somebody is not pulling their weight, the morale of the whole team falls. One particular mistake is for the manager to imply that the team members are all equal when he or she is, ultimately, the boss. Make sure that such points are made clear at the beginning of a project rather than during a crisis.

For all these reasons, there is in social and community work a concept of 'supervision' whereby the manager meets regularly with individual staff to assist them in planning and undertaking their work and learning from it. This process is vital for the development of good practice and to assist staff members to cope with the frustrations of the work. (See Kadushin and Harkness, 2002, and also Bluckert (n.d.) for an introduction to supervision.)

On occasion, the supervisor will have to take difficult decisions or direct staff. When taking such decisions try to consult widely beforehand and then act decisively. Remember, though, that people in authority often do not realise how easy it is to abuse their power. A chance remark or a mild criticism can seriously undermine more junior staff. Also, w*rite down* compliments to staff, but *say* critical things (unless they have to be written). Most community workers, in my view correctly, seek relatively open and informal relationships with those with whom they work. However, there need to be some limits to this when you are a manager; you need to keep some distance in order to help maintain your authority for instance. Also, it is usually wise to try to keep our private and professional lives reasonably separate.

Inexperienced workers, especially, require experienced supervisors. Meetings with the supervisor will usually cover the work undertaken in the previous month or so and at least a verbal evaluation of it; plans for future work; and any problems the worker may be facing. With new employees, students on placement and at times of staff reviews, the emphasis needs to be on what the worker has learned, what they think they do well and less well, what new areas of knowledge and skill they think they need to gain and how these objectives can be reached. I often also ask them about their feelings in relation to the job. This can often throw up useful points, for both the supervisor and the worker. Supervisors are, in my view, not doing their job properly if they studiously avoid the 'personal', i.e. attitudes and qualities. On the other hand, they have to be careful not to overstep the boundary between that part of the personal which relates to professional effectiveness and the entirely private concerns of the member of staff. I also often ask the person I am supervising to determine the agenda. This gives them the space to raise issues which are of concern to them and often gives me an opportunity, later, to add my own view. When they have had their say they are usually prepared to listen to what I wish to tell them.

If a worker has been getting appropriate supervision but their work has been and still is unsatisfactory, point out (and write down) exactly what is not adequate, and indicate what an adequate performance would consist of. (But do ensure you compliment them on the aspects of their work which are good). Try to get the worker to accept what needs to be done and to agree to the steps which will improve their performance. In this process ask for and listen carefully to their explanation of the situation. If a worker is not performing well, try to indicate this early at a supervision session rather than conveying it as a bombshell at an annual review. Supervision also needs to include an opportunity for the worker to comment on the support offered by the supervisor and the agency.

If two workers are working on the same project, they can sometimes learn a great deal by undertaking and reflecting on it together. Nevertheless, supervision is essentially individual.

Managing 'volunteers' in neighbourhood community work

Some community groups require services which neither the worker nor other members of the community can provide. For instance, members of a disabled club with which I once worked required help with shopping and transport. There may also be projects which a worker wishes to initiate, such as a youth club, which no local people seem able or willing to take on. If it is done sensitively, volunteers from another locality can be successfully involved in many of 'your' community activities. In Britain the National Centre for Volunteering provides many useful leaflets on managing volunteers.

If volunteers are needed for complex and responsible tasks, it is necessary to spend a good deal of time helping them to think through the implications of the work. For some activities it is important to take up references carefully, and, increasingly, to undertake 'Criminal Records Bureau' checks on them. Unless you spend a considerable amount of time with volunteers before they start work, during which you will also be assessing which kind of activity would be most suitable for them, you may wish to give them simple tasks first, such as delivering a newsletter, after which they can be moved on to more difficult tasks. Note though, that more volunteers leave because they are underused than leave because they are overworked. (You have to think hard how to use them best.) Consider, too, how to provide continuing support, through a regular group, perhaps. Volunteers need to understand that, if their work is to be of value they need to attend reliably. They also have needs, for out-of-pocket expenses and training, for instance. In short, they need a contract and to be managed. A few really good volunteers eventually become colleagues who develop and manage their own area of interest without a great deal of supervision or support.

Local activists as paid (community) workers?

When local activists become employed in 'their' communities, they bring a great deal to the work. But they may have a rather subjective view of the situation. They may also have local 'enemies'. Community activists may be excellent voluntary workers, but, in that situation, they could play to their strengths. Professionals sometimes have to work on projects which they find uncongenial and operate according to an agency's requirements. If local activists are to be employed as community workers, they may need substantial help to become enablers rather than leaders and to develop relevant analytical and report-writing skills, for instance. This transition takes time, training and continuing support. While community development work consists of transferring skills and confidence to other people, doing this is a high skill in itself. We are not doing anybody any favours if we pretend that these 'facilitating' skills are 'common currency' and employ people who cannot do the job. Having said this, the divide between the 'facilitator' and the 'local leader' is a fuzzy one, summed up by the Chinese saying: 'When excellent leaders have been at work, the people say "We did it ourselves." ' For the kinds of reasons outlined above, Swansea Council for Voluntary Service trains local community leaders to be paid community workers, but then encourages them to work in communities other than their own.

From volunteer to paid worker?

Grace, a local resident, carried out a great deal of advice work in her own home, and we eventually began paying her to run two sessions weekly in our advice centre. These sessions gradually increased, and, after another three years, we employed her full-time. This was the length of time that (we thought) she needed in order to build up her skills and confidence and become accustomed to the culture of a professional agency. On the other hand, Jack, the leader of the adventure playground had a local voluntary helper, Greg. When money became available for a second playleader, Greg applied. When he did not get the job, he caused a great disturbance, physically assaulting Jack, who had to close the playground for a time and ban Greg!

Local management?

Some community workers consider being employed by a community group the ideal, since one is accountable directly to the people with whom one is working. However, community groups tend to be short-lived, have difficulty in managing money, and do not always take decisions well. They may also have a conservative leadership which is easily threatened and has an authoritarian approach to managing staff. If you are employed by a community group, you may get no guidance and you may have to support the group rather than get support from it. You may not get paid regularly and have to work out your own salary and National Insurance contributions. You may not be allowed to work with organisations in the locality with which your employers are not in sympathy. Finally, community groups often have quite enough to do without having to manage staff. It *can* work, but go into it with your eyes open.

Conclusion

I once attended a training course on statistics, where the tutor, using a blackboard, did various calculations in arithmetic. However, as these calculations became more complex, they turned, to my amazement, into algebra. I had thought, naively, that arithmetic and algebra were completely different branches of mathematics. It is the same with community development and social planning – one leads on to the other.

Points to ponder

1. Do you think there is a place for 'social planning' approaches in community work (and why/why not)?
2. Have you ever had the experience of managing anybody, e.g. children, volunteers, or paid staff? What have you learned from this?
3. What do you have to bear in mind most when project planning?

Further reading

Brager and Holloway (1978) *Changing Human Service Organizations*.
Kadushin and Harkness (2002) *Supervision in Social Work*.
Rothman (1976) 'Three Models of Community Organization Practice'.

7 | Community work, social change, and broad-based organising

Collaboration (or 'working the system')

Specht (1975) identified four broad 'modes of intervention' in relation to promoting social change: collaboration, campaign, contest and violence. A collaborative approach is applicable when there is consensus about the issue between, say, the community and the Local Authority. In such a case, the community worker does research, writes reports, sets up joint working parties with people in the 'target system' and negotiates a changed procedure, using the power of argument, good presentation and the influence of allies. Effective collaborative work grows best from the careful building of contacts over a long period with key people in the target system. You also need to find the 'right way in'. A community organisation had been trying to contact the council leader. A contact of mine was on close terms with the leader and I asked him to set up an informal meeting between the leader and the group. As a result, the group received a more sympathetic hearing than they would have if they had merely written a letter, because the town clerk might have prevented the matter from being presented to the leader in the way the group wanted.

In order to bring influence to bear on any organisation you need to build alliances, starting with those most sympathetic to your cause and gradually converting more of the relevant people inside and outside the organisation. You need to know who your opponents are, and to work out ways of countering their arguments. Also, use the written word effectively. A chief officer once told me how the housing committee had made a 'daft decision' (his words). His reaction was to write a report pointing this out, and he got it changed at the next committee.

If you want to change your own organisation, it is important not to overestimate your support. Your contacts may agree with your position but not do anything on your behalf. Or, they may have less influence than you, or they, think. Also, 'progressive' ideas are more likely to be listened to if they come from someone who is seen as conservative, than if they come from someone with a more radical image. So, find the right people to present your arguments to those who are likely to be resistant.

If you are employed by a large organisation, you will have access to both information and influential contacts. Discover how the various parts of your organisation (and others) work, their sensitive points and how they are likely to react to particular kinds of proposal. You will inevitably be bound by the limitations which your own agency imposes, and you have to be 'canny'. A student on placement asked the housing manager to attend a public meeting, but he refused. I advised the student to talk quietly with a councillor with whom he already had some contact. He did, and as a result the housing manager was *told* to attend the meeting by the councillors! (However, an employee doing this would also need to be careful not to be found out – senior officers don't like being manipulated.)

Be aware that 'gains tend to erode'. By the time a changed procedure has been in place for a year, the main supporter of it in the sponsoring organisation may have moved on, and their successor may see things differently. Therefore, once the change has been approved, make sure that: it becomes agreed policy; adequate resources are devoted to it; and, if appropriate, staff are in post to operate it permanently. You will probably also have to perform a 'watchdog' function to ensure that the system does not revert to old ways of operating. When Albert Einstein told the US President that Germany was probably building an atom bomb, the President said he would set up a committee on the matter! (The 'dead hand' of the bureaucracy.) The system you are trying to change may find ways of adapting without changing for the better.

You may also become so conscious of the constraints that you are afraid to test the imagined limits because everyone is scared of upsetting a particular politician. You can get 'sucked in', too, by the often pervasive feeling within large public organisations that it is impossible to improve the situation, so why bother? Or you may become so immersed in day-to-day 'wheeler dealing' to achieve minor objectives that you lose sight of strategic goals. 'Working the system' involves compromise and incremental gains. It requires the ability to see and exploit opportunities within a constantly changing political environment. It is the 'bread and butter' of the social planning approach to community work.

Campaigns and contest

In a classic article, Rothman (1976) identifies three models of 'community organisation' practice: (1) 'locality development', similar to 'my' (generic) community development work; (2) 'social planning'; and (3) 'social action'. In social action, one group pressurises another group to make a concession or change a policy. The scope, in Britain, for paid workers to engage in social action is limited. Nevertheless, sometimes it is possible, for instance: where the worker is not funded by the 'state'; where the community worker is acting clearly as a facilitator to an autonomous group; and when community workers and others form alliances to bring pressure to bear, perhaps working in their own time.

In a 'campaign', the campaigning group pressurises the other party to do something it is resistant to doing. But the campaigning group plays by the rules of the game, consults, collects evidence, lobbies, holds law-abiding demonstrations and generally publicises and builds its case. 'Campaigns' merge with 'collaboration' at one end and with 'contest' at the other. A group trying to influence a particular decision may commence with a collaborative approach and, if it is not successful, move through campaigning to contest. If the campaign or contest is won (or even lost), then it is necessary in most situations for collaborative relationships to be re-established. However, any influence strategy may require collaborative, campaign and contest work at the same time, which, ideally, should be undertaken by different people or organisations co-ordinating their efforts.

Walton (1976) contrasts a collaborative influence strategy (which he calls an 'attitude change' strategy) with a contest (or, in his terms, a 'power') strategy. A power/contest strategy seeks to expose, embarrass and discredit the other side and to polarise the issue in order to build the power of one's own organisation and force the opponents to concede. It can involve disobedience, boycotts, sit-ins, disruptive tactics, strikes, and the skilful use of the media. On the other hand, the 'attitude change' approach involves establishing positive relationships with the other side, empathising with their view of the situation, minimising differences, sharing information, building trust and making attempts to solve the problem jointly. If you are involved in a campaign or contest, consider whether a powerful enough coalition can be built both to persuade (or force) the opponent to concede, and to sustain the victory. If you are unable to build this power, which is by far the most common situation, you need to think carefully about how far you are prepared to alienate your opponent, and you may decide to use campaign rather than contest tactics. Also, if the group is taking a contest approach on one issue, but has a useful co-operative relationship with the other side on different issues, or needs the support of other players who are uneasy with a contest-type approach, this may jeopardise the achievement of other or future goals. Workers dependent on state funding need to think through carefully: whether they can become engaged in campaigns and contests at all (either in work or non-work time), if so, how far they are able to take an active as opposed to a background advisory role; and how far they will take their supervisor and employer into their confidence.

In a contest, some of your tactics will be confrontational and disruptive. But, once the council chamber has been occupied a few times, this tactic begins to lose its force, and one needs to consider other methods: petitions; a continuing barrage of letters asking different (and difficult) questions; or processions which attract the media because they contain tableaux depicting the issue in question, for example. Always prepare your tactics with care. Although a hastily planned demonstration, executed while people feel like fighting, can sometimes win the day, mostly it does not. Also, vary your tactics, take the opposition by surprise, and keep the initiative. Remember though, that, the battle of ideas still needs to be fought; every opportunity must be taken to present well-researched argument, using experts when appropriate. You will also need to become experts on the issue in question.

Whether you are in a collaborative, campaigning or contest 'mode', build support behind the scenes through informal networking and alliance building and try to get the issue of concern on relevant agendas. Understand who the most powerful people are, who has influence on them and how they are likely to react to a particular approach. Think early about whether you are in a situation where both sides stand to win something, in which case you may be able to persuade the other side without a confrontation, or whether you are in a situation where, if you win, they must lose. In the latter case, an approach based on persuasion probably stands little chance.

In reality, for most community workers and projects, the 'contest' mode is most useful when the other side will not meet you, listen to your arguments or in any way recognise that you have a right to be heard. In that kind of situation, kicking up a fuss in a way which also attracts media attention may get you in the door. But, generally, if you do not eventually convince the other side by your strength of argument (or, in exceptional cases win a legal or quasi-legal case against them), you will not win (or at least hold on to any gains) by contest tactics alone.

Negotiation

If you or the community group's representatives are very angry or upset during a negotiation, you won't be able to negotiate effectively. A community worker helping a group to negotiate must ensure it is clear about its negotiating strategy. Spend time preparing its members in detail, using rehearsals, and role plays. Try to predict the other side's likely response (and prepare your response to the response). I once accompanied some residents to the local bus company HQ. We had a list of several problems with the bus service. To our surprise, the company said, 'Yes, we agree. How should it be changed?' We didn't have an answer, not having thought that far ahead!

In the first negotiation, group members may be nervous and unsure. One community worker took some tenants, the day before, to the rather plush committee room in which the negotiation was to take place, so that they would not be over-awed by their surroundings. Remember too that 'the other side' is likely to feel nervous. They may also be inexperienced, and there may be ways of exploiting this.

Fun?

It's great if a campaign can be fun. However, the preparation, the organisation-building, the letter-writing and the waiting can't always be fun. Nevertheless effective community workers give attention to making the work as enjoyable as possible. Americans seem very good at this, ending serious meetings with the singing of an old civil rights song, for instance.

Broad-based organising

The vision of many community workers and activists is that community/citizen action can create a just and equal society. However, while small 'victories' happen and while community action can influence the 'spirit of the times', generally speaking, it has come nowhere near realising that vision. I believe there are seven main reasons for this:

1. Community organisations are relatively powerless, especially ranged against large ones, whether these are government, the 'religious right' or big business.
2. Community organisations 'fight their own corner', but may be vehemently opposed to other groups 'down the road'. At worst, they seek their own benefit at the expense of other groups or communities which have greater need.
3. Their leaders generally fail to 'develop' their own people, and sometimes put them down strongly.
4. They tend to become dependent on state funding, which severely limits their scope to engage in campaigns.
5. They tend to be ephemeral. When I was a fieldworker I had great difficulty in keeping community groups alive.
6. They tend to be reactive, not 'proactive'; they may campaign against, say, hospital closures, rather than working towards positive health service improvements.
7. Finally, they often rush in without thinking things through and get involved in un-winnable issues.

For these reasons I had come to the conclusion by about 1980 that the 'social action' side of community work had no future. However, in Los Angeles in the early 1980s. I discovered 'broad-based organising', which I, virtually at once, came to believe offers the possibility of overcoming many of these difficulties. The following account is closely based on the research of Lina Jamoul (2006).

What is broad-based organising?

A broad-based organisation is a permanent, diverse alliance of civil society institutions, working in specific localities to effect social and economic change. Broad-based organisations are alliances of other organisations: churches, mosques, trade union branches, schools. Through one-to-one 'conversations', institutions are recruited to broad-based organising based on their values: love, justice and a commitment to building a broad-based organisation. Through campaigns, action and reflection, organisers train and develop people as 'public beings' and build power for the alliance and its members.

Broad-based organisations run on relatively small budgets with money spent on organising, not service delivery.

The Citizen Organising Foundation (COF)

This mix of politics and community work was introduced to Britain via the Citizen Organising Foundation (COF) in the late 1980s. Neil Jameson (now Director of COF), then employed by the Church of England Children's Society, along with many community workers, activists and others passionately concerned with social justice, thought that, if poverty and exploitation were to be effectively addressed, it would mean altering dominant power relations. But how to do this? The Labour Party was in disarray and out of power. Even when in power, it had failed, for whatever reason, to do much in that respect. Unions had also had little effect, and their influence was declining.

While I was in the USA in 1984, I attended broad-based organising training, organised by the Industrial Areas Foundation (IAF), the organisation which Saul Alinsky (a famous American 'organiser') had established, and was invited to see if broad-based organising could be established in the UK. On my return I held some meetings with a few individuals, mainly in churches, but without any success. Neil Jameson heard of my endeavours and visited me. Neil contacted Eric Adams of the Barrow Cadbury Trust. Eric was disillusioned with the very limited effects of community development efforts in the 1970s, in which he had been involved. From this base, several others, mainly social workers and church leaders, formed an embryonic group, mainly due to Neil's untiring work and, later, some modest funding from the Barrow Cadbury Trust. I came up with the name: Citizen Organising Foundation.

Eventually Neil was appointed the first COF organiser and set up a broad-based organisation in Bristol in 1989. COF's 'project' was assisted by the IAF which, since the 1970s, has consistently grown as a movement with, in 2006, 56 affiliates in 21 states. Its veteran organisers have developed, refined and taught the methods of broad-based organising, what they call the 'art of politics'. COF has also successfully established three broad-based organisations in London under the umbrella of 'London Citizens', and one in Birmingham (Birmingham Citizens). London Citizens, one of the largest and most diverse networks in London, is made up of the East London

Communities Organisation (TELCO), South London Citizens, and West London Citizens. COF has found that the best base for broad-based organising is faith-based organisations.

The main tenets of a broad-based organisation
Institutional membership and financial independence
Broad-based organising is based on the idea that, in order to build power effectively, an alliance of existing organisations is vital. Thus, a broad-based organisation is made up of member institutions that pay substantial annual dues (up to £2000 p.a.). These institutions (sometimes referred to as mediating institutions because they are not public or private sector, and not kin or friendship networks either) are drawn from civil society. The (high) fee level is to encourage real ownership. A broad-based organisation will employ only one or two professional organisers, who facilitate, encourage and develop the commitment and energy of its membership. Another reason why the payment of dues is stressed is that independence from government is regarded as essential. State funding is not taken, and organisers prefer to rely on their own membership for money and the control that comes with it. Thus, broad-based organisations give institutions an opportunity to act on their values through a process they themselves control.

The function of these (mediating) institutions is to provide for 'their people', whether in terms of spiritual nourishment (faith institutions), protection in the workplace (trade unions), or educational and personal development (schools). Underlying these functions is a set of values characterised by love, justice and mutuality. One of the priests involved in London Citizens remarked that the message of faith communities is that: people can live differently; faith communities should be spaces that engage people's desires for a different world; and that they can act as islands of hope in the face of poverty, alienation and disengagement. Belonging to a broad-based organisation enables these institutions to be involved in politics in a way that stays true to their values – a source of power and direction. Broad-based organising also draws on these 'mediating' institutions for practical reasons. COF's aim is to organise as many people as possible into a collective for power and justice. Such institutions are places where people are already gathered and organised – a good starting point.

Diversity

Institutions join a broad-based organisation mainly because they understand that, working with others, they can realise their vision of justice for 'their people' more effectively than they can alone. Also, they come to value the opportunity to work with people they would not otherwise meet. In order to be effective, therefore, the membership of a broad-based organisation should reflect the diversity of the area. Both London and Birmingham Citizens are organisations that include a wide range of people: Catholics, Anglicans, Methodists, Pentecostals, Evangelicals, Sunni and Shiite Muslims, Buddhists, atheists, school and university students, academics, cleaners, nurses, teachers, priests, nuns. Broad-based organising gives these constituents a reason to go beyond the walls of their institutions and form a public relationship with each other. This diversity ensures that broad-based organisations do not become parochial and narrow. Those in London and Birmingham Citizens also recognise that they make up the constituencies which national politics fails to connect with (young people, Muslims, low-wage earners, migrants) and this gives them a sense of power and legitimacy.

Active, collective leadership

Activists in a broad-based organisation are called 'leaders' and are identified by COF's organisers as people who not only have a 'following', but who can 'deliver' that following, i.e. get them to turn out in large numbers in a disciplined way. Organisers work hard to find and develop leaders – the people inside the institutions who have imagination that the world can be a better place, who are angry in the face of injustice, but are able to make strategic decisions about action. Mediating institutions are filled with such people, and COF's job is to tap into their potential by bringing them into public life. The viability of a broad-based organisation depends on sustaining a core group of leaders who will stay with the organisation and come to 'own' it.

A campaigning organisation

'Action is the oxygen of the organisation', claimed Alinsky. Broad-based organisations campaign on a multitude of issues. These issues are based on combining the self-interest of members with notions of the common good. London Citizens' Living Wage campaign was not only in terms of justice for low-waged cleaners – the wider injustices, pressures and societal strains of poverty wages were also highlighted (Wills, 2001, 2004). A broad-based organisation cannot take on all social and economic problems, and it cannot deal with the root causes of those problems directly. That is the business of national governments. But broad-based organising can achieve and sustain meaningful victories. And, since COF builds sustainable organisations, the work can continue permanently. This work involves the dignity of people, assisting them to develop the power to act for themselves and to bring about change, having more control over the issues which affect their lives. Through broad-based organising they also gain the benefits of solidarity and fellowship. By campaigning, therefore, COF organisations develop leaders and followers, effect some social change in favour of the poor but also develop people's individual capacities for purpose, meaning and personal power.

Winnable issues

In a successful COF campaign, a distinction is made between general 'problems' that are huge, multifaceted and overwhelming, and particular 'issues' that are immediate, specific and winnable. Before members agree to take on a campaign, research is carried out among constituents on their most pressing social problems (often known as a 'listening exercise'). In the collective process of turning 'problems' into 'issues', as leaders discuss possible, specific solutions to their problems, a power analysis is carried out. Who are the potential targets for the campaign? What official has the power to make things happen? This can often be a complicated exercise, and it highlights the role of research before embarking on a campaign.

In a campaign to make Whitechapel Road in Tower Hamlets a cleaner and safer place, TELCO found there were almost too many agencies responsible for the road. These included: several Council departments; a private cleaning company; Transport for London; the police; the 'regeneration industry'; and a major hospital. Each one refused to intervene in what it saw as another agency's responsibility. TELCO decided to focus most of the pressure of the campaign on the Council, since it was an elected institution.

In deciding whether to develop a campaign or not, leaders will ask if the organisation is powerful enough to negotiate with the relevant authorities and win. When TELCO was first established, organisers and leaders identified low wages as a huge problem in East London – people were just not earning enough to live on. However, the organisation did not have the capacity to take on the power players that could deliver a living wage in East London, and so that was not the first campaign to be taken on. Instead, TELCO focused on building a stronger base out of smaller campaigns until it was powerful enough to risk taking on some of the largest corporations operating in East London as well as the Mayor. Broad-based organisations start from small, incremental, winnable campaigns that strengthen the organisation and build solidarity among the leadership. Over time, they are able to take on campaigns that effect bigger changes.

Action–reaction–evaluation

COF has a slogan, 'every action is in the reaction'. This means that, when actions are planned, careful thought is put into the kind of reaction they are trying to elicit. As part of the campaign to clean up Whitechapel and make it safer, TELCO organised a high profile crime survey. Just by being in the area and asking people about their experience of crime, leaders and organisers attracted more police to the area. As part of every action, an evaluation takes place among members. The process of learning is arguably the most important part of a campaign, both because it helps individual leaders and the organisation to develop, and also because it lays the basis for more effective campaigns in the future. Evaluations look at the reactions of the campaign 'targets'; the press; and crucially, the members themselves: how people feel; what people have learnt; what they are going to do as a result of the action. COF campaigns have been successful in winning on issues and in developing leadership skills in people precisely because of this circle of action–reaction–evaluation.

The uniqueness of broad-based organisations

A training organisation

In the past two decades, COF has developed a training curriculum, based on the IAF model and its own experiences. COF organisations regularly run evening and weekend workshops as well as two national training weeks a year. The most important learning, however, takes place by people taking an active part in campaigns. They are not run on an advocacy basis by a small group of professionals, but, rather, are grounded in the actions of hundreds of people. Some people may be seasoned leaders in their church or union branch; for others it may be the first time they have been involved in public life. Through public speaking, directly negotiating with officials and organising actions, people learn the skills needed to negotiate their way through public life. For example, London Citizens' Living Wage campaign, one of the organisation's most high profile campaigns, is based on the self-organisation of hundreds of low-waged workers who have: shared their experiences with each other; shared their experiences with their supporters through public assemblies; and have been central in organising actions aimed at public and corporate bodies. Many of them have had the experience of directly arguing their position with politicians, business leaders and managers.

A relational organisation

COF organisations nurture a culture based on relationships, trust and accountability. The foundation of all broad-based organisations is the 'one-to-one' tool, based on the belief that real democracy begins not with elections, but with 'conversations'. One-to-one conversations, initiated by the organiser, build relationships among people in the organisation, creating a politics which is based at first on self-interest. Then slowly (through taking actions and risks together), it turns into a politics based on relationality and solidarity. The 'one-to-one' is an intentional conversation aimed at getting to know something of substance about another person. This includes a bit about their background, what their prime interests are, what they spend their time doing and why, the motivating forces in their life and who they are connected with. It is a two-way conversation where both people share things about themselves and enquire about the other. COF considers one-to-ones to be the 'art of politics' and has trained many hundreds of people to carry these out. All campaigns are underpinned by people sharing their stories. These stories become firm foundations for long-term relationships inside the organisation. People may be attracted to the organisation based on the possibility of it helping to address the issues they are concerned about. However, those who stay long-term do so, at least in part, on the basis of the comradeship they develop.

The role of the organiser

Much of an organiser's time is spent developing relationships. COF organisers carry out 15–20 one-to-one conversations a week with leaders, members and potential members. They meet with people who head up their member institutions, with people inside those institutions, trying to identify those who might join and those who could become leaders. In COF's experience, people enjoy coming out of their institutions and meeting other people. However, they need to be constantly reminded and cajoled to do so. People in civil society institutions are often busy and under stress, bearing many of the burdens of deteriorating neighbourhoods. Churches, mosques, schools and trade union branches are under pressure, whether it's declining membership, increased state surveillance, large classroom sizes, higher demands on performance, or subcontracting and privatisation. They struggle to cater for their members as best as they can under difficult conditions. Organisers help people see beyond their busy day-to-day work, in part, by facilitating meetings where leaders from the different institutions get together to discuss the direction of a campaign or to reflect together on the pressures they face.

Because a broad-based organisation cannot function without talented leaders, an organiser's job is to look for such people inside its member institutions. Through one-to-one conversations organisers identify people who are passionate to make a difference, and who are connected to other people inside their institutions. An organiser is also always on the look-out for new member institutions. He or she will meet the priest, head teacher or branch secretary as well as spend some time in the institution, to get a feel of it. Once an institution has joined, continuing diligent work is necessary to find leaders who will carry the work along inside it. An organiser develops leadership skills in others by encouraging people to take leadership roles inside the organisation or for a particular action. This can include, for instance, public speaking in assemblies, chairing large meetings, leading negotiations with officials. When it comes to public action, the organiser will ordinarily take a back seat and encourage the leaders to take centre stage. Organisers also identify people for the COF national training, which is delivered by all the organisers from London and Birmingham Citizens, giving trainees a breadth of experience.

Establishing a broad-based organisation

One of COF's aims is to see broad-based organising spread. Its newest organisation is West London Citizens which grew out of an invitation from the Westway Development Trust. An organiser, Catherine Howarth, spent a lot of time getting to know the civil society landscape of West London through one-to-ones. When she had met with a substantial number of people to find out if there was a desire to set up a broad-based organisation, a 'sponsoring committee' of key leaders was established. West London Citizens was not established officially until Catherine had been working with the different groups for a year and a half. After Catherine identified key institutions and leaders to be part of the organising effort, 'community dialogues' in the different boroughs of West London started. In four boroughs, representatives from very diverse groups (including the Muslim Cultural Heritage Centre, Ramgarhia Sabha Gurdwara, Chelsea Methodist Church, Transport and General Workers Union (London Hotel Workers Branch), and St Francis of Assisi Roman Catholic Community) came together over three evenings to discuss the most pressing problems for them, their families, their institutions, and their neighbourhoods. They then talked about the possibilities of tackling those problems collectively. Out of this deliberation, representatives from West London attended the COF training and visited events held in East and South London to discover more about broad-based organising and decide whether they wanted to set up their own organisation. Finally, in 2005, West London Citizens had its founding assembly with 700 people representing 22 institutions and, in 2006, voted on its first campaign initiatives as a new organisation.

Achievements of the COF organisations

COF has made inroads on a number of issues. In East London, the organisation has: campaigned successfully on waiting times in Newham General Hospital; lobbied Tower Hamlets Council effectively to put litter bins and install street lighting on Whitechapel Road; and democratised the process for the regeneration of Queen's Market in Green Street by holding a public inquiry on what users and workers in the market want for their area.

One of COF's most successful campaigns has been the Living Wage campaign. London Citizens managed to combine long-term vision of economic change with strategic, concrete victories towards that goal by winning the issue in different sectors of the city. The first target was the health sector in East London, and the second was the banking sector in Canary Wharf. Once gains were made in hospitals and banks, the organisation had built a reputation strong enough to go to the Mayor. After an 'accountability' campaign the Mayor agreed to set up a Living Wage Unit at City Hall, which, in 2005, recommended that employers pay their workers a living wage of

£6.70 per hour (the national minimum wage was then £5 per hour). London is the only city in Europe to have a 'living wage' figure. Next in the campaign came university campuses and the hotel sector. Over the years, the campaign, with a mixture of short-term gains in the different sectors and a longer-term vision, gained momentum.

COF organisations have also built relationships with power holders in the areas where they organise. This has never been easy, with political and economic elites resisting when being confronted not only by the demands of COF organisations, but also by a myriad complex pressures and other campaigning groups, enmeshed as they are in a political process over which they have little control. Often the initial struggle is not over the specific demands, but over elites accepting broad-based organisations as legitimate entities to do business with. COF organisations have had unprecedented success in getting relationships with some of the most powerful people in London. One trade union official remarked, 'I want to understand how TELCO got Sir John Bond, the chairman of the HSBC Bank, out of his office to talk with you!' The relationships that COF groups have with power holders are often conflictual and multiple, characterised by tension and agitation. They sometimes feel like a tug of war. These negotiations, however, often end with respect and some degree of mutual understanding, unlike the relationships of many other organisations with power holders which tend to be characterised either by a completely oppositional stance, one that refuses engagement with 'the system', or one that buys wholesale into the system's agenda, achieving very little for the communities represented in the process.

Targeting a major bank

When TELCO first started targeting HSBC to become a living wage employer, nobody from the bank would meet with TELCO. TELCO did not just want a meeting with someone from the public relations department; they wanted a meeting with someone with power to make decisions. In 2002, TELCO held their first picket of HSBC's annual general meeting (AGM), and a few people bought HSBC shares. Priests, nuns, Muslim clerics, low-wage workers, students and a local celebrity stood outside the meeting hall, while the leader of the delegation, a parish priest with a loud voice went inside with one of the organisers. During the chairman's opening remarks, the priest interrupted the proceedings, condemned poverty wages as immoral and put a public request to the chairman – 'Will Sir John Bond meet with TELCO to discuss the problem of poverty wages in East London?' There was no way the chairman could say no to an ordained minister, publicly, in front of his shareholders and the press.

Just because TELCO got a meeting didn't mean they had won the campaign. Most of the meetings took on a circular nature. The bank would claim it was the cleaning company's responsibility since HSBC didn't directly employ the cleaners; the cleaning company would say HSBC pays for the contract and they would have to put more money towards the contract in order to increase wages; HSBC would close the case by saying wages are set by market forces. At HSBC's next AGM it was Abdul Durant, a cleaner who worked in the HSBC tower in Canary Wharf, who interrupted. Abdul told the chairman, the shareholders and the press what life was like living on £5 an hour and having to raise five children. In response, the chairman told Abdul that people with his living standards shouldn't have five children! Next day, the *Independent* newspaper ran with the headline, 'The cleaner, the chairman and the £2 million differential'. The public exposure helped the campaign enormously. (The action is in the reaction!). This was how TELCO balanced its relationship with HSBC's chairman, combining a willingness to negotiate in meetings with a willingness to make those negotiations public, trying to establish a constructive relationship while not being afraid to inject tension when needed. In the end it was not moral or economic arguments that convinced HSBC, but the threat of a campaign of mass withdrawals of HSBC accounts, combined with growing adverse press publicity. Days before HSBC's next AGM, the bank issued a press release taking responsibility for subcontracted cleaners, increased wages and improved working conditions. TELCO leaders showed up again at this AGM and publicly thanked HSBC for doing 'the right thing'.

Growth of people

The best successes of broad-based organisations are not the ones that hit the headlines, but are found in the experiences and growth of people who get involved. All the COF campaigns, no matter what their nature and demands, have the same basic aim, that is, to develop leadership potential in ordinary people and their capacity for public life. Through training and having responsibility for major campaigns, making decisions, evaluating and learning from actions, people develop public skills in ways that have repercussions beyond the contributions they make to the broad-based organisation and their own institutions. When sixth formers took part in a campaign to make political candidates standing for the election of Mayor accountable, it gave them invaluable skills and a close perspective on London politics. Their involvement also gave them a sense of their own power and achievements:

> You see people around you being prominent in society, making a real difference and you think 'I could never do that'. This makes you realise that things like this are stepping stones to getting to that stage.
> (School pupil and TELCO leader)

The students who got involved in TELCO found themselves immersed in deep discussion about political candidates and who they were going to vote for, whereas before their involvement they would have been completely disconnected from the election process. Their experience also made them hungry for public life, and they planned to get further involved in student politics when they started university.

Part of this development of people is the rediscovery of an important part of our human capacity, often forgotten. German philosopher Hannah Arendt (1958) called it the 'capacity for speech and action'. She lamented its decreasing quality since 'the world does not provide a proper space for its exercise'. COF organisations try to do precisely that, provide a space for the exercise of public life. Because this public space is independent of government and business, it is possible to act proactively. In general, groups made up of disadvantaged people tend to act reactively to political and economic conditions. Their only source of power seems to be in opposing the often drastic changes in their neighbourhoods that they have little control over. Acting proactively means shaping the political and economic agenda, not merely reacting to it. In London Citizens' biggest gathering of 2,000 people, one of COF's veteran leaders, Monsignor John Armitage, stressed the fact that, before the Living Wage campaign, politicians were talking about the 'minimum wage'; now London Citizens and its allies had managed to shift the terms of debate to its own agenda.

The future?

COF has now been established for over 15 years and it has had many ups and downs in its development as a nationwide project. During the 1990s, it oversaw the development of broad-based organisations in Bristol, Sheffield, the Black Country, Wales, Merseyside and London. Of those, only the London group has survived. Perhaps it is understandable for ambitious and experimental projects to peak, trough and sometimes die. There are risks involved in setting up a broad-based organisation, and its sustainability is not a foregone conclusion. Two factors are central to sustainable broad-based organising: funding and organisers. Because broad-based organisations don't rely on government funding, and because it has proved impossible to raise all the money necessary to sustain an organisation from membership dues, COF groups are heavily dependent on foundation money. It has largely been through the hard work of its director, Neil Jameson, that COF has survived. Birmingham Citizens has emerged as a likely stable and permanent entity, while London Citizens has grown and flourished over the last few years. In order for COF to grow and for broad-based organisations to take permanent hold elsewhere, foundations need to invest in this unique type of community work on a long-term basis. Organisers also need to be found, trained, mentored and become committed to broad-based organising.

While broad-based organising, at last, seems to be taking root in Britain, I remain slightly surprised that community workers committed to 'radical change' have not generally espoused it. The nature of political and institutional reality is such, it seems to me, that broad-based organising provides the best, though by no means the perfect solution to the quest to bring about social change which benefits excluded people through citizen involvement. It also offers some hope that the seven major limitations of community action (see p. 126) can, at least to some extent, be overcome.

Further information about broad-based organising

Alinsky (1972) *Rules for Radicals: A Pragmatic Primer for Realistic Radicals.*

Chambers (2003) *Roots for Radicals: Organizing for Power, Action, and Justice.*

Gecan (2002) *Going Public.*

Howarth and Jamoul (2004) 'London Citizens: Practising Citizenship, Rebuilding Democracy'.

Pierson and Smith (2001) *Rebuilding Community*.

If you want to consider becoming an organiser with COF, or just want more information, go to www.cof.org.uk.

Note also that there are several other 'organising traditions' in the USA, based on Saul Alinsky's principles, for instance, ACORN: http://ACORN.org

---

Points to ponder

1. What are the key things to take into account in developing 'influence' strategies?
2. Do you think that broad-based organising offers a good way to create more social justice for disadvantaged people? If yes, why? If no, why not?

Further reading

Wilson (1984) *Pressure: The A–Z of Campaigning in Britain.*

8 | Advanced practice

The work described here falls into four general categories: (1) engaging in community economic development and running private non-profit organisations; (2) working as a manager in large bureaucratic organisations; (3) 'partnership working'; and (4) highly skilled work in difficult situations.

Community economic development

Community enterprise

The idea of a community business or a community enterprise (the two phrases tend to be used interchangeably) is that a community group identifies both a need and a market, for a recycling scheme or an odd job service, for instance. It then carries out a feasibility study, obtains capital, draws up a business plan and hires staff to carry out the work. The aim is that sustainable jobs will be created for local people, also benefiting the community by providing goods and services. In practice, community enterprises often grow organically, responding to need/opportunity, rather than in a planned way.

Community enterprises have sometimes received start-up grants on the assumption that they would generate a revenue stream and become self-sustaining businesses. However, many remain grant-dependent. (See Twelvetrees, 1996, 1998a; Harris, 1998; and Pearce, 1993.) This would not be a problem if the funders recognised that such initiatives need continuing subsidies to provide what might be a useful community service and some jobs, but mostly they do not. To a certain extent, community enterprises have not always approached what they have to do in a businesslike way; the feasibility study may be 'wishful thinking' with no real market research; there may have been a business plan once, but it is never really used or updated; they may have hired staff who needed a job as opposed to staff who had the skills to do the job in question (a dilemma here is that relevant skills may not exist in deprived areas); or they may have carried out a feasibility study which indicated that £20,000 of start-up capital was needed but have gone ahead even though they only had £5,000. (But what do you do if you only have £5,000?) Another scenario is that some community enterprises (e.g. training organisations) get quite big on contracts, but they don't make enough money to reach sustainability without them and collapse when the contracts finish. Sometimes, too, one underpaid staff member over-works, does all the jobs and gets burnt out. Also, staff who are too busy don't have the time to go on relevant training, even if this exists.

Having said this, some extraordinary women and men do manage to sustain and develop community enterprises in unpromising circumstances and make a useful contribution to a local community. Moreover, in places where sponsors and funders recognise that, for a subsidy of, say, £20,000 per year, they will get both some jobs and needed community services, community enterprises can prosper. If you wish to establish a community enterprise, visit a few first, ask questions, especially about where their cash flow comes from, and think long-term. Try to ensure there is serious backing from a major player.

There are problems with success, too. A council estate-based community enterprise hit on a means of colouring concrete and became very profitable. Eventually, one of the workers bought the business and ran it himself in a conventional way, eventually relocating out of the area. Assuming you don't wish such relocation to happen, how do you prevent it? This is where development trusts come in.

Development trusts

Development trusts are community-owned, 'private non-profit' bodies and also businesses which aim to regenerate a neighbourhood in a range of ways. They may: own some economic enterprises; engage in joint ventures; provide financial services to local businesses; run business development programmes; operate managed workspace; manage training schemes; run youth development programmes; provide social housing. Development trusts also need to be seen as partnerships, with local government and others, in a joint effort to improve an area. When they start off, development trusts need grants, mainly to employ staff. However, over time, they are able to earn a proportion of their income through trading. They are often effective at ensuring that an annual grant of, say, £100,000 results in a turnover of three times that amount.

Nevertheless, a development trust operating in a deprived area will find it difficult to establish a self-sustaining economic initiative unless it engages in activities which bring an *assured* return as opposed to an *unpredictable* return. Examples of an assured return (all of which have both advantages and disadvantages) are:

- a large financial endowment which can be invested to generate interest with which to pay staff;
- the *gift* of a physical asset (such as property or land) where substantial income can accrue through renting out part of that asset;
- contracting with another organisation to undertake particular tasks (with the development trust taking a percentage as profit);
- agreeing with a major buyer of a product that a certain proportion of that product will be bought for a substantial time at a good market price (for example, a childcare facility offering 20 places where a large employer agrees to take 10 of these at the market rate).

The Development Trusts Association in England now recommends that development trusts should seek to obtain physical assets (usually buildings) at no or very low cost which they can use to generate income through rents. Some development trusts have reached a degree of economic sustainability via this route. However, in order to generate enough money to employ a reasonably sized staff team, the asset needs to be worth at least £2.5m. It would also need to be in an area where what it offered could be effectively marketed. For instance, in Tredegar, Wales, a managed office space was created at a cost of £400,000; the gross annual rent from this was £20,000; and £10,000 was expended in management costs. The remaining £10,000, while useful, did not keep the parent organisation alive. (Note also that some 'assets', e.g. old buildings, can become liabilities.)

There is a debate as to whether development trusts in disadvantaged areas should aim to become self-sustaining through trading. Poor people need services. And most services will never make a profit. So, I have reservations about this. However, according to David John, an expert in this field, about 50 development trusts in the UK are now fully self-sustaining. The most successful 'think outside the box' about how to make money and have developed many symbiotic links with private business. They operate many ventures including: car rentals, theatre schools, training schemes, sub-post offices, restaurants, art galleries, community transport, youth hostels, care homes and travel agencies.

Development trusts act as brokers, facilitators and co-ordinators between the community and a range of other organisations, as a result of which those other organisations deliver better programmes than would otherwise be the case. They also attract substantial resources into the community. The co-ordinators of development trusts are always establishing relationships with key players, attending working parties and working up ideas with others. This rather invisible work is a vital building block for local development, and it would be costly if one had to pay for it separately. Development trusts, as independent entities, are able to act and earn money in ways which are not open to governmental organisations. Also, in so far as development trusts are public/community partnerships and address multiple issues, they lay a basis, in some cases, for a comprehensive approach to local development. There is no legal structure for a development trust as such; they can be thought of as neighbourhood-based voluntary organisations as well as community companies. Bear in mind, too, that development trusts will not automatically promote community development or 'develop people; if a development trust doesn't have an agreed vision about community development, this will not happen. Finally, because they are not private companies with their own assets, development trusts can't usually get hold of money quickly, e.g. to buy a property.

Setting up a development trust usually takes about two years. I recommend carrying out a community profile as a first step. Assuming it concludes that a development trust should be established, then that proposal and the community profile itself must be discussed both in the community and among other agencies, allowing the idea of a development trust to be debated. Next, there needs to be considerable investigation into the purposes which that particular development trust would fulfil, and the careful identification of the vision and mission which, with occasional modification, will guide it through its life. Following this, different options for the structure and membership of the development trust need to be considered. While a small group is working out such details, steps need to be taken to keep both the wider community and relevant agencies informed. At the same time, resources to provide staff for the development trust need to be identified, applications made, those resources obtained and staff hired. If an aim is to obtain a large asset, explore this possibility thoroughly. Eventually, the development trust has to be legally established and projects designed and implemented. In reality, work on all these fronts often takes place at the same time, and in practice, the development trust may be built around particular projects which present themselves as opportunities – to take over, refurbish and develop for other uses a vacated school, for instance.

Establishing community economic enterprises – some tips, by Mel Witherden

'First, understand that setting up community-based economic enterprises involves expertise from (and understanding the values of) both community development and business. Neither, alone, is sufficient.

Don't let structures become a distraction. A simple constitution is fine during the initial planning phase. Later, the group will need the partial legal protection of (in Britain) a "company limited by guarantee" or a (more recent) 'community interest company' and may also decide to apply for charitable status. More complex structures involving subsidiary trading companies are rarely needed until there is a significant trading income. Make sure the group receives sound advice from someone who knows about these things (only rarely will this person be a solicitor). The group will probably also need guidance to ensure it does not take bad business decisions. It is a myth that trading will generate large profits to support social activities or eliminate the need for grants. But it should make the organisation more businesslike and independent. The issues which group members have to face may be so unfamiliar that they become confused, apprehensive or unsure. The worker's role is to build confidence, make the goals concrete and the process comprehensible, but without creating unrealistic expectations.

There are two stages to planning for a multi-purpose partnership organisation such as a development trust, on which a group will usually need expert guidance: (1) putting together an overall *community strategy or action plan* which meets the community's needs and incorporates the realistic aspirations of the residents; and (2) producing a detailed three year *business plan* with budgets and targets which shows what will actually be done in the early stages.

The community strategy and business plan must be able to demonstrate to potential funders and supporters that the needs and wishes of local people have been properly taken on board. How this is done – whether by the group or an outside consultant – needs to be considered carefully. The best results come from using a variety of consultation approaches and information sources. The job of consulting with the community is also a not-to-be-missed opportunity for the group: to build up a wish-list from which a small number of achievable projects can be selected; to attract public attention and draw in new members; to develop team working; to take ownership of the project; and to gain management experience by monitoring the work of its development worker or consultant.

Support workers need to know about market research, job costing, cash flows, marketing, etc. But they will have to speak in terms that won't alienate group/community members. They will also need to build the capacity of the group members with planning and training sessions, covering the following:

● the (critical) role of the business manager, who must be trusted to pursue commercial opportunities without the board breathing down his or her neck;

● mutual trust, clear responsibilities, unambiguous targets, and sharp management reporting arrangements are all essential to building the right board–manager relationship;

● the need for opportunism and risk-taking;

● the importance of dynamic leadership;

● the absolute requirement for monthly financial monitoring, preferably in a small finance committee.

The challenges mentioned above never disappear. Complex and dynamic community organisations are in a state of constant change and rarely achieve the staff resources they need. Support workers should try to make groups aware: that the future is unpredictable; that they should hunt down appropriate outside expertise if they need it; and that securing the right help at the right time may be extremely difficult. Getting plugged in early to support agencies, networks and personal connections could save them from disaster later.'
(Personal communication)

Community workers and development trusts: some dilemmas

According to Ben Reynolds, if you work with a development trust (especially if you are employed by the Local Authority) it may not be clear who is your master. You may find yourself as a development trust member, in which case are *you* the member or is the Local Authority the member? If the latter, are you actually *representing* the Local Authority? You will certainly find that people outside the 'community sector', e.g. Local Authority officers, just don't understand that sector. They may expect you to be able to get the 'community' to do what they want the community to do. And what do you do when the community members want one thing and the Local Authority wants another? The trustees may well have different values from you and want different things from the organisation, but you can't direct them – you are not in charge of them. And their motivation may not be altruistic. How do you deal with trustees who are behaving inappropriately e.g. criticising the organisation in public? You can send them on training but, however much training you give, some people can't seem to learn appropriate skills. And it's particularly difficult to change attitudes.

You need continually to be thinking about the role of the board and how to develop them. You need a strong leader of the board with whom you can work closely. However, you may need to put a good deal of time into helping him/her develop appropriate knowledge and skill. Also, what about the board's responsibilities with regard to employment law, health and safety and Criminal Record Bureau checks as *voluntary* board members? Whose responsibility is it when things go wrong? Yet if you took no risks nothing would ever get done. Try to clarify such issues before they become crises.

Running a development trust, by Mike Durke and Anthony Brito

'When you are running a development trust, recognise that, first and foremost, you are a business. You need to survive through grants, rental income, trading, fees for service, etc. When setting up the development trust, the potential members must design it to do what *they* want – there is no blueprint. There is also a tension between managing the "business" and facilitating collaboration between stakeholders, which require different skills. It is difficult for one person to do both. Also, if you are going to do community development work on the ground, you need yet another person. So, to run a development trust successfully you really need a business/board manager, a partnership development worker (with agencies) and a community development worker. A good development trust will also, through: contacts with staff in government agencies; outreach work in the community; and the active partnership which it constitutes, formulate the views of local people so that public agencies make a better contribution to the area.

When you have a board to oversee getting things done quickly and effectively and, sometimes, large budgets, you have to develop its expertise and ensure continuity. You need a small board for this, definitely fewer than ten. However, such a "professionalised" board may exclude local people, thus reducing volunteering and local involvement. So you may also need a wider open forum, meeting less often, which has a dialogue with the board. And you must be able to call on people to help, without them having to be on the board. Some agencies will join the board, but others, such as the police, will not, though they may come to meetings and give advice. Also, think through the purpose of meetings carefully. If you have large agendas and people from different backgrounds on the board, the meeting will take a long time. Local people may wonder why they have to get their heads around charity law, for instance. Conversely, health professionals may wonder why they have to sit through meetings discussing the next carnival until "their" two-minute slot arrives. The whole thing will have to be held together by the co-ordinator. You need to work continually to get appropriate people onto the board, keep them informed and ensure they have the skill to advise you and set policy.'
(Personal communication)

Community economic development – a redefinition

In deprived areas, up to 70 per cent of the whole population may be outside the labour market and not benefit much from schemes which are only job creation focused, especially if these are part-time, temporary and poorly paid. So, I define community economic development as any activity which increases the wealth of the members of a particular, usually disadvantaged, community. It can, therefore, include actions by community groups, the voluntary, public or private sectors to: establish, run or provide advice and assistance to local economic enterprises or local entrepreneurs; make low-cost credit available; ensure community members get relevant training; provide or run managed workspace; provide better local shopping facilities; get people to where jobs are; create community-owned, income-generating assets; and many more. In one sense, therefore, community economic development merges with both generic community work and 'anti-poverty' work (increasingly given emphasis now by Local Authorities in Britain). But, looked at another way, some of the elements of community economic development are properly carried out by economic development agencies. Because, for poor people, the economic and the social are inextricably linked, community economic development needs to be one element in a comprehensive approach to excluded communities.

Social enterprises

Social enterprises are 'socially owned' companies which have some similarities with development trusts. Their board or owners are a group, which could be a co-operative or a community of need. They have to trade in order to create income. They are committed to creating social benefits, for instance giving away their profits to charitable causes.

The best social enterprises are developed by one person who is so 'bloody-minded' they make it work. They have the same ambition and ruthlessness which are necessary to succeed in the private sector. They always ask: 'Is this saleable?'; 'Can we make it pay?'; 'Who will buy it?' (David John, personal communication).

Running a not-for-profit agency – the example of a Council for Voluntary Service (CVS)

A CVS serves voluntary organisations by providing, among other things, advice, funding guidance, information, training and (sometimes) a volunteer bureau. Carol Green, who runs such an organisation, told me she tries to work according to the following precepts:

1. As a good business person, you need a strategic view. What is likely to happen in the future? Where are things going? Where will something take you? What can you afford to neglect? What is money likely to be available for next?
2. It is crucial to be well connected and for others to have a degree of respect for you. Keep all the channels of communication open and have contact with the key individuals or constituencies regularly.
3. Have a good understanding of your organisation's money. Your finance person might not understand the politics and *you* will

have to argue for resources outside your organisation, not them. If there is likely to be inconsistent funding you may have to cut jobs. The longer you put this kind of problem off, the bigger the problem you will create. But try to move the good people into new areas.

4. Know the law – what you can and can't do – especially in the current era of litigation, tribunals, etc. You won't have an HR and finance department, or somebody else setting the rules; you'll have to do it pretty much all yourself.

The community worker as a manager in a large bureaucratic organisation

Today, community work is gradually becoming institutionalised, and some community workers find themselves managing a range of different workers, especially in Local Authorities. If you are not prepared for this, it may come as a shock, because the culture of such organisations is often in opposition to the ways in which community workers operate. You have to get used to 'procurement' procedures, 'delegated powers' forms and the jargon of formal project management and performance indicators. The things you need to do in order to survive this experience and to use it effectively are as follows.

Leadership and team building

Agree team values early and make sure, too, that you live by them yourself. It's also vital to ensure that new team members are made aware of these. One way of identifying appropriate values is to have a team exercise listing inappropriate behaviours. You can then move on to identifying appropriate ones.

The old mode of leadership was 'telling people what to do'. Modern leadership is more consistent with community work values. But it still needs the use of appropriate authority. The effective leader is able to 'look' in several directions at once, e.g. to: sponsors/funders; his/her staff; end beneficiaries; his/her own learning; other departments and agencies. You can motivate your staff by recognising them, praising them, being clear about what you expect from them and creating an open atmosphere where constructive criticism and disagreement are encouraged. You also need to ensure there is good communication in all directions. However, if you tolerate poor work, the staff who are performing well become disgruntled.

Good managers are prepared to coach their staff (including assisting 'sub managers' to manage). Make sure you have timetabled sessions with each staff member which they know are about their own development. Here, use the skills of the coach to help them assess their own work and approach to it, and to identify their learning needs. But first of all you need to have established a trusting relationship with them. They will 'give you a lot' if they see you are really interested in them. (See Adair, 1987.)

Conflict of many different kinds occurs in a team. This can help people re-evaluate and grow but it can also be destructive. If you are a team leader you must be prepared to deal with this. Conflicts cause strong emotions. So, in order to resolve conflicts you need to find ways of taking the emotion out of the situation, such as temporarily halting a meeting. Then, find out exactly what is causing conflict and hear different parties' views on it. Finally, suggest, or get the parties involved to suggest solutions. If none can be found, you need to 'rule' how the situation should be resolved and not be afraid of this. Make sure you remain impartial and fair You then have to put in place a continuing means of ensuring that the problem causing the conflict is addressed, e.g. by directing or coaching staff, moving them around and spelling out, where necessary, what you want to see happen. Be aware of your own emotions too. (See Thomas and Kilman, 1996.)

Communicating well

Good communication depends on listening. To do this, focus on the words of the speaker and try to connect with their feelings. Note, too, that we don't always say exactly the right words to communicate precisely what we mean. So, you might repeat back to the speaker what you believe they have said in order to check you've got it right. Similarly, when you are saying something, as the manager, you need to be sure the other person knows what you mean, possibly by repeating it in a different way or by asking the other person to repeat it back to you. If you disagree with someone, don't 'put them down' but acknowledge their ideas. Write important things down. When I'm coaching I often talk in parables or metaphors, so that staff will see the point or message, without me either telling them what to do or explaining literally what I mean. I sometimes use scenes from films or stories from books to illustrate a point.

There is both a formal and a 'psychological' contract with employees. The latter is about assumptions, expectations, culture, the give and take and the small customs which make an office run. For instance: somebody with childcare responsibilities may be allowed to take time off flexibly when their child is ill; being able disagree with your boss; knowing the actual limits (as opposed to the official limits) to what you can do. A good psychological contract is what makes a group of people a team. An inappropriate psychological contract is difficult to change. The psychological contract cannot be completely written down, though having clarity about what is and is not OK is vital.

Try to know what makes your staff 'tick'. What motivates them? You can do this at a team meeting, by asking them. Generally, having autonomy, being listened to and being praised motivate people, but staff differ slightly in this respect.

Handling difficult situations

1. *Sickness*. Some staff struggle into work when sick. Others stay home when scarcely ill and you suspect they are feigning it. It is important to monitor sickness and do a 'return to work' interview with everybody when they come back. That way you cannot be accused of picking on certain individuals. This can also enable you, sometimes, to identify issues early, problems at home for instance, which it is useful for the manager to be aware of. If you think sickness is not genuine get guidance from your own supervisor or HR department. If you indicate that further time off for sickness will be investigated, you might see an improvement. When a staff member returns to work from stress or a long illness, you may need to make special arrangements for them, initially, at least.

2. *Poor performance*. I find that the hardest thing when dealing with poor performance or misconduct is judging what kind of position to take and when. The situation is often not simple in that the employee may have a sick relative or be having domestic difficulties. In many cases a quiet word can be enough. But if behaviour doesn't change you have to be more directive – 'You will do such and such'. You may also have to offer coaching or training, or suggest the staff member gets external advice and help. If behaviour still doesn't improve, you may need to move towards a formal disciplinary situation. Another difficult thing to work out is whether

or not to signal that this will be the next step if the behaviour doesn't change, because it may seem like a threat, be counterproductive or trigger a grievance being taken out against you. When moving towards a disciplinary situation you need to be sure of your ground. So, make sure you consult carefully with the HR department, and follow the rules to the letter. You don't want to face a tribunal later on for having got the procedures wrong. Write down everything, both to cover yourself and to spell out to the staff member exactly what you want them to do in order to improve. Hold regular meetings to check progress. Raising the performance of staff who present difficulties, whether you are directing them, coaching them intensively or are in a disciplinary or quasi disciplinary situation, takes ages.

Problems with poor performance and conduct tend not to go away, and it is important to address these early; otherwise the problems and attitudes which go with them become entrenched (see ACAS, n.d.)

Performance management

I explain to new staff what I expect of them and what they can expect of me, in effect summing up the 'psychological contract' and the culture I wish to engender. I also hand this to them on paper. You could also get your team to consider such expectations and suggest modifications, perhaps in a team meeting. When your team is adopting targets, it is best if these can be worked out together and not imposed. Sometimes they are imposed from above, and you just have to accept them and perhaps work to change them. Getting staff to work to imposed targets which they don't 'own' is difficult. The process of working out targets needs careful thought, sitting down together and discussing ideas, going off at tangents sometimes, asking 'what if'. Only through this process can you set appropriate targets. A good action planning process also requires the same approach. Often, in my experience, targets are not only imposed in Local Authorities, but poorly thought through and even unattainable. If this happens, make sure you go back early to your superior and get them clarified – don't try to work out what you think is meant – you'll probably come a cropper (I have!).

There also need to be as few targets as possible – the 'vital few'. Try to make sure, too, that you are a 'learning' team. One of the biggest problems in government today is that change is so fast, with imposed performance indicators, that the 'rate of learning is slower than the rate of change', spelling disaster. A related point is that slow, step-by-step change is nearly always better than dramatic change, which, if it goes wrong, creates massive problems and cannot easily be rectified. Finally, make sure that you and the team produce evidence about achievements, both to enhance your morale and to show others what good work you have done, especially if the work is somewhat invisible (see Revans *et al.*, 1998; Argyris and Schön, 1974; Senge, 1990).

Some tools

Most community workers have learned about project planning, performance management, etc. through trial and error. However, there are many useful tools to help with this. One I use a lot is 'RAG' (Red, Amber, Green):

Red = won't work – put on back burner
Amber = possible – explore with view to implement soon
Green = yes – everything in place, so implement now.

Other tools include:

● a cause and effect diagram;
● process flow mapping;
● asking key questions (what, why, where, who, when, how);
● stakeholder analysis;
● risk analysis.

Problem solving

The pressures in local government are such that quick and poorly thought through action is sometimes taken when there is a problem, often compounding it. It is vital not to rush to a solution. First, analyse the problem. Then search for possible solutions, evaluate them, allocate resources and 'do it'.

Recruitment

This is the most important thing you ever do. There are four 'rules':

1. Be absolutely clear that everybody agrees what the staff member will do. Put it in the job description and make sure you test for

that as practically as possible in the interview. Telephone referees, rather than relying on written references alone

2. Give it lots of time; it must be your top priority to get this right.
3. If in doubt, don't appoint.
4. If you can, enforce a probation period, extending it if things are not working out and offering training. Do not be afraid to terminate the position during the probation period if the member of staff does not perform appropriately. (All this means that you have to monitor and work carefully with new staff to be sure they come up to scratch, and have the necessary evidence to take appropriate action if they do not.)

Project management

Project management is primarily a 'mind set' requiring certain attitudes or qualities which can be cultivated. These include: having a vision; having drive; being organised; being clear about aims and objectives; ability to analyse steps along the way; ability to pick up problems early. You also need to give proper time to this. The bane of the life of many Local Authority officers is that they have a service to run and they are asked to run a project on top of this. They can't do both, and huge problems occur. Again, there are lots of tools to help you, often available now as software packages. These include: stakeholder analysis; network analysis; work breakdown structure and project schedule; project initiation document; statement of requirements; workflow diagrams; timeline and dependency (GANTT) charts; and force field analysis. While I have not used many of these myself, except in a limited way, some close colleagues use them all the time and they can be very powerful.

Ensure you take into account both the 'hard Ss' and the 'soft Ss' (Table 8.1).

Table 8.1 The soft and hard Ss

Soft Ss (people skills)	Hard Ss (task-related skills)
Leadership	Project definition
Communication	Project control
Managing people	Project planning
Negotiating skills	Risk management
Motivating skills	Review
Team building skills	Quality assurance

In project management it is generally wise to separate out the people who are sponsoring, funding or directing (in an overall way) the project from the project implementation team. This assures good accountability and does not waste the time of top managers on operational issues. A few final points to remember are:

● When projects fail, it is mostly through poor analysis at the beginning.
● So, write down assumptions about the project at the start because everybody will have slightly different ones.
● Give lots of effort to getting 'buy in'.
● Build slack (time/money/backup) into the system because of unexpected delays or problems e.g. staff getting sick.
● Get the right project manager.
● Encourage people to ask 'stupid' questions.

(See Brier *et al.*, 1994; Rodney Turner, 1993; PRINCE 2, n.d.)

Commissioning services

How often have you had a haircut or repairs to your house and not got what you expected? It's the same with project commissioning. Today many services are commissioned externally, but what I cover below also applies to internally commissioned projects. In order not to get the wrong 'haircut', you need carefully to do the following:

● Identify what you currently offer (i.e. where you are now).
● Identify gaps.
● Work out what stakeholders and potential beneficiaries want/need.
● Consider whether you can do it best in-house or on a contracted out basis.
● Make everything explicit.
● Decide.
● Agree a contract, with milestones.
● Have regular meetings to monitor performance.

I once commissioned a project costing £120,000 from another body. I drew up a two-page contract which I sent to our legal department to peruse. It came back thirty pages long six weeks later. But they were probably right to extend it.

Managing change

As a community worker you are largely facilitating change 'from below', but as a manager you may find yourself implementing it from above. The five prerequisites for change are: vision; skills; incentives/benefits; resources; and a good plan. Without these you get: confusion, anxiety, false starts, frustration or inefficient change. You need to take account both of the soft Ss and the hard Ss (see Table 8.1). But probably the most important thing is spending time explaining the change and getting 'buy in' from staff, if at all possible. If you don't involve the people near the ground who know the problems in practice, it will probably not work well. They are often in a position to sort out mistakes if you have their goodwill. Some people may lose and others gain from the change. Try to make it 'win-win' and think hard about how those who will lose can be compensated.

Above all, remember that, as the change is implemented, performance is likely to drop. There will be low morale until people find ways of making the change work and feel comfortable with it. Staff need to be supported through a process which can involve shock, denial, confusion and frustration. Finally:

- Be clear what is not negotiable.
- Brief people regularly.
- Continually uphold the need for change.
- Get the team to come up with ideas about *how* to implement it.
- Remember that change is a process, not an end point.

(See Burnes, 2000.)

The budget

You will probably find yourself managing a large budget. You should know what should be spent monthly (budget profiling), so that you can anticipate where an overspend may be and where money may be saved, as well as what the pressures are likely to be in the future. While staff leaving can often create an underspend, such events are counter-balanced by extra expenditure which you haven't thought of. Have regular meetings with your finance person to ensure you keep on top of this, and spend time carefully going through the figures.

Some practical applications, by Mandy Jones

'I manage fifteen community work (and other) staff. You can't treat everybody the same. Some need to be told what to do; others less so. You need to know how to approach each to get the best out of them. The targets we are "given" are usually quantitative. But we need to measure, e.g., changes in attitude. I make sure I meet with colleagues not working in my area; otherwise local issues get on top of me. An informal lunch with these "friends" is a lifesaver. Traditional "project managers" have no idea about how to involve the community, and they create all sorts of problems as a consequence. Short term funding is disastrous. You just can't plan. It is unsettling for staff and destructive for the community. You lose the people who have most experience. You have to deliver on the "external" funding organisations' pre-specified aims. But, I would rather go in without money, build capacity and then ask for money.

The aims of the Local Authority often clash with those of the community. We were looking at the development of an industrial heritage site. The Local Authority only wanted community involvement to help it get a government grant. Eventually the community pulled out. We supported them on this. Local councillors think they know best – "I am the elected representative: I know the community". They can be narrow-minded, talk all the time and don't accept other people's views. One once said to me at a public meeting: "Remember whose name is on the bottom of your pay cheque." You need to "manage" councillors, often to "sweet talk" them. Some staff are great at this, some hopeless. If you don't get this right they will scupper everything you do. But a good councillor is a real asset.

The community may criticise a worker in a partnership meeting. I (as manager) let them criticise the project but not the worker. The criticism may or may not be valid. The opposite of this is where the community say the worker is wonderful because he's sitting down with them drinking cups of tea all day. But I know he's as lazy as hell.'
(Mandy Jones, personal communication)

Cross-boundary and partnership working

Today the work of many agencies is dependent on co-operation across boundaries, requiring the establishment of a variety of inter-agency partnerships and working groups. Most managers in British public services are now involved in such initiatives. Also, there are many staff whose job is to facilitate such partnerships and to seek to ensure that the strategies, plans and actions agreed by them are successfully implemented and reviewed. To some extent these partnerships and related arrangements deal with 'wicked issues' (see Rittel and Webber, 1973), which more traditional organisational processes do not easily handle. Some characteristics of 'wicked problems' are: solutions cannot be applied in a linear fashion; outcomes from actions are difficult to predict; there is a poor link between outputs and outcomes; some 'solutions' exacerbate the problem (the 'law' of the opposite effect); you don't know if a particular solution will 'work' until you have tried it; if a particular solution 'works' you may not know why; the resources (including intellectual resources) needed to act on the problem are shared among many agencies.

With regard to the ordinary partnership member it is obvious that there are effective and ineffective partnership players. Worker 'A' hardly ever attends partnership meetings, doesn't respond to requests for information, sticks rigidly to their departmental imperatives etc. But worker 'B': chats a bit before and after meetings; goes the extra mile to provide that additional information you need but is not so vital to them; thinks 'how can we solve this together' rather than emphasising the difficulties. The role of the (more or less) full-time partnership co-ordinator is, essentially, facilitating 'the mutual adjustment of behaviours of actors with diverse objectives'. The qualities they need include: being respectful of others; tolerance; being committed to ultimate service users; diplomacy and tact; being a good networker; being a good listener; emotional intelligence. Their technical skills include: facilitation; organisation building; negotiation; group work; mediation; dispassionate problem analysis; project planning skills; knowing how organisations (including partnerships) work; evaluation skills. Effective 'boundary spanners' seem also to have wide experience and knowledge of different agencies (Williams, 2002, 103–24).

There are many different types of partnership. Some consist of only two individuals working closely together. Others consist of several stakeholders meeting to inform each other of their planned actions and seeking to ensure that all of these fit together well. In such partnerships individual members continue to undertake their existing work, using their own resources, because of their need to remain accountable to another authority, perhaps. Other partnerships collectively allocate (but don't directly spend) extra resources to develop new programmes. Yet others become formal organisations with several staff working directly for them. While you need to be clear which kind you are involved with, the problems they face are similar.

Some issues in partnership working: a case study

A very large amount of money was to be made available from the European Union to regenerate a council housing estate. The Local Authority set up a 'partnership' which involved agencies and local people, developed proposals and redeployed staff to consult the community and run programmes. However, there had been a history of conflict between that estate and the Local Authority, and there was lack of trust between the community representatives who emerged and the council. When initial proposals were brought forward from the community, Local Authority officers who agreed to develop them further sometimes found it necessary to modify them. However, they tended not to explain this fully to the community representatives or consult carefully. The community representatives did not always understand the proposed financing or design of a programme. Several quite reasonable projects were stopped because some of the local people on the partnership thought the council was merely pushing through its own pet schemes. Different community representatives sometimes attended consecutive partnership meetings, so, a project which seemed to have been agreed one month was vehemently opposed the next. Certain community groups were also in continual conflict with others.

Partnerships and partnership working – a contradiction in terms?

Most public/community partnerships get weighed down with: numerous performance indicators set by government; different members fighting for resources; and complex bureaucratic procedures. The focus of such partnerships should not be on these things at all, at least initially, but on starting small and building up trust.

(Bill Jenkins, personal communication)

Good partnerships tend to arise when a few people, at least, are in a good (professional) relationship with each other over a long period and are determined to use their time, respective skills and available resources to collaborate in order to achieve a jointly agreed vision and aims. (See Fosler and Berger, 1982). The need for trust becomes obvious when we look at: work teams (especially in dangerous industries, such as mining), sports teams, orchestras, marriages. Effective partnerships are also characterised by people enjoying the experience of creating something together. So how do we make partnerships for community regeneration work?

Making partnerships work

The reality of partnerships for community regeneration is that things often go wrong. For instance, you jointly decide to establish a particular project but fail to achieve it; or when established it does not meet the needs which it was expected to meet. In this kind of situation those involved have to, without recriminations, look at what went wrong, learn lessons and try again either with the same project or with something else. Developing a partnership well cannot easily be done by somebody with a strong allegiance to any one organisation. The partnership facilitator's task is, first of all, to get to know all the potential actors and to understand fully their positions, hopes and desires. If there is potential conflict within a partnership a great deal of work needs to be undertaken outside formal settings – in one-to-one meetings or in very small groups, for example. Here the worker, once he or she has developed trust, needs to be prepared to explain, a hundred times if necessary, the view of one party to the other, suggest compromise solutions or smooth egos. The partnership facilitator should also ensure that the capacity of the partnership to act effectively is continually strengthened.

When a formal partnership is first being established it can often be useful if a vision and a mission are collectively agreed. When particular projects are suggested, they can be compared with the vision and mission and the work generally reviewed in relation to these. Different professionals often see a situation slightly differently, because their starting points are different. Therefore, in initial meetings each of the stakeholders should be encouraged to take some time to describe their own organisation, and perhaps their personal perspective too, outlining what they want from the partnership. While it is illusory to expect all stakeholders to want the same thing, it *is* realistic to ensure that they all understand what each other wants. If you don't do this, the group may become clogged with people talking at cross-purposes due to different unstated assumptions about goals and means. This process, which needs to be undertaken with sensitivity because some individuals and organisations may not be entirely sure what they want or may be reluctant to reveal it, may also need to be repeated occasionally. Facilitating informal contact between partnership members is also useful, because that is how relationships develop.

Successful partnerships also need specified goals. If these are agreed at a particular meeting and written down, then everybody has, in a sense, signed up to them. They will need to be reviewed from time to time, too. It also needs to be decided who will carry out particular pieces of work to meet particular goals. Clearly, the community cannot be involved effectively in a partnership unless it is well organised. In a deprived, 'unorganised' community I would recommend that a community development process is engaged in for at least two years before a wider partnership is established.

Highly skilled work in difficult situations

Community work in divided communities

The world today sees many communities, in effect, fighting each other: Muslims and Christians, black, brown and white, Catholic and Protestant, Palestinian and Israeli. Community work has much to offer such situations, and there is a need for good handbooks and case studies to show how this is best done in differing contexts. I have taken the Northern Ireland situation in order to illustrate what seem to be successful approaches, and I hope that readers who operate in different contexts will be able to draw out universal lessons. This section also needs to be read in conjunction with the subsequent sections on 'promoting community cohesion', 'anti-discriminatory practice' and 'equalities work'. The following account is closely based on the views and experiences of Avila Kilmurray.

Division and conflict in local communities may sometimes become so intense that they become the predominant context within which community work takes place. This is particularly obvious where divisions turn into violence, and where conflict is based on wide-scale alienation of certain groups or communities. Whatever the specific circumstances there is a need for community workers to recognise both the causes and the impact of marginalisation and alienation. For conflict to be addressed, it must be honestly acknowledged. This is not always easy for a community worker as there is always the apprehension that doing so will make matters worse. There are a number of insights that are useful to remember when seeking to map such tensions:

1. Individuals and groups within apparently 'single identity' communities can hold differing viewpoints, which will change over time depending on the progression of the conflict.
2. In order to be able to make a realistic assessment of community views, it is important to probe beyond the accepted local institutions, whether these are the religious leadership, the school principal, or business interests.
3. The 'scapegoating' of community conflicts on criminal elements, delinquent youth, or political extremists (almost all portrayed as unrepresentative) can be misleading.
4. Seeking the causes of conflict and alienation within local communities, rather than in the relationship between them and state institutions and culture, can also be misleading.

It is important to work with a range of individuals and groups within a community in order to get a sense of the complexity of views and to identify shared experiences and grievances. Engaging local people in a 'Future Search' exercise, where they reflect on their community life history as a prelude to identifying priorities for future development, is a useful tool to promote dialogue. This allows a diversity of voices to be heard.

There is a tendency for people to be called on to take sides, thereby silencing the voices of those who are unhappy with the prevailing 'certainties'. Consequently, one of the most critical tasks in working with communities that are beleaguered as a result of violent division is to create a safe space for discussion and the expression of different views. At the height of the 'Troubles' in Belfast, a community activist set up a weekly discussion forum, called 'The Common Grumble', as an attempt to encourage dialogue. In other circumstances neutral spaces outside the community can be used to organise both intra- and cross-community discussions. Community workers in neighbourhoods where deprivation is compounded by violence, have to do the following:

1. Develop sources that can provide an understanding of the main opinions within the community.
2. Adopt a 'self-effacing' role which refuses to be put in the position of representing the community.

3. Work both with community members to highlight injustices as experienced by the community and also to prevent the external 'demonisation' of the community.
4. Give 'leadership from behind' without being manipulative.
5. Adopt a judicious approach to the expression of personal views – particularly when these may be political.
6. Know when to 'keep the head down and ear to the ground', while still maintaining a position of integrity in relation to the local community.

One difficulty faced by community workers in these circumstances is the competing demands they often face. For instance, a worker may have a structured work plan, agreed by their agency, which is thrown up into the air if there is a riot, as the local community may want the worker to prioritise their work to respond to the local crisis. In order to avoid a conflict of loyalties it helps to negotiate role clarity at an early stage.

Many community workers who work in divided societies are highly motivated. However, such motivation can lead to frustration at the slow pace of change. There is also the need to recognise that government policies shift and change, and that community development risk-taking encouraged today may well be demonised next week. Consequently, community workers need to keep an eye open to shifting political priorities at the macro level to ensure their work is not deemed part of the problem. They must be aware of:

● national and local government policies – both declared and actual;
● any security implications;
● issues at community level;
● the attitudes of the broader voluntary sector.

The locally based community worker may have to be guide, encourager and trail-blazer to give cover to other statutory and voluntary agencies that otherwise may be apprehensive about working in the situation. The community worker can sometimes arrange formal and informal meetings between local people and the representatives of external organisations in order to make explicit the local needs, while at the same time humanising relationships between these parties. The adverse perception of an area can often prejudice people against those who live there. One of the complexities facing workers in such communities is to know when it is timely to speak out. As in all community work, it is generally more effective if groups of local residents are empowered to speak out rather than the worker, particularly if he or she is not local. Invariably in situations of conflict, local communities themselves throw up the most amazing activists.

In Northern Ireland, workers should not take their holidays over the tense summer marching months or during the anniversary of a particularly emotive event. However, it can make sense to organise an outward bound challenge event for local teenagers at such a time. A 'frontline' area, where violence is common, runs the risk of 'drawing in' people from the wider area, attracted by the conflict. Consequently, the local community worker might seek to be in touch with a broader network of workers and activists in the surrounding areas. However, it is vital that such issues are discussed with the local group or groups, since community workers can only go as far as the local community will let them.

Support also needs to be gained for Community Action Plans – both in terms of 'regular' issues and with regard to conflict-related issues. Such plans should ideally be negotiated long before any suspected periods of tension since crisis management is generally the worst form of planning. It is never easy to get community groups to honestly address sensitive and controversial issues. Consequently, it may be useful to use an accepted external facilitator, so that the community worker is not seen to be drawn into a particular agenda. Essential for the agreement of an effective Action Plan is the inclusion of all the groups making up the community. If local groups feel no ownership of the Plan they can thwart it. Such inclusion may be difficult with regard to those people actually involved in violence, but there are always local intermediaries who 'know their thinking'. Such channels of communication are invaluable; if conflict cannot always be prevented, it can often be modified. The following initiatives have proved invaluable during periods of open conflict in Northern Ireland:

- A mobile phone network where workers and activists on various 'sides' agree to phone each other in order to check out, or defuse, rumours. (Rumours are perhaps the most dangerous mechanism for aggravating violence.)

● Establishing telephone contact on a regular basis with vulnerable community members to check they are safe. An extension of this is where a named neighbour is available to visit them. (For example, an elderly person may not be able to collect essential medicine during a riot.)

● Identification of, and community group solidarity with, local residents who might be seen as targets during a period of tension.

● Organisation (with careful stewarding) of festivals to defuse periods of potential tension.

● Negotiation with local activists to remove/replace contentious symbols. (Judicious negotiation tends to be more effective than unilateral action.)

● Coinciding with school holidays, the organisation of diversionary activities for young people when pubs are closing or crowds likely to gather.

● Identifying the young people most likely to encourage their peers to become caught up in violence and encouraging them to become involved in positive activities.

There also need to be longer-term strategic interventions, which can be grouped into three main categories:

1. *Encouraging discussion and dialogue.* This entails ensuring there is space for all views to be heard and challenged. There is little point in discussion being limited to reiteration and reinforcement of a single interpretation. So-called 'single identity' work is important, but primarily to ensure that there is self-confidence for communities to tell the story of their own experiences and to share their fears and aspirations. Where communities find it difficult to articulate the latter, they feel more alienated. One of the most important formats through which community perspectives can be shared is through arts and drama. It is particularly important to ensure that the voices of those who have been most hurt as a result of the conflict are heard, although they cannot be allowed to have a veto on change.

2. *Proactively opening up opportunities to engage and interact with the 'other'.* This is difficult but equally critical. Sometimes initial links can be made through networks of community activists around issues of common concern. Local women's groups often take the lead here. For instance, the 'Women's Information Day

Group' held a meeting, once a month, for local women's groups in various communities throughout Belfast. Meeting in alternate venues between Nationalist/Republican and Unionist/Loyalist areas, they provided transport and a crèche to bring women together across the sectarian divides. Were people scared at times? Yes. On some occasions did the members fall away? Yes. But the initiative was maintained on a consistent basis nonetheless. In other cases neutral venues for cross-community meetings were arranged outside specific aligned communities.

3. *Brokering in the necessary support and skills to underpin such strategies.* During periods of tension it can be useful for any community worker involved in such meetings to encourage the participants to agree to some ground rules to ensure confidentiality and safety. It can also help to have external facilitation, but the local people involved must feel comfortable with this. Those cross-community dialogues that work best tend to be characterised by a consistency of participation over a long period of time, allowing trust to build and prejudices to be questioned. The local participants must, however, dictate the pace and have control over both the subject material for discussion, and how the meetings are communicated back into their own communities. The main role for the community worker may be in making the initial contacts, brokering in the necessary resources, skills and support and identifying potential follow-up activities. For example, where a community 'on the other side' has developed a project of interest, they might arrange a visit or a speaker. Another useful role can be in supplying information about the challenges faced in other areas – to question the tendency of local communities caught in conflict to see themselves as 'the most oppressed people ever'.

It is crucial that a network of support is in place for workers, in order to help them develop competence in this area of work and to prevent burnout.

Community development and community cohesion

Every few years in Britain, and in other countries, too, there are clashes between communities, based ostensibly on 'race' and religion, and the government has now set up a Cohesion and Faith Unit to seek to reduce these. According to Gilchrist (2004), the most important factors to take into account are as follows. The underlying causes of inter-community conflict are complex and relate to Britain's colonial history, discrimination and poverty. Work to reduce such conflict needs to be based on an understanding of the histories of specific communities and their perceptions of themselves, other communities and the majority community. There is a need for a long-term approach which enables communities to work together and to establish mechanisms for managing disputes and tensions. There needs to be a (transparent) core value of 'seeking justice'. Inter-communal grievances and real inequalities need to be seriously addressed if progress is to be made and sustained. (That is, it is not helpful merely to bring people together.) Also, strong supports of a community development kind are needed both for building up the capacity and understanding of communities and facilitating positive interactions between them. You can't make an effective impact in this area without a good (political) analysis of the nature of the relationships between different communities and their position vis-à-vis the state. Additionally there is a huge amount of work to do in order to ensure that public authorities develop culturally sensitive services and anti-racist strategies to tackle the exclusion, disadvantage or oppression of certain communities. But policies need to be devised and explained too, by means of well thought out consultation and communication strategies; otherwise positive action to benefit a certain community can fan the flames of conflict.

It also needs to be noted that it takes several years to move from building up shared community confidence to a point where members of communities in conflict (or potential conflict) are prepared to meet and work together on joint issues. Separate provision (for example, for people from different ethnic origins) can be a vital and empowering step along the way to integration and racial equality. However, communities sometimes have 'self-styled' community leaders who seem to prefer to foster conflict and reinforce difference. Community development work has much to offer in facilitating the emergence and development of leaders who represent their communities responsibly and can be held accountable.

We have to not only encourage (and celebrate) diversity, but also facilitate integration if we want better community cohesion. Community workers have the skills, and should help communities to manage diversity and change and learn strategies for achieving negotiated and equitable compromises. We also need to recognise and understand heterogeneity *within* communities, in relation to age and gender, for example. Based on an understanding of power differentials and cultural differences we need to know how the quality of life is unevenly experienced in different communities, and to assist people in addressing these issues. This process can generate fear and hostility as people's 'comfort zones' are challenged. Mistakes are inevitable and community workers need to find their own sources of information, advice and support in order to learn from and improve their practice.

Promoting reconciliation in general

Community development work with excluded groups often seems to be part of the reconciliation process for resolving intra-community conflict (see, for instance, Gilchrist, 1998, pp. 100–8; Ndolu, 1998, pp. 106–16). It is only necessary to mention a few of the techniques of promoting reconciliation (see Acland and Hickling, 1997) to indicate the similarities between this and community development work:

- Identify exactly who the parties are and talk to them separately.
- Be aware of what role you want to take up before you act.
- If you take a 'third party' mediating role, this needs to be accepted and agreed to by the other parties.
- Do not take sides.
- You need to feel comfortable with the techniques you use.
- Allow plenty of time.
- Find out the causes, the history, what people really feel.
- Reflect back what you hear to check that you have got it right.
- See the world from the eyes of each of the groups you are working with.
- Break groups up into smaller groups if necessary.
- Ensure that all participants understand that this is a problem-solving process.
- Understand that decisions have to be reached with both groups meeting together and make this clear.
- Agree ground rules early on.

Anti-discriminatory practice

Members of community organisations sometimes act in discriminatory ways against ethnic minorities, older or disabled people, for instance. Consequently, some community workers have sought to develop anti-discriminatory practice. Alison Gilchrist (see Gilchrist, 1992, pp. 22–8) argues that community workers need to:

- recognise that the marginalisation of certain groups is a reality at all levels of society;
- understand that we all need to find ways of working which empower and include excluded groups and individuals;
- seek to ensure that the organisations in which we work or are involved do not discriminate against such groups;
- combat discriminatory behaviour or systems;
- encourage others to combat them.

Alison (who was white, middle-class and relatively young) helped community groups in an inner city neighbourhood of Bristol establish and run a community centre. She found that, in the middle of the area which now accommodated significant ethnic minority populations, the community association which employed her was run largely by local white people, including several influential working-class people who had lived there all their lives. In effect, other groups (especially black groups) were excluded, though not by conscious intent. Alison worked, with others, for six years to change this situation and to encourage the organisation also to address several dimensions of oppression (for instance, disability and sexual orientation). She had some success, but it was challenging work. From this experience she developed the following guidelines.

1. Work to create a less discriminatory situation (and attitudes) must be strategic and have time and resources allocated to it.
2. Understand the detail and dynamics of the local context.
3. Understand that there are three kinds of causes of discrimination:
   (a) *Psychological*: prejudice, hostility, ignorance, different cultural values.
   (b) *Practical*: access issues (for example, no interpreters), lack of facilities (for instance, childcare), lack of transport, access to information (for example, problems with language, use of jargon), cultural requirements not being catered for (Muslims not drinking alcohol, for instance, or allowing boys and girls to mix).

(c) *Political*: institutional and legal power, informal decision-making networks.

4. It can be useful to divide up the anti-discriminatory practice strategy in three main ways and to decide which approaches you are going to try to take, when, how, and in what combination.

(a) *Empowering the 'oppressed'* through: outreach; consultation; targeting; creating positive images; providing access to information and decision taking; arranging separate provision; providing support; supporting 'self organisation'; and showing solidarity.

(b) *Challenging the oppression* by: providing training and education; encouraging cultural awareness; persuading the discriminators to change policies procedures and practices; engaging in confrontation and other conflict tactics; making connections between oppression which the 'oppressors' may also suffer and that of those who they are oppressing; and identifying common areas of concern between the two (or more) groups.

(c) *Celebrating diversity* by: being positive about different choices and cultures; creating opportunities for people to work successfully together around shared issues; organising events which enable people to meet informally (for instance, cultural or sports activities, meals or trips); and enabling people to learn from each other's experiences or perspectives.

5. Adopt targets: 'This summer I would like to see at least three disabled children using the play scheme regularly.'

6. Monitor progress and evaluate how the work develops, being sensitive to change and flexible in response to criticism.

7. Consult continually with the people who you are trying to help and ask them what they want to see happen.

8. Educate yourself about the situation. (Alison had to recognise that the Muslim requirement to pray several times a day had an impact on the organisation of a meeting if Muslims were to attend it.)

9. Work out who is likely to be deterred or prevented from participating by a particular arrangement.

10. Start on the gentler, more persuasive, 'chatty' approaches and only move to confrontational approaches later.

11. Recognise that anti-discriminatory practice takes time and resources and that the allocation of these will need to be justified.

12. Create a good professional support system for yourself before engaging in such work, and find allies.

As a result of her work, a greater tolerance of diversity was created and, in some cases, the value of this was recognised. Some people were certainly empowered and began to look at themselves in new ways. A great deal of energy was generated and discussion opened up. There was much learning on both sides and, in some cases, greater understanding. More needs and aspirations were met. The end result was fairer access to power and resources. However, Alison also found that she had stirred up some antagonism and suspicion towards herself, as well as conflict within the group she was working with. Some members had drifted away. Several people had had their feelings hurt. Consequently, she had to spend time with them, in their homes sometimes, helping them work through these. In the process of anti-discriminatory practice some people's genuine needs and aspirations were neglected. Some people got labelled as racist. She also found that:

- some black people said she was not doing enough;
- some white people said she was doing too much and neglecting *their* interests;
- some *black* people said she should not be doing this at all!

She was also aware that the worker could easily abuse her own power. In her attempts to change the views and behaviour of some residents she might well be perceived as disempowering and unsympathetic to their needs and experiences as white working-class older people. Also, as resources are always scarce, it may be necessary to take them from somewhere else in order to carry out anti-discriminatory practice.

The anti-discriminatory practice worker needs to play a range of roles: enabler, organiser, challenger, advocate, developer. It is important to work out which one you are adopting when and with whom, and to play that role honestly and openly. While community workers often operate with groups in relatively non directive ways, in order to address the issue of inequality you sometimes have to be challenging and, in a sense, judgemental. Reflecting on her role, Alison concluded that it is vital to be clear about one's mandate. A continuing concern is always the question of 'tokenism' – for instance, inviting members of the black community to join the management committee without the deeper change of attitudes among its existing members which would bring about and sustain change.

Anti-discriminatory practice also includes:

- making sure that communities acknowledge and accommodate difference;
- being aware of class differences;
- being aware of language (for instance, calling an initiative a '*parents* and toddlers' group);
- checking whether a piece of work is likely to be discriminatory in any way;
- ensuring that funding applications incorporate money for positive action measures;
- seeking to include people who are normally not reached, for instance, Sikhs, travellers, people with cerebral palsy themselves, and not just representatives from the organisations run *for* them, recognising that there are also, for instance, gay and lesbian black people;
- seeking to ensure that any improvements are 'mainstreamed';
- seeking to ensure that people from different groups find ways of communicating across their boundaries, which can result in mutual understanding;
- putting people from different parts of the community in touch with each other and enabling them to co-operate.

'Equality' work in large institutions

Local government and other public services today are rightly concerned that all potential beneficiaries receive the services they need, irrespective of gender, race, location, age, etc. There is also now much legislation, in Britain and other countries, which requires such organisations to ensure as far as possible that services give equal benefit to all groups. Anna Freeman who worked as an 'equality' officer in one Local Authority told me that her work included:

- working with the Police, the Race Equality Council and others to create a 'race equality strategy' and to prevent and tackle racial crime and related problems;

- ensuring equal opportunities procedures were fully complied with in staff selection, promotion and training;
- ensuring disabled people, people with small children or people without much knowledge of English could use council facilities and services;
- carrying out audits and collecting statistics to assess the Local Authority's progress on equality;
- working to ensure greater understanding of the service needs of different groups;
- seeking the views of, for example, disability or ethnic minority groups and inviting them to send representatives to relevant working parties;
- producing strategy documents on: gender, disability, ethnic minorities, etc;
- providing advice and training to Local Authority departments and committees on equal opportunities issues, and requiring each department to state how it proposed to take equal opportunities forward;
- setting up a helpline for the victims of racial harassment;
- working with other organisations to promote equality of opportunity.

Anna summed up her approach in this way:

> You can't move people on by hostility and pointing the finger at them. People generally want to be nice people and are afraid that you are searching out the racist in them, so I make efforts to be approachable. Spend time finding people with whom you can work – don't spend time worrying about the shortcomings of those you can't work with. Examine an issue from all sides before you act. If you are not careful, particular action in relation to one kind of disability may make things worse for another. Try to discover from service users themselves what they want. Don't reinvent the wheel. Seek out examples of good practice from elsewhere. Finally, there is a bottom line – you don't meet racism half way.

Conclusion

If you can do all the kinds of community work described in this chapter and those preceding it, you are getting near to becoming the complete worker. But what about 'specialist community work? This is what we look at next.

Points to ponder

1. Are there common factors of 'advanced practice' which you can identify from this chapter?
2. Which are, for you, the most challenging aspects of advanced practice, and why?
3. What are the key characteristics of effective 'partnership working'?

Further reading

Brier et al. (1994) *Project Leadership*.
Gilchrist (2004) *Community Cohesion and Community Development: Bridges or Barricades*.
Scottish Centre for Regeneration, *Partnership Working: A 'How to' Guide* (n.d), (www.pt.communitiesscotland.gov.uk).
Twelvetrees (1998a) *Community Economic Development: Rhetoric or Reality?*
Williams (2002) 'The Competent Boundary Spanner'.

9 | Specialist community work

This chapter explores community work approaches which are different or narrower, at least in some ways, than those of 'generic' work in small geographical communities. There is, however, disagreement about the concepts of 'generic' and 'specialist' community work.

> My view is that the purpose of community work is to empower individuals and communities by learning through collective action. Much of what might be seen as specialist isn't significantly different from what might be regarded as generalist, except that some specialist knowledge of an issue or the target community might be required.
>
> (Charlie Garratt, personal communication)

For me, however, 'specialist community work' is a necessary part of a theoretical framework. Additionally, of course, generic workers become, in a sense, specialist when they work with a particular need or issue related group in a geographical community. Therefore, some knowledge of different dimensions of 'specialist' community work is useful. Perhaps most importantly, I try to show in this chapter that aspects of community work need to be central to a wide range of social interventions. In a sense, therefore, I am suggesting that all human service workers need some of these skills.

Types of community work

Generic, neighbourhood-based work – a recap
The 'generic' neighbourhood worker works with groups which have a clear connection with place, and it is in this geographical sense that 'community' has its strongest meaning. Some of these groups – for instance, residents' associations – have a broad range of concerns and can, potentially, consist of all the residents of the locality. Others, for example, single-parent groups, are communities of need within

the geographical community. The generic worker potentially works with any of these groups, and on any issue.

Specialist work with communities of need

Some workers are employed only to work with specified 'communities of need', usually over a wide area. Such 'communities' consist of people who share a particular condition or circumstance and are usually excluded from access to resources, good services and power. Depending on the context, people from ethnic minorities, disabled people, older people, teenage parents, gay men and lesbians, and many others, can be thought of as communities of need. I call the workers assisting such 'communities' *specialist community workers, working with a community of need*.

Specialist 'sectoral' workers

Other community workers focus on community work only in relation to a particular service or issue, for example, housing, health, or the environment. I call these workers *specialist sectoral community workers*. Having said this, these workers may also be operating in relation to communities of need and place.

Specialist work with a community of interest

This is the name I give to those workers whose work focuses around a particular interest, e.g. sport or the arts, though they undertake this work with both need and geographical communities.

Some general issues in specialist community work

The theoretical framework for community work (and community development work in particular) has been developed almost entirely in the context of work in geographical communities. This may be because what I call specialist community work is often undertaken by members of need communities themselves or by 'sectoral' service professionals who are untutored in community work principles. As a consequence, less emphasis is probably placed on the empowering and organisation-building role of the outside enabler, which is the cornerstone of 'classical' community development theory. Having said this, the main principles of work with neighbourhood-based groups apply also to specialist community work and especially to work with communities of need. (See Chapters 1–4.)

However, if you are organising, say, visually impaired people, there may not be enough of them at neighbourhood level to form a group. But, if you are organising across a large town and into its hinterland, there is no equivalent, in Britain, at the city/county level, of the ward councillor who can take up issues for you. When you do bring members of need communities together, there tends to be a hub, probably meeting in a town centre, but a large periphery of people who can't easily get there. Considerable organisational resources are needed either to take the meeting to outlying areas or to transport people into the 'hub'. For all these reasons, any organisation you establish may not have much influence. Also, how do you reach the members of 'need communities'? People with Parkinson's disease or women suffering domestic violence, for instance, often have to be contacted via the professionals who work with them. But, which professionals, and do the professionals know them all? Do they trust the professionals? By contrast, people who live in the same neighbourhood may already know each other and meet in pubs, outside the primary school, at the doctor's surgery, and so on. If one of them misses a meeting, the local grapevine will probably let them know what happened and the date of the next one. They will be served by the same elected representatives. They may be of a similar class and culture and will share *many* of the same needs. By contrast, the particular characteristic which the members of need communities share may be the *only* thing they have in common. All this makes it more difficult to 'organise' them.

The three types of specialist workers mentioned above will generally be employed in: housing agencies, senior citizens' organisations, health organisations, economic development organisations, etc. Their managers and colleagues will share a particular culture, which they will mostly absorb, too. They won't generally see themselves as community workers or have knowledge of community development work, and, indeed may have moved into their current role from being a mainstream service deliverer.

How not to engage with the community

An employment office had linked well with community groups in a neighbourhood community development project and was having some success getting excluded people into jobs. Then, a government

> programme was announced which suddenly 'threw' large amounts of money at that neighbourhood. A specialist team came in, 'brushed aside' the employment office staff, failed to liaise with local community institutions, and withdrew after two years when the money ran out, leaving a mess.

When agencies with no history or knowledge of community development processes initiate programmes which are supposed to promote community involvement, or depend upon it for their success, they usually fail to consult the extensive literatures on the subject and neglect to use experts in the field. They invent their own 'brand', resulting, often, in poorly thought-out programmes. There are huge training implications here for human service professionals.

Similar problems happen with 'consultation'. A three-month project engaged primary schoolchildren in examining their inner city neighbourhood, and they came up with many proposals to improve it. Brilliant! However, when the consultation facilitator departed, there was nobody to work with the children and others to seek to implement the proposals, some of which were contentious. Disillusion all round! Many service providers now do consult with service users routinely, which is to be welcomed. It is also reasonably easy to do. However, acting on what comes back is often difficult, and more thought needs to be given 'up front' to what it will take to respond effectively, and resources (including skilled staff time) allocated as appropriate for 'follow-through'.

For the reasons outlined above, workers whom I might call specialist community workers often take a social planning approach, and don't engage in community development work at all. Therefore, their work to develop services to such groups tends to have as its starting point what the agency believes is needed (perhaps, today, based on a needs analysis). However, a service to a disadvantaged community (of need) will generally not work well unless the beneficiaries are able to influence it. And they will not easily be able to do this if it is a 'top-down' service with a minimal amount of consumer involvement or consultation (or if consultations are not heeded) or if it does not invest in empowering the 'beneficiaries' to speak and act for themselves at least in some respects. However, specialist community workers employed by non-statutory agencies, such as Women's Aid, Mind, Age Concern and the like, often have or can create a degree of freedom to use community development approaches, if they so wish.

If you are a generic neighbourhood-based community worker, it is usually easy to know when you are working with agencies (i.e. taking a social planning approach) rather than with local residents. The corresponding community development approach with a non-geographical (disadvantaged) 'community', especially beyond neighbourhood level, is to get into contact with people either through their representatives (e.g. the parents of children with learning difficulties) or through the professionals who work with them. However, the 'professionals' may also be members of such groups. For instance, while one of the leaders of a self-help group of cancer sufferers was a health visitor, who was primarily there in a professional capacity, she also had cancer. Similarly, an organisation was established by a community worker employed by a social services department to seek to improve housing and work opportunities for people with learning difficulties. The majority of the committee consisted of parents, and it contained no individuals with a learning difficulty. Several of those parents were long-standing volunteers with 'Mencap', and one of them was now also employed by that organisation. Other committee members included a bank manager and a health service representative. The social services department community worker was a full member of the group and also had a child with learning difficulties.

In such situations, the roles which professional community workers are called upon to play can be confusing and conflicting. On the one hand, you may have brought people together to form the organisation by using your 'enabling' skills. On the other, you may also play a major organisational role and be, in effect, its secretary or chair. You might, in addition, become the main employee of such an organisation if it goes on to receive money to employ staff. You could well share the same circumstances as the 'ordinary' group members (for example, be from an ethnic minority). Different roles, e.g. chief employee, enabler and leader are difficult to combine, and clear thinking about these is vital.

The specialist (sectoral) community work conundrum

Specialist (sectoral) community workers often find that the needs/ wants of the community or group do not fit neatly into their sector of work. For instance, what does the health-focused community worker do when the community wants to run a carnival? Specialist sectoral community work depends, in part, on the community already being organised. If it is not, a worker, on environmental issues for instance, might need to spend two years helping the community to organise itself. This would have to be around issues its members cared about, and these would not necessarily be the concern of the (specialist) worker. Where community groups exist but want a specialist (sectoral) worker to assist them on projects which are outside the worker's strict brief, the worker has to decide whether to become 'generic' for a time, whether to try playing a leading or directive role as opposed to a facilitating one or whether, ultimately, to refuse to work with that group. This is another reason why specialist sectoral workers, often take on more of an organising/social planning role rather than a community development role.

Notwithstanding the above, I believe that what I call specialist community work is self-evidently needed, particularly to help service agencies link well with the communities they serve. The problem lies in the fact that often nobody is doing the generic community development work 'up front', work which needs to be done if the different forms of specialist (especially sectoral) work (and other service interventions) are to be really effective.

Specialist sectoral community work – some examples

The following section includes some practice insight boxes written by experienced specialist community workers on the problems of working in their particular field.

Community work and housing

In Britain, the growth of community development work is closely associated with the expansion of council housing after 1918. In the 1970s, many community workers learned the job on council housing estates, where they assisted tenants to campaign for improvements and to improve opportunities for social and recreational activities. Until the 1980s, that work tended to be either 'against the (local) state' or in relative isolation from it; Local Authorities (the landlords) either ignored tenant action or reacted negatively to it. There was no real acceptance that community involvement was valuable. Today, it is recognised that council estates need the active involvement of tenants, and there are several organisations, for instance, the Tenant

Participation Advisory Service (www.tpas.org.uk), which provide advice about effective tenant involvement, run training courses and make policy recommendations. Many Local Authorities have also employed tenant liaison or participation workers. Mostly, such (specialist) workers have a fairly restricted brief, e.g. facilitating tenant contributions to housing policy or dealing with tenants' problems. It's also interesting to note that some (private non-profit) 'registered social landlords' now employ community workers in recognition of the fact that their tenants need assistance to organise themselves to represent their interests. Such community workers also tend to play a more generic role by working with tenants on issues such as economic development, the provision of play facilities, environmental improvements and so on. Finally, in Britain, council housing is now often being transferred out of the control of local government, and, in some cases, community companies are being formed, city-wide, to receive and manage the housing stock. Clearly, there is a major role here for community workers to help build such companies.

Crime prevention and community safety

A partnership approach to community safety, by Sue King

'The Morgan Report (Home Office, 1991) emphasised the importance of strategic partnerships to address local crime and introduced the concept of "community safety", which is wider than crime prevention. In 1993, the Home Office produced *A Practical Guide to Crime Prevention for Local Partnerships*, which offers a useful structure for community safety planning. It focuses on: defining the problem via a crime audit and review of current policy and practice; preparing an action plan; implementing the project; and assessing achievements. Later, the Crime and Disorder Act (Home Office, 1998) required police and Local Authorities to create "community safety" partnerships comprised of a mixture of public, private, voluntary and community bodies.

If a partnership is established to initiate social and economic regeneration, in my view, its first step should be community safety and crime prevention measures that will improve the quality of life, reduce fear of crime and actual crime and start the return of the "feel good" factor. Before capacity can be built in our communities, these basic crime and community safety issues must be addressed.

A regeneration strategy was agreed by fifteen agencies in a Welsh town and the whole strategy was underpinned by crime prevention and community safety measures, including: creating and supporting neighbourhood watch groups; burglary prevention work; closed circuit TV; youth work; engaging a community artist; graffiti clean-ups and other schemes in which the community was involved. Within two years, there was a reduction in the fear of crime by over 50 per cent, and burglary had reduced by 69 per cent. Subsequently many community development measures were initiated, following a strategy agreed by residents' groups, with partner agency support. None of these initiatives would have been possible if the community had not started to feel safer and taste a better quality of life.'
(Personal communication)

Sue's position, above, is that crime prevention approaches have to take place before community development initiatives. Others would tend to argue that they can both take place at the same time.

Community work and youth offending, by Eddie Isles

'You have to both tackle the crime issues in a community and take that community with you; it is a complex "twin track" process. We analyse the crime data and we map the high risk areas. We bring together the incidents and the addresses of the known offenders and victims, which leads us to priority areas. This enables us to target areas of greatest need. We then talk to parents, professionals and young people, with the aim of getting the young people into preventative and engagement programmes, e.g. family group conferencing, youth action groups, peer education, sports, etc. Young people who are involved with crime want what we all want: a stable family, a job, a supportive community. Therefore, as well as working with young people involved with crime, we have to find ways of re-integrating them into the community and getting the community to "forgive" them. To do this we link with whatever is on the ground at local level: neighbourhood groups, multi-agency partnerships, etc. Involvement with such groups helps us explain to the community the nature of the programmes we run, to get support for them and even to recruit parents as volunteers. The kind of intelligence you get from community groups is different from that which you get from officials and statistics.

All this requires patient build-up and a long-term perspective. Community groups often shout us down first of all because people are sick of graffiti, annoyance, burglaries and car theft. But, if we persevere, we usually get a degree of community "buy in" to solving real problems. After a few meetings local people start giving positive suggestions as to how to make progress. This is a good example of "top down" meeting "bottom up", and it works!'
(Personal communication)

Community work and the environment, by Chris Church

'Links between community work and environmental activity were once limited, but this is changing. The lack of linkage may have been partly due to the focus on national/global policy issues by environmental groups, who have also been accused of caring little about poverty and of being mostly made up of well-off professionals. However, environmental action can build local engagement. People who never dream of going to a residents' group may happily plant daffodil bulbs round the base of a tower block or take part in a clean-up day. Such activities can open the door to longer-term engagement.

The developing focus on sustainable development, arising from the Rio Earth Summit (and Local Agenda 21 (LA21) that came from it) had a core principle within it of the need to integrate environmental, social and economic issues (CDF, 2003). The LA21 programme was taken up by almost all UK Local Authorities, but there was no central support. So, while LA21 initiatives did offer ways to link workers in different fields, most were not followed through. Nevertheless, some projects did start to link environmental and community development, and many LA21 networks have now merged into (Local Authority-wide) Local Strategic Partnerships, often serving as the environmental sub-partnership.

Engagement has recently been improved by the growth of what has been described as the Environmental Community Sector, consisting of environmental organisations working on local infrastructure and engagement. Some of these are linked to large organisations such as Groundwork UK, but many are individual projects, collaborating through issue-based networks such as the Community Recycling Network or the Federation of City Farms and Community Gardens. These groups have also built some links with voluntary community sector organisations, such as the Community Sector Coalition. Now, organisations concerned

> with transport, energy, conservation, and food growing are developing community-level networks and projects and are usually keen to work with and learn from community workers. In 2006, a new governmental initiative, Community Action 2020, began to focus on enabling local communities to take action on environmental issues, and a number of voluntary community sector bodies are supporting this work. It includes a training programme aimed specifically at community workers. As the poorest communities often have the poorest environments, the idea of "Environmental Justice" has now been recognised by the UK government and taken up by some socially progressive environmental organisations. The availability of Geographic Information System (GIS) mapping means that it is possible for community organisations to assess the quality of their environment. This can offer powerful support to any campaign to improve the quality of life in a neighbourhood.'
> (Personal communication)

Environmental community work, if we can call it that, is not simple. Unless, say, there is a polluting factory, the environment may not be high on the agenda of most excluded people. They might be more concerned to chop down the 'ancient woodland' for firewood, for example! Thus, there is often (quite properly) within environmental community work a top-down element involving organising, leading, educating and expanding people's horizons.

Rural community work

People in rural areas have similar needs to people in urban areas, often compounded by feudal attitudes about who participates and who decides, isolation and 'invisibility'. Community workers in rural areas may cover twenty small communities, and they cannot work with them all in depth. Transport is often so problematic that it is impossible for many community group meetings to be held. Henderson and Francis (n.d., 1992, 1993) argue that rural community work needs to contain three elements which are not necessarily those on which an urban project would be based:

1. *Working from a distance.* Here the worker:
   - monitors relevant issues, by reading local newspapers and reports of council meetings, for instance;
   - identifies trends and gathers information, about, say, the closing of village shops;

- works as a lobbyist with other agencies in order to influence policies towards the area;
- acts as a bridge between communities and professionals, providing information and 'interpreting' both ways;
- supports networks of existing community groups by providing advice, information and training.

2. *Focused indirect work.* Here the worker:
- selects carefully which communities within the whole area and which issues to focus on in depth;
- supports community leaders in the culture and skills of community development work so that they, not the worker, work with individuals and groups within the community;
- assists existing community groups to broaden their horizons, expand their agendas and act more imaginatively;
- plans and negotiates withdrawal from an early stage.

Focused indirect work can easily be carried on alongside 'working from a distance'; it allows some in-depth work with particular communities or on particular issues while not neglecting the majority.

3. *Direct community work.* Here, the worker is able to see the whole process through: making contacts and building trust; helping people to form new groups; strengthening existing groups and building alliances; creating wider community strategies; and using other approaches described earlier in this book.

In some parts of Europe, LEADER projects (programmes with tourism, economic development, agriculture, environmental and community development staff operating as a team) have conferred integrated benefits on their target areas. They represent a good model to be copied in other areas.

Community work, health and well-being

People's health is determined primarily by the quality of their social relationships and the equity of the distribution of material resources . . . The experience of health is captured as being energised, being loved, loving, belonging.

(Labonté, 1998)

Poor people are unhealthier and die earlier than the non-poor. Belonging to strong networks and the absence of feelings of loneliness and isolation contribute markedly to better health and longevity (Labonté, 1999). Inequality, rather than poverty, seems particularly bad for health (Wilkinson, 1996). For these reasons, some health agencies are now establishing health promotion projects at local level, and governments are establishing health promotion strategies with some of the following elements: local health audits; home-safety groups; accident prevention schemes; anti-drugs and alcohol projects; healthy eating groups; exercise clubs; health discussion groups; smoking cessation courses; sexual health projects.

Some such schemes move beyond strictly health issues and cover, for instance, transport, welfare rights, and the establishment of community meeting places, thus, virtually turning into generic community work projects. This makes a great deal of sense, because the evidence suggests that, unless action is taken at community level to empower and involve people in issues which concern them, the health of the most excluded will improve little. It is difficult, however, to show the links between such interventions and improved health, because the results may come many years later and because there will be many other variables affecting the outcome. Also, local people may not ask for such programmes, so there is again a top-down element. This raises the classic dilemma of specialist/sectoral community work – where do workers decide not to become involved in a project because it is outside their field? According to the above analysis, health promotion workers should really become community and anti-poverty workers. Those establishing such projects need to consider this problem during the project design stages rather than face the issue two years in. Goosey, an expert in this field, provides more information in the following box, showing how community work on the ground needs to be matched with higher-level strategies.

Reducing health inequalities, by Sandra Goosey

'There are mixed views within the Health Service as to the appropriateness of community work being undertaken by health professionals. Health promotion specialists are usually committed to this approach, but are often compelled to label action as "community health development" in order to legitimise it. At senior level, there is still limited understanding of, or investment in this approach. The contribution that could be made by health professionals is often unable to be maximised, due both to the ever increasing caseload of individuals and the fire-fighting nature of the work, and to a lack of confidence, experience and specialised training in community work. Nevertheless, many "health social care and well-being strategies" (in Wales) aim to give attention to specific groups who are disadvantaged with regard to health at local level. However, funding for community health development is generally based on short-term grants; consequently, a longer-term strategy is difficult to achieve.

In Wales, a number of specialist health teams have couched their work in the wider principles of the "Ottawa Charter" (1986). This provides a framework through which local public health teams can work with partners in providing a city- or county-wide approach, particularly focusing on specific communities, in order to contribute to regeneration and reduce inequalities. Here is an example of how this approach is utilised in one city in relation to improving the health of children:

1. Healthy public policy: contributing to the planning, development and implementation of strategic plans and new commissioning structures.
2. Re-orienting the health service: establishing a strategic health partnership for children's services, and developing sexual health services for young people in non-health settings.
3. Creating supportive environments: developing health improvement programmes in a variety of settings (e.g. promoting a network of "healthy schools").
4. Community participation: delivering health promotion workshops on e.g. substance misuse, smoking cessation, personal hygiene and promoting community events, e.g. festivals.
5. Developing personal skills: building public health skills in professionals, building community capacity in disadvantaged areas, supporting the development of community groups, e.g. food co-ops and credit unions.'

(Personal communication)

Community social work

The phrase 'community social work' was coined by the Barclay Report (1982) which suggested that social workers should work in indirect as well as direct ways to help clients, especially as 'social care planners'. Community social work is particularly associated with decentralised forms of organisation – often called patch social work – where social workers operate in specific neighbourhoods (see Hadley and McGrath, 1980; Hadley *et al.*, 1987). A community social work approach has to be department-wide. Moreover, managers need training in it as well as field staff. There also has to be clarity as to whether individual workers are aiming to be, on the one hand, community social workers or, on the other, specialist community workers. Community social workers use approaches and attitudes central to the philosophy of community work to help *their individual clients* more effectively. In particular, they get to know the community they work in so that they can, for instance, involve the local Age Concern group in supporting a lonely elderly person. On the other hand, a (specialist) community worker in the social welfare field would be aiming to: strengthen local support networks; develop new or modified organisational arrangements to ensure that better welfare services were provided; and involve beneficiaries in determining those services. These are very different roles.

In Britain, community social work does not now really exist, at least in the public sector. Nevertheless, there is a compelling case, particularly in the context of 'prevention' and work to reduce social exclusion, for the social work profession to apply community social work techniques, in some situations at least.

For a community social worker, or team, once the relevant managerial arrangements have been made, which may take a great deal of time and effort, the next step might be to conduct a relevant community profile. You will be most interested in data such as: the numbers of older people at risk and existing community support networks; playgroups; senior citizen clubs. After constructing the profile, you should work out what you can reasonably expect to achieve by working in new ways and then plan it. Ways always need to be found of keeping in contact with what is going on in the locality, and team members should divide this work between them. There are, of course, a variety of ways of developing contacts; doing one morning a week in an advice centre, or dropping in to a senior citizens club. 'Patch' community social workers soon find that they know quite a few people in the area, who provide helpful information. Workers then begin to see themselves as merely part of the support system for particular clients. Consequently, when a particular need arises, the worker may have a range of contacts who can assist or they may start referring aspects of some of their cases, to their new community contacts. And these contacts start referring aspects of the cases which they cannot deal with to the social worker. While this can be difficult, because of child protection and other safety and confidentiality issues, it can certainly be done, especially in relation to individuals and families who are not facing severe difficulties. When I was a field-level community worker a colleague from the same agency adopted, in part, a community social work approach, and it worked well.

However, once outside the bounds of the normal professional relationship, we are less secure and more vulnerable. We also question established practices and try to respond to needs over and above those which come as conventional referrals. We may be called off the street to advise on a problem, asked to transport furniture, arrange a holiday, set up a group for teenagers. Even if we say we cannot help, should we try to find someone who can? You can quickly find that you have an enormous informal caseload and that you are dabbling in a great many areas, all of which require more time if they are to be undertaken properly. How, if at all, should you record this work? How do you react when an informal contact complains that you are spending a lot of time with Mrs Jones (one of your 'regular' clients) and hardly any with him? We need to be hard-headed, to be able to say 'no' and to have worked out what we are doing, with agency backing. Finally, as it takes a long time really to get to know the area and build up trust among people, a worker needs to be prepared, if possible, to stay in the job for a reasonable amount of time, two years, at least.

Community work and community care

From the mid-1980s in Britain, there was a strong governmental emphasis on 'community care', as a result of which many individuals with, for instance, learning difficulties, mental illness or severe physical impairments, and who had been in residential care, were 'rehabilitated' in the community. In this process, rarely was the question asked as to whether assisting such 'at risk' people collectively to articulate their own needs would result in a better quality of life for them. They and their carers (carers are another 'community of need', but not discussed in this book) are often severely disadvantaged. Some of them also suffer discrimination, when a 'group home' is proposed in a residential neighbourhood, for example. If community work is to do with empowering disadvantaged people, it surely has a contribution to make to 'care in the community' for such groups, as Barr *et al.* argue:

> The principles of community development apply to community care, both in terms of collective empowerment of care users and carers . . . and in relation to the role that people in neighbourhoods might play in supporting community care . . . Reception into residential care often relates as much to the breakdown or lack of a network of support as to the person themselves . . . Generally, little work is done to prepare communities for the de-institutionalisation of people and the impact which this may have on neighbourhoods . . . If care users are to participate in society, then an educative process on the rights, needs, difficulties and disadvantages they experience needs to take place . . . Attention also needs to be given to work with established community organisations to encourage anti-discriminatory action . . . It can be argued [that] the success of a commitment [in care planning] to quality assurance may depend upon empowered consumers who can articulate their concerns, exercise choice and protect their interests in an organised manner. (1997, pp. 12, 13, 16)

Barr *et al.* also comment that 'community care' potentially offers job opportunities to people in community-run enterprises, including some care users themselves. Indeed, there are now many examples of such enterprises.

Communities of 'need' – some examples

Community work with women, black (and multi-) ethnic minority communities

There are now many writings on black ethnic minorities and, for instance, women's role in society. It is also interesting to observe that much community work writing is 'gender blind'. For instance it has often been noted that women tend to be strongly represented at the lower levels of community organisations, and may have started things off. However, men tend to take the senior roles in more formal groups, such as development trusts. But, turning this around, I once heard a fascinating account of how a city-wide skills service had been remarkably effective at getting people with no qualifications onto training courses, and so I asked how many were men. None! The professional worker needs to know how to work with particular categories of people, whether the worker is a member of that 'category' or not. For instance, in *Women and Community Action*, Dominelli (2006) recognises that the role of men in relation to women's organisation is not well 'theorised'. Also, if women are organising around, for instance, rape or sex trafficking, clearly one would expect the organiser, if there was one, to be female. Similarly, in Britain, workers with black ethnic minority communities are usually not white British, which probably makes it easier for such communities to identify with and respond to them, and vice versa. With regard to gender, all workers will be conscious of the sex of those they are working with and will, possibly unconsciously, alter their approach, according to the dominant sex of the group and their expectations or knowledge of the norms and behaviours of its members. It must have felt different for the young mums whose coffee morning I used to facilitate as a 30-year-old male worker than if a female was running it! It certainly felt very different to me than it would have been working with a similar group of men. All of us work with groups whose characteristics we don't share, at least to some degree. Consequently, we have to do as much as we can to empathise with other people in the situations they face if we are to be effective. This applies particularly if we are, or are perceived as being from a more powerful or dominant group. According to Alison Gilchrist, empathising with different 'others' is easier if you do the following:

● If you don't share the circumstances of somebody who is in an oppressed or marginal situation, listen especially carefully to what people from that group are saying.
● If you are, in relation to them, privileged, acknowledge your own privilege.
● Be more willing than you might otherwise be to acknowledge that your 'norms' are not the only 'norms'.
● Recognise that 'hidden power' and status systems support the status quo.
● Educate yourself about others' cultures and experiences.
● Try to be aware of what you don't know.
● Develop your listening skills.

Personally, I have found some of the insights and techniques from Rogerian counselling theory useful in terms of listening to and empathising with others (see Rogers, 1961–95).

With regard to work in multi-ethnic communities Alex Norman, an experienced African-American community organiser, working in the USA has some helpful comments:

> Whatever color s/he is, the worker needs to have an awareness as to whether ethnicity plays a role. This includes the worker's own ethnicity and that of those with whom s/he is working, whether these are agency personnel or local people. You need to try to understand the culture of those you are working with and their possible psychological position or positions. Then you can take this into account in your interactions with them. For instance, 'Latinos' have a culture which often means you have to work through men rather than women. A white female community organiser, working with African-American women, once said, 'OK, girls, are we ready to go?' She learned the hard way that a white person calling an African American a 'girl' was generally regarded as denigrating by such women. So, you need an awareness of the 'person in the environment', and you need to be aware of how you may be being perceived. When I work with 'whites', I usually need to consider 'class' (which may or may not play a role); when I work with African Americans, I have to be prepared to take race and class into account; when I work with, e.g. Cambodians, I need to take race, class and culture into account. Each encounter is different, and the issues which the racially and culturally aware worker needs to be aware of may or may not be an issue for those s/he is working with. Because I had a certain experience with a particular group of people last time, this doesn't mean it will work the same way next time. Stay 'open'.
>
> (Personal communication)

Community work with disabled people

In the first box below, Elinor Evans describes what is, to me, community work with disabled people, but, interestingly, she does not regard herself as a community worker. In the second box, Andi Lyden describes some of the issues workers face when working with disabled people.

Disability development work in a council of social service, by Elinor Evans

'I have a "social model" of disability, I am concerned about how society "disables" people who have impairments. I support a "disabled forum" in a large town/county consisting of: groups and individuals; disabled and non-disabled; and carers. I seek to create "community" around the social model, and then we look at barriers which people with impairments face and which "disable" them. Forum members might discuss, e.g. continent services, access issues, tactile paths, direct payments or independent living campaigns. I also try to strengthen mechanisms to involve users in social care planning with service providers. Recent legislation in Britain places a duty on statutory bodies to promote "disability equality". This enables the forum to be pro-active. We lobbied the Local Authority about poor wheelchair access and the police about disabled parking spaces. In the forum, disability groups and disabled people create the agenda. I try to ensure that forum members themselves respond to requests for information and involvement. When there is not enough time to get a group together I ring around – I see myself as a facilitator. However, agencies want a "one-stop shop" in relation to disability; they want to talk to me, partly because they think (wrongly) that I will be more "reasonable".'
(Personal communication)

Work with disabled people – a personal experience, by Andi Lyden

'If you're trying to do community work with disabled people and people with disabling illnesses, you have to create the idea of "community". It's much harder than in a neighbourhood. Also, each person's experience of a particular impairment will be different – for instance, whether you are well or not, whether you have always had the condition, or not. There are also many different kinds of disability (and combinations, e.g. Welsh-speaking blind people who need books in Welsh Braille); people with learning difficulties and their carers; amputees; people suffering traumatic stress disorder; paraplegics; the "association of partially sighted lawyers". They all need different levels of help. Disabled people may live regimented lives, added to which the systems we have to support them often make them dependent, as do, in some cases, their carers. The expense and logistics of getting people (plus their carers, sometimes, for whose transport you might also have to pay) to meetings are often too great, and not recognised by, say, the Local Authority, which wants their views. Halls may not be accessible. And, once there, they want to have fun, and not discuss the Local Authority's disability policy or organise a campaign. If you want to discover their needs, it's best to meet with them informally. We had a big coffee morning once and they "discussed everything" – they weren't afraid to say things in that setting. You need to see how disabled people and their carers perceive things. For instance: disabled people sometimes feel guilty about their situation; benefits for a disabled person become part of a family's income and are depended upon; if a disabled child disappears, there's a hole there – you are taking away the family's *raison d'être*. You have to accept the motives of disabled people and their carers as a reality.

While putting disabled people in charge, transferring power and authority is difficult - nevertheless, in the process, people learn skills. In some cases, those with high expectations (often only one or two) develop the skills to get things changed, and I can sometimes work with and through them. You particularly need disabled professionals, as employees, "raising the bar" of expectations. Then, when these people are in groups of disabled people they are by implication saying, "Look at me, I did it, so can you." If people are angry enough they will overcome most barriers.

Opportunities to change things arise from big organisations such as Local Authorities asking you to put them in contact with a group to consult with on disability issues. This gives disabled people a chance to get their voices heard. And I can put things into words which the Local Authority accepts. So, you are using the expertise of these groups about their own situation to change other organisations. A Local Authority may propose to offer a service to, say, people with learning difficulties. I know it won't work, but I can tell them how to make it work.'
(Personal communication)

Community work with children and young people

Henderson (1998) describes three approaches to community development work seeking to achieve benefits for children: (1) face-to-face work with children; (2) work with adults to benefit children; (3) work which is intergenerational (that is, involving both children and adults) from which children benefit (see also Hasler, 1995, pp. 169–82). There are several examples of successful community development work with young people. For instance, Burke (1995, pp. 28–9) describes a project to facilitate young people collectively deciding their own priorities and forming a group which realised some of these. Also, youth workers increasingly see their role as being to assist young people (sometimes individually, sometimes collectively) to determine for themselves what choices they need to make in life and to find ways of solving their own problems.

In some ways it's easier doing community development work with teenagers than adults, because they are often prepared to take direction, on how to chair a committee, for instance, more readily than adults do. I once assisted a group of teenagers to take up public transport issues. I used to meet with the officers of the group, who had been elected earlier, help them to design an agenda, and got them to think about what they wanted out of the meeting. I sat close to the chair during meetings and made quiet suggestions to her as the meeting progressed. When we reviewed things afterwards I helped her work out what to do next. There are, however, some differences in working with young people as opposed to adults. Teenagers have lots of energy and tend to 'lark about' a lot, for instance. So you need to make meetings quite short and allow a bit of space for fun. Similarly, if you want to find out what teenagers think, you might do this best in an impromptu fashion on a minibus trip rather than in more formal ways, though other methods can also be used (especially modern ICT).

The growing literature on how to facilitate the participation of children and young people does not generally present itself as community development theory. Also while it does not, on the whole, focus on work with 'committees' of children and young people, it is consistent with the values of community development. Additionally, some of the literature focuses on games and exercises (which can be great fun for adults too), which imbue children and young people with insights, skills and confidence. Some examples of children and young people participation are: children and young people producing an interactive video on drugs; children and young people in residential care designing a questionnaire and feeding back the results to managers; a play development worker meeting with children under 12 to discover what they want to change about where they live; children and young people holding a debate in the council chamber; children and young people being assisted to present a local community centre management committee with their views about their needs; a youth worker facilitating the establishment of a children and young people forum. Note, however, that you need many skills to do this work: community work skills; skills of working with children and young people; and a battery of skills for facilitating participation, especially games (see Funky Dragon, 2002; Wales Youth Agency, n.d.; Dynamix, 2002).

The participation of children and young people is also now mandated, at least in some respects, by the UN Declaration on the Rights of the Child (Article 12). In part consequence of this there is now a flood of publications on how to go about this, in Britain, at least (see, for example, Kirby et al., 2003). There is also, in Britain, an emerging body of knowledge about how to organise and support school councils (of pupils). See www.schoolcouncils.org for more information here. Where these work well, literally thousands of children and young people are organised to discuss and take some action on matters of concern to them, largely relating to matters such as bullying, school meals, etc, but also, in some places, the school curriculum and neighbourhood issues.

When it comes to the participation of say, the under-fives, there is also an emerging body of knowledge. (See, for instance Miller, 1997, 1999; *Children Now*, 9–15 Nov, 2005; pp. 20–1.) These publications give examples of approaches to listening to very small children and babies, adducing evidence that 'listened to' babies grow up psychologically stronger. While this is largely about horizontal rather than vertical participation, it is participation, nevertheless.

Community work with people with very limited capacity

Community development work usually means working (mainly) with the leaders of a community group and encouraging people to take leadership roles. Consequently, most community development work is carried out with adults who do not have, in general, severe personal incapacities. This begs the question as to how far community work can be carried out with very young children, elderly people who are mentally infirm, or people with severe learning difficulties, for instance. With such 'communities', the scope for promoting autonomous collective action is extremely limited. However, it is here that the values of love, justice, respect and self-determination come in. In working with such 'communities', an approach which was based on these values (together with appropriate consultation and, possibly, 'self-advocacy' and social planning approaches) would be consistent with a community work approach. But it could also be argued that, with such groups, community work was no different from good social work, or other human service provision. Therefore, what might be considered community work with such groups, is not easily distinguishable from other forms of work. It is also worth noting here that, if the circumstances of people are or have been extremely difficult, you need to address these issues before such people can engage in collective action. One example would be asylum seekers who are suffering trauma through having been tortured.

Working with communities of interest and need together

An organisation called 'Community Music Wales' has a good track record in involving often disaffected young people in learning, playing and performing music. Similarly, people organising street theatre, local video projects, 'artist in residence' schemes, and the like, are sometimes effective at breaking the fatalism which often pervades deprived communities. The potential benefits of involving people in arts at community level are well summed up by the following statement:

> Arts programmes have been shown to contribute to enhancing social cohesion and local image; reducing offending behaviour; ... promoting interest in the ... environment; developing self-confidence; enhancing organisational capacity; supporting independence and exploring visions of the future ... [However] the models of success and key factors in replication are insufficiently known.
>
> (Joseph Rowntree Foundation, 1996, p. 1)

Ben Reynolds makes a similar point:

> In other areas it is perhaps now accepted that a particular
> approach works; but the arts are continually having to
> demonstrate that community-based arts development is a
> viable notion in its own right and makes a real contribution
> to community regeneration, social well-being, community
> cohesion and a sense of purpose for individuals.
> (Personal communication)

Interestingly, the case for community work and sport is easier to make. There are sports development officers whose job is to encourage the taking up of sport, often in disadvantaged communities. There is also an almost endless number of development officers promoting all kinds of 'interest', from fishing, to minority languages. Whatever we call them, these officers certainly need community work skills.

Conclusion

Clearly, community work principles and skills can and need to be applied widely. The work in several of the 'sectors' described above is also, it seems to me, striking by its similarity. Some 'specialised community work' is still peripheral to the main business of the sponsoring organisation, badly planned and funded, with the workers poorly prepared, managed and trained. Other workers are now better resourced. However, many are still not well integrated with other specialist or generic projects or services in the same community and do not link 'upwards' to related policies, programmes and strategies. The sheer number of different approaches to meeting the needs of communities (of both place and need) from the bottom up, at least in part, seems to me to indicate that community work, in its many forms, is an idea whose time has come, even though what may legitimately be called community work is often not labelled as such. However, if the potential benefits of these various approaches to meeting the needs of excluded communities are to be fully realised, a more comprehensive and properly thought-out approach is required. This is the subject to which we turn in Chapter 10.

Points to ponder

1. Do you think it is valid to have a theoretical category of 'specialist community work'? If yes, why, and how would you define specialist community work? If no, why not?
2. Do you think this chapter has used the term 'community work' too widely? If so how would you restrict it?

Further reading

Dominelli (2006) *Women and Community Action.*

Hadley *et al.* (1987) *A Community Social Worker's Handbook.*

Hoggett *et al.* (1997) *Contested Communities: Experiences, Struggles, Policies.*

Mayo (1994) 'The Shifting Concept of Community'.

Rogers (1961–95) *On Becoming a Person: A Therapist's View of Psychotherapy.*

Willmott (1989) *Community Initiatives: Patterns and Prospects.*

10 Community work and public policy: towards comprehensive strategies

Organised communities tend to be healthy communities, in every sense of the phrase. (See Putnam, 2000.) It is also clear that community workers help create organised communities. But can stronger communities and community workers effectively help in addressing major issues of deprivation? There now seems to be evidence that community work is a vital prerequisite for small area 'regeneration'. The main aim of this chapter is to look at this evidence and to indicate what effective community work strategies might look like. Consider this statement: 'It is only big programmes (e.g. the opening of a factory with a thousand new jobs at a reasonable level of pay, and the provision of substantially better schools, health services, housing and so on) which can make a significant difference in deprived geographical communities.' If only things were so simple!

In the past fifty years, in many countries, large-scale schemes have attempted to create and attract jobs, provide better education, training, health, housing, and leisure opportunities. But there is not a lot of evidence that these programmes make much long-term difference (for good!) to the poor people who already live in those communities. In London Docklands, a renewal programme rebuilt the area and attracted new industries. But the local people could not afford the new housing. And the new jobs were not relevant to their, perhaps outdated, skills. The upshot of the programme was that large numbers of the existing population not only did not benefit but were also, in some cases, forced to move away as the area was 'improved'. There are many other such stories, borne out now by a plethora of evaluations, though lessons are slowly being learned.

The problems of regenerating highly deprived or remote communities, and those suffering from industrial decline, sometimes seem intractable. New industry will often not come to such areas. If a new business *is* established, it sometimes has to draw its labour force from other, better-off areas whose residents have skills, motivation and transport. The attitudes of many of the residents of deprived areas, who may have poor educational qualifications, may be such that they will neither apply for any new jobs nor go on training courses which are designed to make them 'job ready'. Additionally, in disorganised communities with, possibly, high crime, poor parenting, high substance misuse, coupled with distrust of the authorities, effective services cost a great deal more. Alienated people, especially young people, will also often not take care of public facilities provided by the state, which often get vandalised. All such factors contribute to a cycle of exclusion and alienation which vitiates the potential benefits of regeneration efforts.

Traditional regeneration programmes generally last about three years and then finish. They rarely (and cannot really) affect the underlying circumstances which enable the life chances of disadvantaged residents to be permanently improved. The 'model' which such programmes usually apply is, I think, the 'business investment model' where capital investment is provided which is then supposed to stimulate the creation of more jobs, services, wealth and confidence in a self-sustaining way. That model is not relevant, at least on its own, to the needs of deprived communities, because poverty and exclusion are inherent within capitalist society. (I say this not to make a political point – I can see no other way of organising democratic societies in a competitive global economy – but to emphasise the structural difficulty of the task of regeneration.) Therefore, an alternative model of regeneration is needed which recognises that the problems of deprived communities are usually enduring and, therefore, require enduring solutions. Let us now examine some models which seek to base neighbourhood regeneration on a community work approach.

The People in Communities (PiC) Initiative and Communities First

In Wales, in 1998, the PiC programme was initiated by what is now the Welsh Assembly Government (WAG). (See PiC, 2001.) PiC supported a handful of communities to devise action plans for comprehensive small area regeneration. This support took the form of WAG paying for a co-ordinator who would work with a local partnership to this end. The aim was to test ways to make local service delivery more effective. Local areas (covering up to 15,000 people) were to set up partnership boards, and lessons were to be applied more widely from the results of the initiative. This programme, which included the appointment of 'social inclusion champions', was generally about seeking more joined up delivery in order to provide holistic solutions to thematic issues that cut across service areas, capacity building, establishing trust and networks. The evaluation includes the following lessons.

Flawed in practice

The idea was far-sighted but the implementation was flawed because WAG did not put in place mechanisms for learning or disseminating lessons. The short time in which Local Authorities had to respond to the request to nominate local areas, and the lack of specific guidance about the principles, left people to bid for what they knew about best (i.e. 'things' and services) rather than consider change processes and experimental approaches. Also, the programme lacked several vital support structures, including a network of senior managers extending across agencies (i.e. beyond the Local Authority). Whatever good work was done at neighbourhood level was limited because many agencies failed to change the way they worked. Additionally, participating organisations tended to see the initiative as a 'pot of money', producing 'wish lists' which could not be resourced.

Experimental

Instead of encouraging a 'traditional' action plan and formal partnership approach, WAG should have asked bidders to outline how they would engage with front line agencies and the community to develop experimental approaches to service delivery. Delivery plans would then 'evolve'. Much more support and guidance were needed for co-ordinators than they were offered. They also needed skills in engaging not just with residents, but also with officers, in order to build a bridge with management.

Process change

The evaluators concluded that there needed to be an emphasis (reflected in job descriptions) on: building trust and networks; changing attitudes, cultures and structures of delivery; measuring short-term impact, primarily through lessons learned; broadening the role of the social inclusion champion to be proactive; and developing networks of senior management which identified opportunities as well as responding to requests from co-ordinators. The guidance should have made clear that PiC represented small amounts of money to 'pilot' changes in existing regulations, rules and practices of service delivery. It should also have emphasised building on existing partnerships and previous initiatives. The evaluators recommend that any action plan has to address the barriers to joint working and to be based on an understanding of how partners can work together *prior to the action plan itself* being drawn up.

Recommendations

The evaluators also concluded that WAG guidance should do the following:

- Make sure contracts and job descriptions emphasise 'soft' outcomes.
- Ensure employers think through line management of co-ordinators carefully.
- Ensure the job description for the co-ordinator it is not too extensive.
- Ensure a group of middle managers is in place to identify and seek to overcome barriers.
- Scale the programme down to the resources which WAG can muster to support it (or outsource it).
- Emphasise that the kinds of lessons wanted were, e.g. identifying barriers and coming up with solutions, and exploring the inconsistency of partners' rules and regulations that prevent activity progressing.

Their final recommendations were that it is vital for WAG to promote a culture which values learning lessons, where no blame is attached to failure and where lessons are disseminated frequently. The monitoring framework should be developed and piloted *with* the local partnerships and 'sold' to all parties. The evaluation plan needs to include both baselines and an action research element. Consultation needs to evolve organically and be continuing. Consider consulting people when they are involved in doing something else they like, but remember that local people do not always have wide enough knowledge to comment realistically. Distinguish between (a) an area action plan, i.e. what the community wants agencies to do, and (b) a community action plan, which is what the community does with money it gets. Recognise that there is often suspicion between Local Authority departments themselves and between the community and the council – if the Local Authority employs the co-ordinator this can create distrust. There is a need to create channels which ensure that senior management listen to the front line. Finally, note that, by exposing co-ordinators' line managers to the concerns of the community and to the co-ordinators themselves, they begin to learn (PiC, 2001).

Later, WAG initiated Communities First – a serious attempt to develop a nationwide community development programme, focusing on the most deprived wards. The guidance (WAG, 2002) expected local partnerships to build community capacity and to 'bend' other programmes to benefit the local area. There were, however, several problems. According to an independent consultant closely involved with the programme who I interviewed:

> Initially there seemed to be an emerging commitment to the community development process by WAG, and a serious attempt to learn lessons from other programmes. Given the limited capacity in WAG to manage PiC, it was hoped that Communities First would roll out over, say, three years. Different communities needed different kinds of assistance – while many already had a reasonable capacity for community action, others were 'virgin territory'. Ideally, in year one, you might support: 10 communities which already had high capacity; another 10 which had just commenced the development process; and another 10 which had not started. But it was decided to deliver the programme to 140 communities and to create formal partnerships in each, more or less simultaneously. It was 'one size fits all – wham bam, do it', and, in many cases a disaster. The Local Authority sector is not well educated with regard to this sort of programme. In some places 'old guard' elected representatives hate it and bully workers. Insufficient attention was given to making sure that all players fully understood the nature of the programme. The fact that Communities First was primarily to do with capacity building and 'programme bending' and aimed at getting people to work together to improve

conditions was probably not fully understood by WAG officials and ministers, and certainly not by Local Authority members and officers.

At least with communities with limited capacity, we should have started with low level stuff, i.e. get a community development worker in place, with an office. When partnerships are fully established, they can use larger amounts of money. Instead of this, those managing the programme established complex funding schemes which complicated matters. Getting the capacity in WAG right in order to drive the programme required a sophisticated understanding both by ministers and officials. Extensive discussions should have been initiated across all relevant WAG departments to help them gain this. Communities First required a different concept of governance from the traditional one.

(Personal communication)

This consultant identified other problems too:

- The programme was initially very prescriptive.
- It did little to break down the silo mentality, especially in Local Authorities.
- There was excessive micro-management (one Communities First local co-ordinator had to ask WAG's permission to attend a conference, which was refused).
- Audit played too heavy a role. It became so bureaucratic that, in one area, they had to stop local people using the photocopier.
- The thinking behind this programme was that a community can come together quickly and produce a realistic action plan – that is almost impossible.
- 'Up front rollover funding' should have been provided initially, then verified retrospectively, otherwise voluntary sector projects could close.
- 'Floor targets' e.g. health improvement, job creation, educational improvement should have been looked at five years down the line. The targets for the first period should have related to community participation and partnership working.
- There was no joining up with other and related programmes.
- There was confusion over 'action plans'. The partnerships expected that, when the community had produced an action plan, this would be funded either directly by WAG or out of

existing service budgets. But, with the constant pressure on services, there was no way this was going to happen. Partnership members and co-ordinators got frustrated when, after all the consultation work, the resources were not made available. Co-ordinators desperately required responsive management as well as a small capital budget.

● The guidance should have specified that there should be a single unit to co-ordinate the Communities First neighbourhoods in each Local Authority area, arrange training, evaluation and take care of some of the financial aspects. This might best be a hybrid between the voluntary sector and the Local Authority. The Local Authority should not dominate.

(Personal communication)

A manager of the programme at Local Authority level added:

> WAG did not appreciate the impact of a new programme on existing groups and partnerships. There was not enough groundwork involving other organisations, especially the Local Authority. The accountability structures of the Local Authority vis-à-vis the partnerships were not clear. Co-ordinators don't like being managed by the Local Authority. The 'programme bending' idea requires leadership at the highest level. Local elected representative training is vital. Finally, there is a need for a mechanism to ensure that each local area knows about the cross-area strategies e.g. children and young people, substance abuse etc.

(Personal communication)

Another commentator added:

> The local partnerships need a great deal of support, as do Local Authorities, in working out how to manage the programme. Some Local Authority members felt threatened if they did not control it. Also, WAG need assistance with policy development from experts in this field. Some of the people who come forward to be on local partnerships increase the barriers. For example, they may just see kids as troublemakers. Some co-ordinators play a sophisticated 'double game' – while they work to the formal agenda of the partnership they do lots of good work behind the scenes!

Much of the work of the co-ordinator is invisible. I would also focus on 'partnership working', rather than on 'partnerships'. But, in some areas the partnerships are ends in their own right. Ideally, the partnerships are there to make links between the community and service providers. One of the best Communities First areas has no formal partnership after three years, but there's lots of good partnership working. One co-ordinator spent the first month talking to people in the council. This stood her in good stead later. However, many co-ordinators felt abandoned and controlled at the same time. While 'programme bending' is supposed to be central to the scheme, many co-ordinators don't know what it is. Training needs are high. Incremental gains are important – you can collect a small number of tangible benefits which add up to something big.

There are two problems with linkages with other strategies. First, why should the resources of an organisation with the money which is being spent through a due process be given up to another organisation? Second, the way in which Communities First partnerships speak to mainstream agencies is important. A 'we want the money spent this way' approach may alienate and not be very effective. The important question is how we get a dialogue towards joint planning.

(Personal communication)

Finally, a senior manager within the programme added these points:

Communities First is a non-prescriptive bottom-up, creative, flexible, risk-taking programme. The basic principle is to start small and build up from there. Inevitably you'll have to take risks. You'll have to have a minister who will stick with it. If I was developing a community development programme I would have built on existing projects. This programme 'bites back'; there are all kinds of conflicts and disagreements. The worst are intra and inter community conflicts. The big Local Authority area-wide strategies and partnerships need to get their acts together to link better with each other and to local communities.

(Personal communication)

Theorising comprehensive community work strategies

Having seen some of the issues involved in developing a national/regional community work strategy, it is interesting to note that the theoreticians draw similar conclusions. Taylor (2003) concludes that government policy seems to be based on simplistic assumptions that communities can be turned into agencies for local improvement. However, there are 'dark sides' to communities, and many conflicts and conflicting interest groups within them. Community leaders get burnt out, too. Additionally, regeneration programmes are particularly problematic if they lack a means to ensure that projects developed through large scale injections of funds are sustained. These are huge blocks which prevent better joined up approaches to local sustained service improvement. Moreover, formal partnerships can militate against partnership working. They tend to be dominated by the 'funding game' and lack understanding, often on all sides, about what working together really means. Heavy auditing requirements, detailed accountability procedures and other government regulations leave little room for manoeuvre and detract from partnership working, risk taking and community empowerment. Notwithstanding the rhetoric, communities have not really been involved; there is often a failure to 'count' what residents feel is important and use local knowledge. There are too few appropriately skilled community regeneration staff. 'Lead-in' times have been too short, and sustainability has been low on the agenda. Finally, lack of co-ordination in central government has frustrated the joining up of goals at local level.

Taylor also gives examples of practical (community development-type) techniques (2003, pp. 168–9) which can be used as a means of people understanding their own situation, taking charge of their own lives and beginning to negotiate with service providers. Her basic point is that you need to spend a good deal of effort in developing community networks so that local people can engage with something they understand and which interests and motivates them. Until you have created, at least partially, an educated, empowered and organised community, there is no point in redistributing responsibilities to it or expecting it to engage constructively with service providers on complex issues. In order to ensure there is effective community participation, she argues that you need to develop a diverse pool of community leaders. She notes that the most successful participatory initiatives are where the state invests early in community develop-ment, participation and partnership, and where this investment is given time to bear fruit. However, there needs to be realism about the levels of participation expected. She observes that successful com-munity initiatives run at a moderate rather than an accelerated pace. Also, people need incentives to participate – at least they need to know the results of their participation, and if what they wanted to happen doesn't happen they need to be told why.

In considering what she calls the 'institutional challenge', Taylor concludes that whatever reforms are thrown at them, public ser-vants are good at 'doing what they've always done' (2003, p. 197). She points out that the daily lives of middle managers are governed by performance targets, output measures and budget constraints. The public service ethos also emphasises concern for proper pro-cedures, control, conformity, reliability, consistency and traditional councillor roles. By contrast, the kind of ethos needed to make local partnerships work should emphasise a concern for results, guiding (as opposed to controlling), creativity, risk taking; diversity, and new roles for elected representatives.

As well as providing incentives for partnership working, there needs to be investment in the skills of doing this. There is a need to hold auditors to account and balance the need to ensure pro-bity with the need for speedy and flexible action. You also need to be clear about what a partnership is trying to do. Often there are too many requirements placed on participants, and the com-plexity of some partnerships makes it almost impossible to produce results. It is vital, too, to ensure there is conscious development of informal links of many kinds between communities and part-ners ('bridging' social capital). This requires new kinds of mediators and brokers whose role would be to work horizontally in order to: stimulate the exchange of knowledge across boundaries; make con-nections between potential allies; build on assets rather than focusing on needs; and encourage joint learning. She also indicates (2003, pp. 201–3) various ways in which bridges can be built between community and middle management and the skills of partnership working learned.

There is now wide agreement that better integration at many levels is the key to improved services. Taylor (2000) concludes that it is the creation of common cultures, knowledge bases and synergies that are the powerful tools for sustaining regeneration. However, the small-scale activities which are so important to building community capacity are often marginalised by the complexities of bidding for and managing regeneration funds. Small amounts of money with few strings attached are vital if a solid foundation for community involvement is to be built. She argues for a framework which includes: a strategic vehicle at neighbourhood level; community development support; joined-up mechanisms at city/county level; a strategy to tie neighbourhood management into other regional and national strategies; commitment from everyone to flexible working; and appropriate finance (i.e. not a big bang, followed by nothing!). She also emphasises that we need to combine the 'strong tools' (regulation, inspection, sanctions) with the 'weak tools' (persuasion, systems of learning, building of networks, and setting or borrowing examples). We also need: an incremental approach, plenty of time and a 'tight-loose' framework (i.e. an institutional framework but local autonomy; clear goals, but a recognition that not all objectives can be in place from the start). This would involve: creating new career structures; rewarding people who work across boundaries; and creating opportunities for dialogue and mutual learning. Providing appropriate rewards for community participants is also vital.

Other reports and evaluations tell similar stories about community regeneration programmes.

Community involvement and neighbourhood regeneration

Chanan (2003) notes that reports on area regeneration are increasingly calling for good community involvement, but without giving sound reasons for that. He and Taylor suggest the following: it overcomes alienation and exclusion; it makes the community strong; it maximises the effectiveness of services and resources; it helps join up different conditions of development; community definitions of need, and the actions they propose, are different from those of the planners and often provide holistic definitions from which joined-up solutions can be developed; community knowledge widens the pool of information that can be brought to bear on problems; the social and human capital that community involvement develops helps sustainability; active community involvement is essential to improved democratic accountability.

Chanan also observes that, while government regeneration proposals require community involvement to be promoted, there is
generally little indication in the programme guidance about how
to make it happen. Such guidance doesn't draw on community
development theory and tends to assume that an organised community already exists. There is a lack of indicators for community
involvement, and it is not generally measured.

Drawing on Putnam (2001), Chanan writes:

> [L]ocal residents are not merely ... people who might become
> involved in governance [and] either have or ... lack
> networks ... and the trust which goes with them. The
> building of ... social capital must ... be a major factor in
> regeneration irrespective of the fact that it can ... also
> convert into vertical involvement. ... These low profile but
> continuous types of interaction are the soil in which vertical
> involvement capacity grows. ... The absence or sparsity of
> such networks and activities ... weighs heavily against ... the
> social quality of life and vertical involvement.
>
> (Chanan, 2003, pp. 55–6)

Similarly, Chanan notes that community groups merge providers and
beneficiaries. They are the training and recruiting ground for local
volunteers (though the volunteers might not think of themselves in
these terms) providing the glue which holds society together at micro
level. Chanan finishes his report with a list of indicators of a strong
community life, and, in a later document (2006) now accepted as
official guidance by the UK Government, lists a more comprehensive
set of indicators, together with a questionnaire which can be used to
identify whether these indicators are present.

We can conclude from the above that, whatever else they do,
regeneration strategies need to seek to create a strong community. In
particular, impacting on horizontal participation is usually neglected.
Yet this really does seem to affect everything else. In summary, the
evidence now does seem to be emerging that community development programmes (with their concomitant 'programme bending' and
related elements) are a prerequisite for the effective regeneration of
disadvantaged areas. However, there remain many questions. For
instance, how effective will small area regeneration programmes be
at reducing disadvantage if properly resourced and thought through

community work strategies *are* implemented to underpin them? My own view is that such programmes will ameliorate more effectively, rather than reverse, the natural tendencies in a capitalist society towards inequality and exclusion. But, let's try, and see how far we get. And Chanan asks: 'If community development happens slowly, which seems to be the only way, and gradually infuses top down programmes with a different ethos, how should we proceed? (personal communication). Surely we can't put the "top down" objectives "on hold" for five years?' I'm not sure of the answer to this. We can, however, be certain that there will be many challenges if we do develop community work strategically as an underpinning aspect of small area regeneration. If we do seriously attempt this, research will eventually tell us what difference it makes

Getting the detail right

In the 1980s, in Britain, the Department of Trade and Industry established a number of time-limited Inner City Task Forces. These comprised teams of five or six people, with a budget, whose task was to seek to regenerate small neighbourhoods in several inner cities. (See Twelvetrees, 1998c, pp. 168–74.) When their funding was coming to an end, around 1990, several developed an 'exit' strategy (later renamed a 'forward' strategy) and some sought to create a development trust. GFA Consulting draw out two essential characteristics for effective 'forward strategies'. First, these need to be developed when the initiative *starts*, though they will evolve over time. Second, a regeneration initiative needs to leave behind a capacity to 'bend mainstream programmes'. They argue that, in the long term, the real difference to deprived communities is going to be made by mainstream programmes, applied or 'bent' in the most appropriate ways.

All the above leads me to conclude that the successful regeneration of highly deprived areas requires *all* the following:

1. The recognition by all the partners that a permanent development capacity (i.e. a staff team) needs to be established. This allows a rolling programme of work, consistent with a long-term vision, to be designed, starting with small projects which are quick and cheap to implement, building up to bigger projects as trust and organisational capacity grow.

2. There needs to be an outreach capacity (community development work) which engages with people to increase their confidence, encouraging them to participate in what is going on in the community and, where possible, to contribute to community life – building social capital.

3. There need to be excellent collaborative arrangements between all the public institutional actors, voluntary/private non-profit organisations, the community, and, if possible, the private sector.

4. Formal partnerships need highly skilled staff to facilitate and co-ordinate them. Co-ordinators must be non-partisan and have as their prime objectives the facilitation of partnership working and assisting others to develop and implement wider strategies rather than to meet the narrower goals of one organisation.

5. There must be staff resources to 'bend mainstream programmes' in order to ensure that the big services make a real difference in the area. This work could also involve brokering the assistance of the private sector.

6. At least one of the big players (but preferably several) with considerable finance must be fully committed to the initiative. If not, when times get hard or when the first few years' funding dry up, the venture will die.

7. These approaches need to be supported by a city/county wide structure involving all the key players who are also committed to making changes to policies and practices.

Local Authority-wide community work strategies

In Britain, the resources to undertake community work primarily come from government. Additionally, Local Authorities provide such a range of services that effective community work at local level needs to go hand in hand with the good co-ordination of Local Authority and other services. Thus, Local Authority-based community work strategies need to be concerned with how all departments deliver services and relate to the community; good community work helps facilitate good governance. If Local Authority and other key local players do not adopt a strategic approach to it, community work will continue to be the 'start-stop' phenomenon which it still is in many places. (See AMA, 1993, for guidance on Local Authority-based community work strategies; JRF, 2006 and the

Appendix to this book for more on community work strategies in general.)

Linking community development with support and prevention strategies

In disadvantaged communities, a small proportion of the population, say, 10%, suffers substantial personal problems, including: mental illness; domestic abuse; serial offending; truanting from school; learning difficulties; alcohol- or drug-dependence; or disability. These people, and their children, can be extremely hard to help and need a great deal of assistance. Most community development programmes don't reach them because community groups (at least their leaders) tend to consist of the more able of a given population. Yet these (highly disadvantaged) people and their children often lead unfulfilling lives, and some of them cause grief not only to themselves but to the rest of society if they are not helped effectively.

There are both universal and specialist services, which attempt to meet the needs of such people. While many such schemes are run city- or county-wide, if community work projects are concerned about highly disadvantaged people, such projects should engage with these kinds of schemes in order to assist them to make a better impact. They can do this by: assisting with local links; facilitating networks; (perhaps) mobilising volunteers to assist; and providing the local knowledge necessary to make something work. We are also inching towards a more scientific approach to 'prevention'. The 'Communities that Care' programme (now operating in many countries) aims to measure risk and protective factors for children and young people and to apply 'promising approaches' which have been shown to be effective in preventing dysfunctional and risky behaviour. A survey of the Eastside of Swansea, Wales, in 2001, measured the degree to which these risky behaviours were present in children and young people, and a number of 'promising approaches' aimed at reducing them were put in place. In 2005, a repeat survey showed that these risk factors had nearly all reduced significantly. Community workers are vitally needed to assist with the development of such projects.

Conclusion – linking it all up

There are around 40 different Local Authority-wide strategies in a given city or county in Britain today, and it is impossible for

any one worker to understand them all. Yet community work programmes must link up with them if both the community work and
Local Authority-wide strategies are to be effective. There are four
main ways to do this. First, as we saw earlier, there needs to be
a city-/county-wide mechanism to co-ordinate a community work
strategy. This could facilitate meetings between community work
staff and workers who are operating Local Authority-wide strategies
(e.g. on health, older people). The aim would be for the participants
to identify what they could work on together. Second, the central
co-ordinating mechanism could employ a staff member specifically
to create links between the Local Authority wide strategies and neighbourhood level community work schemes. Third, Local Authority
heads of service could each take responsibility for a particular neighbourhood, in addition to their existing responsibilities, ensuring
things were joined up. Finally, if there are community work schemes
in, say, ten deprived neighbourhoods of the Local Authority area,
each with a co-ordinator, each co-ordinator could specialise in one
or two 'themes', poverty and education, for example, as well as their
own neighbourhood issues. Each would then also work across all the
ten areas assisting the other neighbourhood co-ordinators with specialist knowledge and know-how in relation to that theme. It is also
worth noting that, in Wales, there are compacts between the voluntary sector and local government which facilitate collaboration;
these compacts could also assist with such processes.

It is imperative not to underestimate the difficulty of this work. In
Britain, Local Authorities and other big institutions are struggling to
join up their city-/county-wide strategies for, e.g. 'children and young
people' with, say, 'community safety', and not always making a good
job of it. This is partly because, in my view, certain models are being
relied on too heavily. Traditional planning models are hierarchical,
with all actions flowing from the top, as if one was constructing a
complicated building where everything has to fit together precisely,
in a particular sequence. But you just can't fit, for example, themes to
do with categories of people (older people, travellers or drug users)
neatly under themes to do with services, for example, health, or
with spatial policies covering neighbourhoods or regions. The model
we need has to be more like a dance or a jazz concert, where the
individuals or couples (read 'service agencies') are performing in the
way they judge most appropriate, but in a way which fits with
the whole because *they are fully aware of what is going on around
them.* However, exactly what they will do, especially in relation to

other individuals or couples, cannot always be specified exactly in advance, especially when innovation and risk-taking are necessary. Community work values and skills, which are, in part, to do with work with and between organisations, as an honest broker with no particular axe to grind or service to deliver or defend, coupled with the skills of problem analysis, organisation building, risk-taking and dealing with uncertainty, equip us well to do this work. Additionally, it is apparent to me that the skills which are inherent in the application of the community work ethos are increasingly important for a great many staff in public service today and not just for community workers. I hope that this book has contributed to a wider understanding of these issues.

Points to ponder

1. Do you think that community work is an essential component of small area regeneration programmes? If 'yes', how? If 'no', where are the gaps in my arguments?
2. What ideas do you have for joining up the big 'top- down' services and programmes with 'bottom- up' community development projects?

Further reading

Chanan (2003) *Searching for Solid Foundations: Community Involvement and Urban Policy.*
Taylor (2003) *Public Policy in the Community.*

Appendix

Requirements for a national/regional community work strategy

Let us assume that a national or regional (i.e. not local) government wants to adopt a community work strategy which is implemented at local level and that it is aimed at deprived communities, at least initially. While circumstances will vary in different places and the exact details will need to be worked out in each case, nevertheless, we can now make some points with certainty.

1. Thoroughly read and study the experiences, evaluations and recommendations from previous programmes, and incorporate the lessons.
2. Central/regional government must ensure that it has good access to sufficient technical expertise to design and operate a community work programme. These programmes 'bite back', and, if there are too few skilled staff at the centre, they won't be able to make good decisions.
3. Be clear what the nature of the programme is. A community work programme is not primarily a 'big money' area regeneration programme, but something which creates partnership working, builds local capacity and creates social capital. In this way it lays a basis for sustained improvement which can help service providers and the big regeneration programmes be more effective.
4. Communicate with care to all relevant departments in the central or regional government, taking time to explain that this programme will require different ways of working at all levels. Carry out workshops and exercises designed to facilitate cross-boundary understanding and working in central/regional government.
5. Ensure all relevant central/regional government politicians understand and support the programme and that they discuss it jointly.

6. Explain to politicians and officials that many of the outcomes of the programme will be difficult to rectify and that, inevitably, mistakes will be made.

7. Set up mechanisms across departments to monitor and learn from the programme as it develops.

8. Do not raise expectations too high.

9. Provide continuing training for the staff and civil servants who are to operate the programme.

10. Be prepared to stay with it when things go wrong, as they will.

11. Recognise that the purpose of the programme will be for all organisations, including central government, to change the way they do things. The implication of this is that, when it becomes clear that a particular regulation is hampering the programme, there will need to be high-level discussions about how such regulations can be modified. This will require flexible attitudes in central/regional government.

12. Recognise that there will not be sufficient skilled community workers, local partnership coordinators and 'programme benders'. Design the programme to fit the probable number of such people and put into place a well-resourced, theoretically sound and 'hands on' training programme to produce new skilled staff. Provide in-service training for existing staff and require them to attend it, providing incentives.

13. The programme guidance and job descriptions should emphasise:
    - community development work and capacity building on the ground;
    - network development of local people and of professionals;
    - social planning, programme bending and overcoming bureaucratic obstacles;
    - facilitating collaboration between all stakeholders at neighbourhood level;
    - collaboration between neighbourhood level staff across a wider area, i.e. the city/county as a whole;
    - mechanisms to feed back to the council, health board, central/regional government, training institutions, housing bodies, etc, what needs to be done to make things run more effectively;
    - the establishment of capacity at senior level in these institutions to change ways of working and to adjust cultures so that service delivery is more effective.

14. Recognise that bringing disadvantaged areas 'up' is an enduring challenge, and that permanent teams need to be established at local level, with adequate numbers of staff.

15. Require that all projects report at least annually on their work and that they evaluate against 'soft' targets such as local participation, increased networking, the establishment of new ways of working, how far barriers to joint working have been addressed, lessons learned, etc.

16. Make sure that there is careful distinction between:
    (a) a capacity building plan;
    (b) an action plan which is within the power of the local team or partnership to carry out because of access to resources within their control;
    (c) an action plan which consists of what the major players can contribute, based on agreement with them;
    (d) What can be done with existing resources and what cannot.
    Of these, (c) above can only be worked up over several years in close collaboration with the big service providers and after much preparatory capacity building work has been carried out both in the community and in the statutory bodies. Such an action plan is also a 'rolling' plan; it cannot be fixed in stone.

17. Ensure that there is continuing commitment in the Local Authority and other organisations to the whole process.

18. Ensure there is a well-resourced unit at city/county level to cover relevant universal aspects of the process, e.g. monitoring and evaluation, finance, cross-area coordination, feeding insights back to the power holders, central administration, coordination of grant applications, etc.

19. Be aware of the suspicion from many communities towards the Local Authority, and note the dilemma here. On the one hand, a central unit within the Local Authority has potentially greater access to the top service providers. On the other, it is vital to use the knowledge, contacts, networks and capacity for voluntary effort of the non profit/voluntary sector. There may be a case for a 'hybrid' central unit, part in the Local Authority and part in the 'not for profit' sector.

20. When neighbourhoods are chosen for intervention, design the local initiative around what is already there. (You need to have checked out the competence of the existing structures first, though.) Don't 'parachute in' ignoring the, in some cases, several years of community development work on the ground. Try to

configure your staff team around who is already doing what. If a council for voluntary service or a church already has community development workers on the ground, you might build your local team around them. They could even employ some or all of your fieldworkers.

21. Provide long-term funding for the staff team, and ensure that there are modest amounts of money for the local team or partnership to spend more or less how it wishes.

22. There needs to be a 'light touch' audit. Don't require the submission of every item of expense to the centre for approval. Give the team a reasonable budget which is rolled over each year automatically, which is mainly for salaries plus running costs and special items, then get them to account for it afterwards.

23. Set up a good system of local project support, liaison and consultancy for the project managers and local coordinators.

24. Ensure that those managing the neighbourhood level projects have the skills to do so.

25. Explain continually to Local Authorities, especially to politicians, what the programme is about.

26. Assuming the programme is to cover, say, ten neighbourhoods in a city which contains altogether 50 potential neighbourhoods, give plenty of time for consultation between the Local Authority and other organisations as to which should be the communities selected. The selection criteria should not only be the level of deprivation; they should also be based on what people think are relatively natural communities, what scope there is for partnership working; and the level of intra-community conflict. It might be best to select those communities first of all where there was a good chance of success.

27. If you are establishing a formal partnership, develop this slowly, building networks, understanding and trust.

28. Remember that a formal partnership can only do certain things. You may have: (a) an organisation responsible for undertaking major work, with a director who needs a small expert board or executive committee; and (b) a wider partnership, consisting of a range of organisations and some local people; and/or (c) a much looser forum consisting of anybody who wants to come and which meets from time to time with the more executive partnership or board. Work out what is best for each area.

29. You will need to foster: (a) the engagement at local level of people who won't come to formal multi-issue partnerships, and (b) networks of professionals.
30. An officers' group of middle managers in the Local Authority is needed to ensure that the lessons are learned and changes are made throughout the Local Authority and beyond. Give this a high priority and don't underestimate the difficulties.
31. Encourage risk-taking; treat failure as equal to success but learn lessons.
32. Via 'action research', disseminate lessons frequently, and bring all the partnership coordinators together across the whole territory about twice a year.
33. If there are related programmes, in particular large urban renewal projects, you have to establish carefully thought through linkages with them. In Britain, at the time of writing, Local Authorities are required to develop and co-ordinate (under various names) overarching strategies for the benefit of the whole area. These Local Authority area-wide strategies need to be carefully joined up to more local community development (bottom-up) strategies. To do this will require a system of working groups, liaison workers, inter-partnership communication structures and visionary leadership.

Bibliography

ACAS, Arbitration and Conciliation Advisory Service (n.d.) *Code of Practice on Disciplinary and Grievance Procedures* (www.acas.org.uk)

Acland, A. and Hickling, A. (1997) *Enabling Stakeholder Dialogue: Training for Facilitators, Mediators and Process Managers, Course Handbook*, London, Environment Council.

Adair, J. (1987) *Effective Team Building: How to Make Winning Teams*, Effective 1 (one) Series.

Alinsky, S.D. (1969) *Reveille for Radicals*, New York, Vintage Books.

Alinsky, S.D. (1972) *Rules for Radicals: A Pragmatic Primer for Realistic Radicals*, New York, Vintage Books.

Allen, A. and May, C. (2007) *'Setting up for Success: A Practical Guide for Community Organisation'*, London, CDF.

AMA (Association of Metropolitan Authorities) (1993) *Local Authorities and Community Development: A Strategic Opportunity for the 1990s*, London, HMSO.

Amulya J, (n.d.) *'What is Reflective Practice?'* Cambridge, MA, Center for Reflective Community Practice, Massachusetts Institute of Technology (www.crcp@mit.edu).

Arendt, H. (1998) *The Human Condition*, 2nd edn, Chicago, University of Chicago Press.

Argyris, C. and Schön, D. (1974) *Theory in Practice: Increasing Professional Effectiveness*, San Francisco, Jossey-Bass.

Armstrong, J. (1998) 'Towards a Plan for Capacity Building in the UK', in Twelvetrees (1998a), pp. 240–5.

Arnstein, S.R. (1969) 'A Ladder of Participation', *Journal of American Planning Association* 35: 216–24.

Aspinall, T. and Larkins, C. (2004) *Breathing Fire into Participation: Good Practice Guidelines on Supporting Groups of Young People to Participate*, Swansea, Funky Dragon.

Ball, M. (1988) *Evaluation in the Voluntary Sector*, London, Forbes Trust.

Barclay, P.M. (1982) *Social Workers: Their Role and Tasks – Working Party Report*, London, NCVO.

Barr, A., Drysdale, J. and Henderson, P. (1997) *Towards Caring Communities: Community Development and Community Care: An Introductory Training Pack*, Brighton, Pavilion Publications, and York, Joseph Rowntree Foundation.

Black, J. (1994) *Mindstore: The Ultimate Mental Fitness Programme*, London, Thorsons.

Bluckert, P. (n.d.) *Coaching Supervision* (www.pbcoaching.com/article-coaching-supervision.php).

Bower, M. (1998) 'Check Your Postcode for Health', *Western Mail*, Cardiff, 4 September, p. 4.

Brager, G. and Holloway, S. (1978) *Changing Human Service Organizations*, New York, Free Press.

Brier, W., Geddes, M. and Hastings, C. (1994) *Project Leadership*, London, Gower.

Brookfield S.D. (1986) *Understanding and Facilitating Adult Learning: A Comprehensive Analysis of Principles and Effective Practice*, Milton Keynes, Open University Press.

Brown, W. *et al.* (eds) (2004) *The Future of Worker Representation*. Oxford, Oxford University Press.

Burke, T. (1995) 'Making Plans for Alnwick', *Young People Now*, July: 28–9.

Burnes, B. (2000) *Managing Change: A Strategic Approach to Organisational Dynamics*, London, Prentice Hall/Financial Times.

Carnegie, D. (1936) *How to Win Friends and Influence People*, revised edition, London, Vermillion.

CDF (2003) *A Better Place to Live: The CDF Guide to Sustainable Development for Community Groups*, London, CDF.

CDF/CLG (2006) *The Community Development Challenge*, London (downloadable from www.communities.gov.uk).

Chambers, E. (2003) *Roots for Radicals: Organizing for Power, Action, and Justice*. London, Continuum.

Chanan, G. (2003) *Searching for Solid Foundations: Community Involvement and Urban Policy*, London, Office of the Deputy Prime Minister.

Chanan, G. (2006) *Safer Stronger Communities Fund*, available at: www.neighbourhood.gov.uk/page.asp?=1567.

Children Now (2005) 'What are they thinking?' *Children Now* 9–15 Nov., pp. 20–1.

Church, C., Cade, A. and Grant, A. (1998) *An Environment for Everyone; Social Exclusion, Poverty and Environmental Action*, London, Community Development Foundation.

Clinton, B. (2004) *My Life*, London, Hutchinson.

Connell, J.P. and Kubisch, A.C. (1998) '*Applying a Theory of Change Approach to the Evaluation of Comprehensive Community Initiatives: Progress, Prospects and Problems*', in Fulright-Anderson *et al.*, pp. 15–44.

Corina, L. (1977) *Oldham CDP: An Assessment of its Impact and Influence on the Local Authority*, York, University of York.

Covey, S. R. (1999) *Seven Habits of Highly Effective People; Powerful Lessons on Personal Change*, London, Simon and Schuster.

Cox, F.M. *et al.* (eds) (1976) *Strategies of Community Organization*, Illinois, F. E. Peacock.

Department for International Development (2002) *Tools for Development: A Handbook for Those Engaged in Development Activity*, available at: www.dfid.uk

Dominelli, L. (2006) *Women and Community Action*, Bristol, BASW/Policy Press.

Dynamix (2002) *Participation – Spice it Up: Practical Tools for Engaging Children and Young People in Planning and Consultation*, Swansea, Dynamix.

Edwards, K. (1984) 'Collective Working in a Small Non-Statutory Organisation', *MDU Bulletin*, July, 3/4.

Eyken, W.v.d. (1992) *Introducing Evaluation*, The Hague, Bernard van Leer Foundation.

FCWTG (1999) *Defining Community Work*, Sheffield, FCWTG.

FCWTG (2001) *Making Changes: Practice into Policy: A Strategic Framework for Community Development Learning in England*, Sheffield, FCWTG.

Feuerstein, M.T. (2002) *Partners in Evaluation*, London, Macmillan Education.

Forbes, D. (1998) *Voluntary but not Amateur: Guide to the Law for Voluntary Organisations and Community Groups*, London, London Voluntary Service Council.

Fosler, R.S. and Berger, R.A. (1982) *Public Private Partnerships in American Cities*, Lexington, MA, Lexington Books.

Francis, D. and Henderson, P. (1992) *Working with Rural Communities*, Basingstoke, Macmillan.

Freeman, J. (1970) *The Tyranny of Structurelessness*, revised version available at: www.bopsecrets.org/cf/structurelessness.htm.

Fulright-Anderson, K., Kubisch, A.C. and Connell, J.P. (eds) *New Approaches to Evaluating Community Initiatives*, Vol. 2: *Theory, Measurements and Analysis*, Washington, DC, The Aspen Initiative.

Funky Dragon (2002) *The Funky Dragon Good Practice Guide to Supporting Groups of Children and Young People to Participate*, available at: www.funkydragon.org.uk.

Gallagher, A. (1977) 'Women and Community Work', in Mayo (1977), pp. 121–40.

Gecan, M. (2002) *Going Public*, Boston, Beacon Press.

GFA Consulting (1986) *Lessons from Inner City Task Force Experience: Good Practice Guide: Designing Forward Strategies*, Bishop's Stortford, GFAC.

Gilchrist, A. (1992) 'The Revolution of Everyday Life Revisited: Towards an Anti-Discriminatory Praxis for Community Work', *Social Action*, 1(1): 22–8.

Gilchrist, A. (1995) *Community Development and Networking*, London, Community Development Foundation.

Gilchrist, A. (1997) 'Chaos in the Community: The Emergence of Voluntary Associations and Collective Action', unpublished initial draft, 21 July.

Gilchrist, A. (1998) 'A More Excellent Way: Developing Coalition and Consensus through Informal Networking', *Community Development Journal*, 2(4): 100–8.

Gilchrist, A. (2004) *Community Cohesion and Community Development: Bridges or Barricades*, London, CDF.

Gilchrist, A. (2004) *The Well Connected Community: A Networking Approach to Community Work*, Bristol, Policy Press.

Goetschius, G. (1969) *Working with Community Groups*, London, Routledge.

Goleman, D. (1996) *Emotional Intelligence: Why It Can Matter More Than IQ*, London, Bloomsbury.

Goleman, D. (1998) *Working with Emotional Intelligence*, London, Bloomsbury.

Hadley, R., Cooper, M., Dale, P. and Stacey, G. (1987) *A Community Social Worker's Handbook*, London, Tavistock.

Hadley, R. and McGrath, M. (eds) (1980) *Going Local*, Occasional Paper One, London, Bedford Square Press.

Harris, K. (1998) 'Some Problems in Community Enterprise and Community Economic Development', in Twelvetrees (1998a), pp. 36–42.

Hasler, J. (1995) 'Belonging and Becoming: The Child Growing up in Community', in Henderson (1995), pp. 169–82.

Hawtin, M., Hughes, G. and Percy Smith, J. (1994) *Auditing Social Needs*, Milton Keynes, Open University Press.

Henderson, P. (ed.) (1995) *Children and Communities*, London, Pluto Press.

Henderson, P. (1998) 'Children, Communities and Community Development', paper presented at National Playworkers Conference, Leeds, Community Development Foundation.

Henderson, P. and Francis, D. (1992) *Working with Rural Communities*, Basingstoke, Palgrave Macmillan.

Henderson, P. and Francis, D. (eds) (1993) *Rural Action: A Collection of Community Work Case Studies*, London, Pluto.

Henderson, P. and Francis, D. (n.d.) *A Rural Community Work Model: Summary*, London, Community Development Foundation.

Henderson, P. and Salmon, H. (1995) *Community Organising: The UK Context*, London, Community Development Foundation/Churches Community Work Alliance.

Henderson, P. and Salmon, H. (1998) *Signposts to Local Democracy: Local Governance, Communitarianism and Community Development*, London, Community Development Foundation.

Henderson, P. and Thomas, D.N. (eds) (1981) *Readings in Community Work*, London, Allen and Unwin.

Henderson, P. and Thomas, D.N. (2002) *Skills in Neighbourhood Work*, 3rd edn, London and New York, Routledge.

Hoggett. P. *et al.* (1997) *Contested Communities: Experiences, Struggles, Policies*, Bristol, The Policy Press.

Holloway, C. and Otto, S. (1985) *Getting Organised: A Handbook for Non-Statutory Organisations*, London, Bedford Square Press.

Home Office (1991) *Safer Communities: The Local Delivery of Crime Prevention through the Partnership Approach (the Morgan Report)*, London, HMSO.

Home Office (1993) *Practical Guide to Crime Prevention for Local Partnerships*, London, HMSO.

Home Office (1998) *Crime and Disorder Act*, London, HMSO.

Howarth, C. and Jamoul, L. (2004) 'London Citizens: Practising Citizenship, Rebuilding Democracy', *Renewal: The Journal of Labour Politics* 12(3).

Hyatt, J. and Skinner, S. (1997) *Calling in the Specialist: Using Consultancy Methods with Community Organisations*, London, Community Development Foundation.

Jameson, N. (1988) 'Organizing for a Change', *Christian Action Journal*, Autumn.

Jamoul, L. (2006) 'The Art of Politics: Broad-based Organising in Britain', PhD thesis, Geography Department, University of London.

Jones, D. and Smith, L. (eds) (1981) *Deprivation and Community Action*, London, Association of Community Workers/Routledge.

Joseph Rowntree Foundation (1996) *Art of Regeneration: Urban Renewal through Cultural Activity*, Social Policy Summary 8, York, Joseph Rowntree Foundation.

Joseph Rowntree Foundation (2007) *Changing Neighbourhoods: The Impact of Light Touch Support in 20 Communities*, York, Joseph Rowntree Foundation.

Kadushin, A. and Harkness, D. (2002) *Supervision in Social Work*, New York, Columbia University Press.

Kellogg Foundation (1997) *Evaluation Handbook*, Michigan, W.K. Kellogg Foundation

Kelly, A. (1993) 'Learning to Build Community', unpublished draft, Brisbane.

Kelly, A. and Sewell, S. (1996) *With Head, Heart and Hand: Dimensions of Community Building*, 4th edn, Brisbane, Boolarong Publications.

Kirby, P., Lanyon, C., Cronin, K. and Sinclair, R. (2003) *Building a Culture of Participation: Involving Children and Young People in Policy, Service Planning and Delivery*, London, Department for Education and Skills/NCB.

Kramer, R. M. and Specht, H. (1975), *Readings in Community Organization Practice*, London, Prentice Hall.

Laber, R.K. (1997) *Group Process: Working Effectively by Committee*, London, Technomic Publishing Company, USA. ISBN 97818566765015.

Labonté, R. (1998) Lecture to Health Promotion Wales, Cardiff.

Labonté, R. (1999) *Developing Community Health in Wales: A Community Development Approach to Health Promotion*, Cardiff, Health Promotion Wales.

Landry, C., Morely, D., Southwood, R. and Wright, P. (1985) *What a Way to Run a Railroad*, London, Comedia.

Levin, P. (1981) 'Opening up the Planning Process', in Henderson and Thomas (1981), pp. 108–14.

Lombardo, S. *et al.* (2000) *Collaborative Leader: Asserting Yourself Appropriately*, San Francisco, Berett-Koehler.

Mayo, M (ed.) (1977) *Women in the Community*, London, Routledge.

Mayo, M. (1994a) 'The Shifting Concept of Community', in Mayo (1994b).

Mayo, M. (1994b) *Communities and Caring: A Mixed Economy of Welfare*, Basingstoke, Macmillan.

McTaggart, L. (1998) 'Second Opinion - about Heart Disease', *Observer*, 5 July.

Miller, J. (1997) *Never Too Young: How Children Can Take Responsibility and Make Decisions*, London, SCF/National Early Years Network.

Miller, J. (1999) *A Journey of Discovery: Children Creating Participation in Planning*, London, SCF.

National Institute for Social Work (1982) *Social Workers: Their Role and Tasks (the Barclay Report)*, London, National Institute for Social Work/Bedford Square Press.

Ndolu, T. (1998) 'Conflict Management and Peace Building through Community Development', *Community Development Journal*, 33(2): 106–16.

Northern Ireland Voluntary Trust (1998) *Taking Risks for Peace: A Mid Term Review by an Intermediary Funding Body of the EU Peace Process*, Belfast, Northern Ireland Voluntary Trust.

Nugent, J. (1998) 'Building Capacity for Community Based Development', in Twelvetrees (1998a).

Nye, N. (1998) 'Building the Capacity of CDCs: A Model for Intermediary Funding', in Twelvetrees (1998a).

Ohri, A., Manning, B. and Curno, P. (eds) (1982) *Community Work and Racism*, London, Association of Community Workers/Routledge.

Ottawa Government (1986) *Charter for Health Promotion (the Ottawa Charter)*, Ottawa, Government Printers.

Partnership Working: A 'How to' guide (n.d.) Scottish Centre for Regeneration, available at: www. Pt.communitiesscotland.gov.uk

Pearce, J. (1993) *At the Heart of the Community Economy: Community Enterprise in a Changing World*, London, Gulbenkian Foundation.

PiC (2001) *People in Communities Initiative: An Interim Evaluation*, Cardiff, National Assembly for Wales, HRR 3/01.

Pierson, J. and Smith, J. (eds) (2001) *Rebuilding Community: Policy and Practice in Urban Regeneration*, Basingstoke, Palgrave.

Piven, F. and Cloward, R. (1977) *Poor People's Movements: Why They Succeed, How They Fail*, New York, Pantheon.

PRINCE 2 (n.d.) Central Computer and Telecommunications Agency, London, The Stationery Office. Available at: www.prince2.org.uk

Putnam, R. (2000) *Bowling Alone: The Collapse and Revival of American Community*, New York, Simon and Schuster.

Putnam, R. (2001) 'Social Capital Measurements and Consequences', *Isuma* (US) 2:1, Spring.

Raelin, J. (2002) 'I Don't Have Time to Think Versus the Art of Reflective Practice', *Reflections* 4(1): 66–79.

Resnick, H. (1975) 'The Professional: Pro-active Decision Making in the Organisation', *Social Work Today* 6(15): 462–7.

Resnick, H. and Patti, R. (1980) *Change from Within: Humanizing Social Welfare Organizations*, Philadelphia, PA, Temple University Press.

Revans, R.W. *et al.* (1998) *ABC of Action Learning*, London, Lemos and Crane.

Rittel, H. and Webber, M. (1973) *Dilemmas in a General Theory of Planning*, Amsterdam, Elsevier Scientific Publishing, pp. 155–9.

Roche, C. (1999) *Impact Assessment for Development Agencies*, Oxford, Oxfam.

Rodney Turner, J. (1997) *The Handbook of Project Based Management: Improving the Processes for Achieving Strategic Objectives*, London, McGraw-Hill.

Rogers, C. (1961–95) *On Becoming a Person: A Therapist's View of Psychotherapy*, Boston, Houghton Mifflin.

Rolfe, G., Freshwater, D. and Jasper, M. (2001) *Critical Reflection for Nursing and the Helping Professions: A User's Guide*, Basingstoke, Palgrave.

Rothman, J. (1976) 'Three Models of Community Organization Practice', in F.M. Cox *et al.* (1976), pp. 22–38.

Rubin, F. (1995) *A Basic Guide to Evaluation for Development Workers*, Oxford, Oxfam.

SCCD (2001) *Strategic Framework for Community Development*, Sheffield, SCCD.

Senge, P.M. (1990) *The Art and Practice of the Learning Organisation*, New York, Doubleday.

Simpson, T. (1995a) 'A Checklist for Community Enterprise Training', unpublished paper, Wales, Community Development Foundation.

Simpson, T. (1995b) 'What Do We Do Now: The Brief Guide to Project Exiting', unpublished paper, Wales, Community Development Foundation.

Skinner, S. (1997) *Building Community Strengths: A Resource Book on Capacity Building*, London, Community Development Foundation.

Skinner, S. (2006) *Strengthening Communities*, London, Community Development Foundation.

Smiley, C. (1982) 'Managing Agreement; the Abilene Paradox', *Community Development Journal* 17(1): 54–68.

Smith, L. (1981a) 'A Model for the Development of Public Participation in Local Authority Decision Making', in Jones and Smith (1981).

Smith, L. (1981b) 'Public Participation in Islington: A Case Study', in Jones and Smith (1981).

Specht, H. (1975) 'Disruptive Tactics', in Kramer and Specht (1975), pp. 336–48.

Spreckley, F. (1997) *The Social Audit Toolkit*, 3rd edn, Hertfordshire Social Enterprise Partnership, available at: www.social-enterprise.co.uk

Stanton, A. (1989) *Invitation to Self Management*, Middlesex, Dab Hand Press.

Stewart, D.W. and Shamdasani, P.N. (1991) *Focus Groups, Theory and Practice*, London, Sage.

Taylor, M. (1998) *Evaluating Community Projects for European Funding*, Caerphilly, Wales Council for Voluntary Action.

Taylor, M. (2000) *Top Down Meets Bottom Up: Neighbourhood Management*, York, Joseph Rowntree Foundation.

Taylor, M. (2003) *Public Policy in the Community*, Basingstoke, Palgrave.

Tenant Participation Advisory Service, see www.tpas.org.uk

Thomas, K. and Kilman, R. (1996) *Thomas-Kilman Conflict Mode Instrument, Conflict Workshop Facilitators' Guide*, Palo Alto, CA, Consulting Psychologists Press.

Twelvetrees, A. (1996) *Organizing for Neighbourhood Development: A Comparative Study of Community Based Development Organizations*, 2nd edn, Aldershot, Avebury.

Twelvetrees, A. (1998a) *Community Economic Development: Rhetoric or Reality?*, London, Community Development Foundation.

Twelvetrees, A. (1998b) 'Customised Training in Britain; A Success Story', in Twelvetrees (1998a), pp. 175–8.

Twelvetrees, A. (1998c) 'Evaluating the UK Government's Inner Cities Task Force Initiative', in Twelvetrees (1998a), pp. 168–74.

Voluntary Activity Unit (1997a) *Measuring Community Development in Northern Ireland: A Handbook for Practitioners*, Belfast, Dept of Health and Social Services.

Voluntary Activity Unit (1997b) *Monitoring and Evaluation of Community Work in Northern Ireland*, Belfast, Dept of Health and Social Services.

WAG (Welsh Assembly Government) (2002) *Communities First Guidance*, Cardiff, Welsh Assembly Government.

Wales Youth Agency (n.d.) *Working with Youth Groups in the Community*, Caerphilly, Wales Youth Agency.

Walker, P. (1998) 'A Strategic Approach to CED', in Twelvetrees (1998a), pp. 257–63.

Walton, R.E. (1976) 'Two Strategies of Social Change and Their Dilemmas', in Cox *et al.* (1976).

Wilkinson, R. (1996) *Unhealthy Societies: The Afflictions of Inequality*, London, Routledge.

Williams, P. (2002) 'The Competent Boundary Spanner', *Public Administration*, 80(1): 103–24.

Willmott, P. (1989) *Community Initiatives: Patterns and Prospects*, London, Policy Studies Institute.

Wills, J. (2001) 'Community Unionism and Trade Union Renewal in the UK: Moving Beyond the Fragments at Last?' *Transactions of the Institute of British Geographers*, 26.

Wills, J. (2004) 'Campaigning for Low Paid Workers: The East London Communities Organisation (TELCO) Living Wage Campaign', in Brown *et al.* (eds) (2004).

Wilson, D. (1984) *Pressure: The A–Z of Campaigning in Britain*, Soldbridge Books. Available at: antiqubook.co.uk

Wiseman, R. (2003) *The Luck Factor: How to Change Your Luck and Change Your Life*, London, Century.

Zimmerman, D.P. (1997) *Robert's Rules in Plain English: A Readable, Authoritative Easy to Use Guide to Running Meetings*, 2nd edn, London, Collins.

Index